MOVIE WORKERS

WOMEN AND FILM HISTORY INTERNATIONAL

Series Editors
Kay Armatage, Jane M. Gaines, and Christine Gledhill

A new generation of motion picture historians is rediscovering
the vital and diverse contributions of women to world film history
whether as producers, actors, or spectators. Taking advantage of
new print material and moving picture archival discoveries, as well
as the benefits of digital access and storage, this series investigates
the significance of gender in the cinema.

A list of books in the series appears at the end of this book.

MOVIE WORKERS

The Women Who Made British Cinema

MELANIE BELL

**UNIVERSITY OF
ILLINOIS PRESS**
Urbana, Chicago, and Springfield

Parts of chapter 4 on editors in non-fiction film were
previously published in "Rebuilding Britain: Women, Work
and Non-Fiction Film, 1945–1970," *Feminist Media Histories*
(2018), 4 (4), 33–56.

Library of Congress Cataloging-in-Publication Data
Names: Bell, Melanie, author.
Title: Movie workers : the women who made British cinema
    / Melanie Bell.
Description: Urbana : University of Illinois Press, 2021. |
    Series: Women and film history international | Includes
    bibliographical references and index.
Identifiers: LCCN 2020053100 (print) | LCCN 2020053101
    (ebook) | ISBN 9780252043871 (cloth) | ISBN
    9780252085864 (paperback) | ISBN 9780252052774
    (ebook)
Subjects: LCSH: Motion picture industry—Great
    Britain—History—20th century. | Motion pictures and
    women—Great Britain—History—20th century. | Sex
    role—Great Britain—History—20th century. | Women—
    Employment—Great Britain.
Classification: LCC PN1993.5.G7 B375 2021 (print) |
    LCC PN1993.5.G7 (ebook) | DDC 791.430820941—dc23
LC record available at https://lccn.loc.gov/2020053100
LC ebook record available at https://lccn.loc.gov/2020053101

Contents

Acknowledgments

I would like to thank the Arts and Humanities Research Council, whose generous grant supported the research project on which this publication is based. I was also supported by the School of Media and Communication and the Faculty of Arts, Humanities, and Cultures at the University of Leeds, and thank them for their generous research leave scheme, which gave me valuable writing time.

Many people have helped with this book. Librarians and staff at the British Film Institute (BFI), the British Library, and the Brotherton Library at the University of Leeds have been extremely supportive in providing information. I am especially grateful to Dave Sharpe, former head librarian at the BFI, who helped with access to the trade union records at a crucial early stage in the research, and Nathalie Morris at the BFI's Special Collections for her advice.

My gratitude to staff at the BECTU union (formerly ACT/ACTT), with particular thanks to Tracey Hunt, who was so generous with her time and supported the project from its embryonic beginnings. I am also grateful to members of the BECTU History Project for access to interview recordings with filmmakers.

I want to record my gratitude to fellow members of the project team—Vicky Ball, Susan Bradley, and Frances Galt—and the project's fantastic Steering Committee: Julia Hallam, Tracey Hunt, Kate Kinnimont, Julia Knight, Sarah Street, and Penny Summerfield. Your sound advice and kindness were invaluable, and you made the process of managing the project much easier. Research associate Susan Bradley traveled the country to conduct interviews with women in the British film and television industries, and the quality and richness of these recordings is testament to her interviewing skills. I am also grateful to BUFVC, now Learning on Screen, which created the digital resource, and in particular Linda Kaye, who led the digital team.

I have been very fortunate to have friends and colleagues who have read drafts of chapters and provided invaluable comments and feedback: John Corner, Christine Gledhill, Helen Hanson, Julia Knight, Annette Kuhn, Martin Shingler, and Penny Summerfield. For your insights and kindness, I am forever in your debt. I also wish to record my thanks to colleagues at the School of English Literature, Language, and Linguistics, Newcastle University, where this project initiated, and for the opportunity to present early findings at conferences including Screen; the Society for Cinema and Media Studies; the British Association of Film, Television, and Screen Studies; and the International Association for Media and History.

This project took many years to complete, and I'm grateful to family and friends for their advice and practical help, especially Chris Curtis, whose unpaid labor went above and beyond the call of duty and should not go unrecognized.

Finally, my heartfelt thanks to the women who were interviewed for the project—the makeup artists, continuity girls, editors, writers and many others—who generously shared their time, stories, and hospitality with the research team and allowed us to archive their recordings for future generations of writers, historians, and "movie workers."

MOVIE WORKERS

Introduction
Women's Work in Film Production
Concepts, Materials, and Methods

> I was working as a production assistant with an older male
> director who, in the office, praised my strong production skills
> and then, on set, would introduce me as his "assistant," which
> was not my job title but made him look better. It was extremely
> frustrating.
> —Anonymous woman, age 23, production assistant
>   and writer, 2017

> When you're in an all-woman crew you don't realize you're a
> woman; you're just being you in your job. . . . It must be what
> men have a lot of the time.
> —Elaine Drainville, sound recordist, 2015

This book is about work, specifically work done by women in film production in the twentieth century. It is about what that work entailed and
how value was attached to it by the industry, society, and film history. It
shows how the skills women brought to the workplace were learned and
not innate, and that if we look differently at their working lives, we can
write histories that disrupt the present. There is much invested in doing
this. Debates about low and unequal pay proliferate alongside ongoing
concerns about gender and racial bias in the media industries. Women's
contribution to contemporary film production (post-2000) is scrutinized
by journalists, activists, and academics, and tracking surveys provide
much-needed evidence of gender bias and segregation in Hollywood and
Britain.[1] Much of this debate focuses on the more recent years, but this

book's historical perspective offers valuable insight into how workplace customs and traditions became gendered and what that meant for women's working lives.

One of the common misunderstandings of women in film production is that after the pioneering days of early cinema—when women directed and headed up their own production companies—they contributed little of substance to film production until the feminist developments of the 1970s. This book challenges that view as too limiting and instead offers a fresh assessment of women and their work in the British film industry in the decades following the introduction of sound. It focuses on the six decades between 1930 and 1989, when employment in the film industry was tightly regulated by the Association of Cine-Technicians (ACT), the country's leading film union. Mapping women's work by decade, and in fiction and nonfiction filmmaking, this book examines women's economic and creative contribution to film production in the many "below-the-line" roles (that is, craft/technical labor) in which they were typically employed. It draws on unique access to ACT trade union records to sketch a diachronic map of the range and breadth of women's work in this sixty-year period, and on oral history testimony to examine synchronically the concrete reality of women's labor at particular historical junctures. It also situates women's work in the wider context of changing social expectations around women and gender roles. Providing a much-needed examination of the range, complexity, and diversity of the work performed by women, this book recovers and celebrates the scale and quality of their collective achievements while laying bare the prejudices and constraints within which they were achieved. It builds on the excellent scholarship about "pioneer" women in early cinema while revealing how much there is to be learned from the sound period. It also highlights new lines of inquiry in the relationship between women and cultural production, reflects on issues of gender and creativity, and opens up fundamental questions about how we write film history.

Women and Work in Sound-Era Cinema

Thousands of women worked in the British film industry in the decades following the introduction of sound. They worked as "continuity girls," production secretaries, negative cutters, editors, costume designers, wardrobe assistants, makeup artists, publicists, sound wave operators, researchers, librarians, paint and tracers, in-betweeners, foley artists, animation artists, matte painters, and, very occasionally, as directors, producers, and writers. They cut film, answered the phone, booked stars, sourced obscure props, painted sets, styled hair, designed and washed costumes, ran the rushes, painted cels, chauffeured directors, and massaged egos. In sum, no history of the British film industry is complete without an understanding of their work. And yet the experiences of women in these types of roles are almost entirely absent from existing histories of most national cinemas, British or otherwise. It is only relatively recently that academic scholarship has begun to engage with women's work of the historical sound era in any sustained way. Erin Hill and J. E. Smyth have in different and complementary ways extended knowledge of women's work in Hollywood's studios, with Smyth focusing on women in senior executive roles, particularly screenwriters, and Hill analyzing women's below-the-line labor.[2] Their research marks a step change in film history, showing what can be achieved and how much is left to be done. Building on these new developments, this research shows how the absence of women is explained by two interrelated factors: (1) the widely held view that work performed by women was of low status and required no particular skills and (2) established film historiographies. I interrogate these factors in turn before outlining what new approaches are needed to bring women's labor into view.

Concepts of Women's Work

Most women in the British film industry during the historical sound era were "movie workers," a phrase coined by sociologist Leo Rosten in his 1941 study of the Hollywood film industry.[3] Movie workers were referred to as "below-the-line" labor, an industry term used in production budgets where a "line" distinguishes those with creative or managerial responsibilities (typically stars, directors, producers) from craft/technical workers. Those above the line can negotiate salaries; those below the line are paid a fixed wage set by union rates. Commonly mapped onto this is a further distinction between creative and noncreative labor, where those above the line have creative autonomy while those below merely follow instructions. Women in these below-the-line roles make a significant contribution to film production, but, as film historian Sue Harper observes, "secretaries have at all times been the grease which oiled the studio machine, yet there is very little surviving evidence about their labor and its complexities . . . [as] few people thought to document them."[4] Why should this be so?

The answers to this question can be found in how women's labor has been conceptualized. Much of their work has taken place in roles deemed auxiliary, which support others in the workforce (predominantly but not exclusively men) and free them to concentrate on tasks ascribed greater value. For example, continuity girls—a role held exclusively by women in the British film industry—were responsible for recording detailed information about scene setups and relaying this to relevant parties when asked, effectively freeing up directors, actors, and cameramen from the burden of remembering technical details. Similarly, editing—another role heavily populated by women—was commonly perceived as a supporting function, where the job holder acts as a sounding board for the director in the pursuit of his creative vision. Moreover, success in these supporting roles comes through the effacement of one's labor—that is, the benchmark for success is to make one's work invisible to the service of the production. Director Sally Potter describes this as the "invisible labor involved in cinema," and as Potter explains, this is gendered: "Women historically have usually done the invisible work in the home and the workplace."[5] In the production hierarchy, auxiliary roles have low status.

Supporting roles are rendered further inconspicuous by the misunderstanding of them—typically by men—as consisting of purely repetitive and low-skill functions. This (mis)conception is evident in trade magazines, which took the lead in defining the business and craft of filmmaking. These were principally authored by men, who rarely engaged with the work done by women and, when they did, dismissed or ridiculed it. Two examples illustrate the point. In 1940 Britain's leading trade journal, The Cine-Technician, described negative cutting as "routine stuff, done more often than not by girls with no pride or interest in their jobs."[6] Such assessments conveniently forget how poor negative cutting led to torn or snagged prints, which were the bane of exhibitors, and how the work of a skilled negative cutter added to a film's profitability. Similarly, descriptions by the fan magazine Picturegoer of the wardrobe mistress as "the housewife of the studios," whose principal duties were "cleaning and ironing," failed to capture the job holder's advanced skills in logistics, teamwork, and problem solving, which were especially valuable on location, where facilities often had to be improvised.[7]

Indeed, the common intertwining of the domestic with the professional in descriptions of women's work points to another of the key ways in which the work women do is often not recognized as work. The skills and competencies that women bring to their professional roles are often assumed to be natural, a product of their biology rather than the acquisition of a set of skills or a body of knowledge acquired through practice and training. As sociologists of gender and work have argued, "Feminized occupations have been devalued since they are constructed as low skilled, and they are designated as low skill because the skills required are those that women are assumed to possess by nature rather than through recognized processes of acquisition such as apprenticeship."[8] For example, women are commonly assumed to be naturally patient and meticulous, with an aptitude for detail work, and to have highly developed skills in communication and empathy. In the context of the film industry, the assumption of natural attributes explains women's overrepresentation in what at first glance can appear to be very different types of jobs in film production. The continuity girl and production assistant, for example, undertake secretarial tasks that require the same kind of skills in patience and attention to detail that characterizes women's work in editing or paint and trace functions in animation studios. Likewise, the wardrobe mistress, described as someone who can effortlessly tackle "sewing, dressmaking [and] repair work," because these are merely an extension of her duties as a housewife, a role for which she is predestined by virtue of her sex.[9] It is in ways such as this that professional skills in note taking, dressmaking, and cel painting, learned through thousands of hours of practice, are reframed in dominant occupational discourse as natural feminine competences. The effect of this is that women's labor is not recognized as skilled labor and is devalued; as sociologists remind us, this has real material consequences: jobs performed by women tend to pay less than those performed by men.[10] The film industry is no exception, with a production secretary earning roughly two-thirds the salary of a first assistant director, in what are effectively equivalent roles in terms of responsibility and skill. We commonly make the mistake in thinking low pay is a reflection of low skill, thus eliding the process by which "value" has been attached. Pay is not set in accordance to the value of the work done in a straightforward manner, and as labor historians have shown, setting low wages for women helped to *create* the idea that women's work was less valuable than men's.[11]

Closely linked to the idea of women's innate capacity for detail work is the notion that they have natural skills in communication and empathy, making them ideally suited to care for others. Here the research of Arlie Hoschchild on emotional labor has been invaluable in understanding the work performed by those in public-facing roles and is directly relevant to the film industry. Hoschchild defines emotional labor as that which "requires one to induce or suppress feeling in order to sustain the outward countenance that produces the proper state of mind in others."[12] Using the example of the flight attendant, Hoschchild shows how those in that position are required to perform "service with a smile" in order to deliver on the airline's promise of a positive travel experience for its customers. This must be performed effortlessly, as "part of the job is to disguise fatigue and irritation; . . . otherwise the labor would show in an unseemly way."[13] Such emotional labor has an exchange value—it can be "sold for a wage"—but it also places an emotional responsibility on the worker when they carry out their everyday duties. Emotional labor relies on the performance of caring skills (empathy) and the ability to manage emotions, both within the self and others, and is central to the service and welfare industries (nursing, social work), which are dominated by women employees.

Many of the jobs undertaken by women in the film industry are service roles connected to the welfare and care of others, and, as such, the industry has relied heavily on the emotional labor of women in order to succeed. The continuity girl, production assistant, personal secretary, and wardrobe mistress have to display tact and diplomacy, to remain calm in a crisis, and to manage on-set egos if they are to perform successfully in their roles. As this study will show, continuity girls were often at the sharp end of production, as it was their job to tell other crew members—tactfully yet firmly—when something was wrong. Personal secretaries were often given tasks that bridged the public-private divide, such as buying gifts for the director's wife or, more dramatically, being asked to procure an abortionist, a request that compromised them both legally and morally.[14] Wardrobe staff, who worked closely with actors, were responsible not only for dressing stars but also for ensuring the performer arrived on set in the right frame of mind to face the camera. And even those in postproduction roles, such as editors, had to be able to work indirectly through persuasion and suggestion. As editor Anne V. Coates described it, women were well equipped to handle the director in the editing suite because they were good at "disagreeing in a certain way"—that is, avoiding direct confrontation, a skill they had learned, she claimed, through managing "cantankerous personalities" such as husbands and sulky children.[15] Emotional labor and the caring skills, resourcefulness, and discretion that foster good interpersonal relations are an essential part of moviemaking— "the grease which oiled the studio machine"—yet they are rarely recorded in official archives or studio records.

Film Historiography

The myths surrounding women's work as unskilled or biologically determined have been compounded by established film historiographies that work against bringing women's labor into view. This is because they privilege the director as the organizing principle for film scholarship, building as it does on the cherished notion in Western culture of the romantic artist as individual genius. This model is predicated on the concept—or conceit—of a single creative vision and clear authorial signature that can be traced across a body of work. Indeed, the production of a substantial oeuvre comprised of multiple works across several years, and preferably decades, is the motherlode of auteur studies. This model of author/auteurship—which also drives publishing and film festivals—favors men and male-defined notions of long, uninterrupted careers, where success can be measured through screen credits and industry awards. As such, it is poorly equipped to deal with women's participation in film industries or indeed most forms of production, cultural or otherwise. The expectation of what feminists define as "continuous work histories" is the cornerstone of industrialized societies, a model that positions "full-time life-long commitment to employment with minimal responsibilities beyond the economic" as the norm.[16]

This is not women's norm, where the working lives of many were shaped by child care and domestic responsibilities, with employment patterns that varied over the life course. More typical are what social historian Penny Summerfield describes as "episodic" waves of working, where career and family alternatively take center stage in a woman's life.[17] Priority within this model could shift within a relatively short time span. Editor Monica Mead (discussed in chapter 5) used the term "episodic work" to describe contract working in the 1950s, where she typically worked for four or five weeks and then had a few weeks off, a pattern that characterized her working life during the years when her children were growing up. Other women chose professions like editing because, unlike directing, it did not demand extended periods of concentrated effort. Women did not lack stamina, but rather, as Virginia Woolf observes, women's lives are "always interrupted. . . . [They] never have a half hour . . . that they can call their own."[18] Interruptions have real, material consequences. Catherine Martin's research on executive secretaries shows how their working week was a mix of high-level and mundane tasks where "the constant interruptions caused by . . . secretarial duties, ma[de] it difficult . . . to gain more specialized skills or earn promotions."[19] Women's workdays are interrupted and interruptible because their work is deemed secondary to the needs of others. Subtle forms of discrimination are built into the very structure of the roles women perform, their time never their own but always at the service of someone else.

We can see this laid bare in the context of the film industry, where there are innumerable examples of women working intensely in film production for relatively short periods of time (five to six years) before leaving the industry, or shifting from one role (director, producer) to another (editing, writing) on the grounds that it fit more easily around children. Joy Batchelor moved from animation into scriptwriting, art director Peggy Gick from features into shorts and commercials, while editor Lusia Krakowska left the film industry for teaching, where she specialized in the care of children with autism. These women, and many others, several of whom are discussed in this book, did not disappear from professional life, but they do have track records that look different from a male-defined norm, with shorter filmographies, often across different media. This makes it difficult to fit them into the gendered frameworks of established film historiography.

How, then, might we address women's absence in film history? This study offers three mechanisms to tackle the problem. First, it mobilizes the concept of the episodic or interrupted career as a lens through which to recover women's occupational labor. Second, it draws on a criterion of success that contextualizes women's achievements within discrimination. Women at all times worked in a male-dominated industry where their labor was valued differently from that of men, and their seemingly "modest" achievements should be understood in this context. Finally, it adopts a more flexible, inclusive model of creativity to accommodate the many and varied tasks women undertook in the performance of their professional duties in below-the-line roles. To do this, I draw on Hoschchild's concept of emotional labor and on two other, less commonly used definitions of "creativity" and "art." One is Elizabeth Nielson's study of costumers, where she found in their accounts of their work an expression of creativity that was "synonymous with resourcefulness . . . a kind of spontaneous adaptability . . . to make do in a hurry with very few resources."[20] I have found this description of resourcefulness-as-creativity a useful way to understand the many ingenious approaches women brought to their working lives, and I use it to recover their work as a form of creative labor. The other is the work of cultural theorist Raymond Williams, who shows how "the original general meaning of art . . . refer[ed] to any kind of skill."[21] This study adopts that definition of skill-as-art and uses it to reposition aspects of women's labor as forms of creative endeavor. My aim here is to show how, by retuning our critical bandwidth into different measures of "a career," "success," and "creativity," we can undo the rigid distinction between creative and noncreative that has excluded women from notice and begin to tackle the related problems facing film history.

Methodology and Materials

There are many innovative approaches to the study of women's film history, not least in cinema of the early period, where scholars have drawn across an impressively diverse range of traditional and often less orthodox sources, including gossip, shipping records, cookbooks, and marginalia.

This process has not only helped to bring women filmmakers into view; it has also opened up questions of evidence and the gaps and silences in the archive.[22] But much scholarship of women in early cinema focuses on senior creative roles (directors, screenwriters, producers), and other materials and methods are needed for a study of women as movie workers. Here studies of contemporary media practitioners provide a guide: research by John Caldwell, Vicki Mayer, Miranda Banks, and others who focus on production workers and production practices in clearly defined media industry contexts. These scholars of production studies typically draw on the traditions, protocols, and research questions of the social sciences, using questionnaires, surveys, interviews, ethnographic observation, and statistical data in their bid to apprehend the social life of present-day media practitioners. These methods focus on how media workers "form communities of shared practices, languages and cultural understandings of the world," the goal being to understand not individuals per se but how media practitioners as communities of workers function.[23] But production studies scholarship focuses on practitioners currently working in media production, and it lacks any historical dimension.

To investigate women in the historical movie workforce, we need a multidisciplinary approach that mobilizes the tools of traditional social sciences with those drawn from a humanities-based film history. To this end, this study brings three main data sources into dialogue: quantitative data (trade union membership records), qualitative data (oral history interviews), and the materials of traditional film history, principally trade and popular film press publications, memoirs, and other sources. Trade union records of the film industry provide empirical data about its workforce, oral histories open up people's experiences of work, while trade and press publications offer a sense of the conversation within the film industry of the day. These sources are discussed in more detail below. This study brings together the sensitivity to unorthodox forms of evidence that characterizes women's film history with a production studies approach to using interviews and statistical data to understand communities of media practitioners. By combining these different methods and triangulating across three main data sources, my ambition has been to draw a more empirically robust yet detailed and nuanced picture of women's contribution to film production than any single source or method could illuminate. This methodology is not about identifying an individual's agency through on-screen textual traces—indeed this type of film analysis is poorly equipped to understand the labor of movie workers—but instead functions to understand the roles performed by women in the film production workforce and the processes through which their collective efforts as workers supported the film industry's outputs. The study lays down a new history of women in a particular national film context, and while British in focus, the research process itself and the implications of its outcome—particularly relating to questions of method—have far wider international applications.

Describing Work: Trade and Press Publications

One of the more valuable sources of primary materials for this study has been press publications, both trade and fan—notably, *The Cine-Technician*, *Picturegoer*, *Documentary News Letter*, and other publications produced for those working or with an interest in the film industry. These publications feature personality profiles, photographs, advertisements, studio roundups, production plans, correspondence, and industry reports, all enlivened with rumor, anecdote, and gossip. *The Cine-Technician*, for example, was published by Britain's leading film trade union and reported not only on key developments in the sector (legislation, government directives, technological changes) but also on the marriages, births, and deaths of notable members of the workforce, as well as social events hosted for industry workers and their children. Sources such as these are not unmediated reflections but should be approached as windows onto the workplace cultures we wish to study. Their lack of impartiality and investedness has significant value for film historians, as, when read from a feminist perspective, they reveal how workplace cultures and their gendered norms, habits, and practices were constructed and contested for their contemporary readership. As Robert Allen and Douglas Gomery argue, trade publications, "being contemporaneous with the events they report . . . provide a sort of baseline chronology for institutional history," and when used in conjunction with other sources, they provide valuable contextualization for understanding women's work in film.[24]

Quantifying Work: Trade Union Records

Along with press and trade publications are the membership records of Britain's leading film trade union, the Association of Cine-Technicians (ACT). This collection of records provides key information about sixty-six thousand technicians accepted for membership between 1933 and 1989, the period of the union's heyday, of which twenty thousand can be classified as film technicians. The records cover a wide range of roles, from directors to negative cutters, men as well as women, and capture data about an individual's name, age, and marital status; the role they held, who employed them, in which department; and how much they were paid. The collection as a whole provides the first comprehensive and empirically based insight into the numbers of women (and men) working in the industry, the kinds of roles they filled, and the gendering of work sectors.

Labor records and employment statistics are a well-recognized source of data for social scientists and labor/economic historians. Feminist researchers have also used statistics effectively to demonstrate women's low levels of representation in the present-day media workforce and to leverage institutional/policy change, but they have been less readily used in film history. This might be explained in part by issues of availability and preservation but also by the types of film history that have dominated scholarship. An aesthetic study written through directors, genres, and film movements (for example, the French New Wave) would have little need for quantitative data of this type. These two factors are, of course, interlinked; the type of film history we write is shaped by the availability of sources, while the preservation of sources is shaped by the types of film history deemed worthy of writing about. But union records have considerable value for tracing the types of forgotten people that make up the bulk of the film industry's workforce.[25] At an immediate level, such records are a form of textual documentation of work, making women's presence in the historical film industry visible and their labor manifest. They can be used to examine structural differences in the workforce—for example, no men got their union ticket through the continuity role, and few women were recruited as sound technicians. In some respects, this confirms what is already known or suspected, but quantitative lists are a persuasive source of evidence, especially when advocating for institutional change. Natalie Wreyford and Shelley Cobb have shown in their research on women in the contemporary British film industry how "numbers gave some sort of credibility to the inequality" experienced by women, making it "speakable, and for some, more real."[26] Chapter 2 lays out in more detail the history of the union, its eligibility criteria, the job levels it accepted, and the impact of this for writing women's film history.

Organizational records offer more than just bare numbers, however. They have what archivist Caroline Williams describes as "rich contextual layers" through which we can glimpse not only an institution's internal dialogue but also how that was shaped by wider social mores.[27] The initial inclusion, and later exclusion, of fields such as marital status on the union's records reflects changing sensibilities and legal prohibitions and constitutes quite a sensitive index of the changes in workers' rights. Moreover, because the forms were completed by workers themselves, they allow us to see the occupational vocabulary they used. Some women used a feminine variant for a job title with a masculine suffix—"draftswoman" replaced "draftsman," for example—or constructed alternative feminine terms such as "editress." These are tantalizing traces of how women used the form to define or claim an occupational identity for themselves as women in a male-dominated business environment. Labor records work at both the macro and the micro level, allowing us to measure who did what and making visible tiny moments of individual decision.[28] Using labor records in this way and on this scale has not previously been attempted in histories of film industries, British or otherwise, and the data and synthesis presented here have the power to transform the field of study.

Qualifying the Work Experience: Oral Histories

Oral history brings a third dimension to our understanding of women's film work. Because women's experiences are often missing from, or misrepresented by, more traditional historical sources, feminist scholars have a long tradition of turning to oral history in their commitment to "uncovering and documenting women's overlooked activities in history . . . [and giving] voice to women who have not been heard."[29] As Polly Russell succinctly describes it, "Oral history methods disrupt traditional academic disciplines[,] and because disruption is central to the feminist project, the two often go hand in hand."[30] Women's individual work histories give new insights into women's experiences of work that, in turn, have the capacity to "reassert women's position as social actors and historical agents," challenging established historiographies that have too often marginalized their labor.[31] This study draws on oral history interviews—both newly recorded and legacy—with women film practitioners from a variety of roles, including continuity, editing, costume and wardrobe, animation, makeup, and sound recording. The interviews provide invaluable insight into the everyday practices, values, and cultures that shaped women's experience of the workplace. Oral testimony is particularly powerful for the ways it brings into view the different forms of emotional labor specific to the film industry. This includes not only descriptions of unpleasant tasks that women found delegated to them—production secretaries made responsible for relaying "bad" news between crew members—but also how those tasks were described. A continuity girl's recollection of being "in a state" over a misplaced prop and the possibility of a scene reshoot suggests how one of the principal functions of her job was to "worry" so that others did not have to.[32]

Archiving Women's Work: A Feminist Intervention

The decision to work with oral history was motivated by two feminist goals: (1) to put women's voices on the historical record, attending to descriptions of their work in their own words, and (2) to archive the recordings for future research and public dissemination, thereby creating a lasting record of their labor. To this end, the oral history interviews and the trade union membership records have been archived at a digital repository titled "Women's Work in British Film and Television" (available through learningonscreen.ac.uk).[33] Support for the repository came from public funds provided by the Arts and Humanities Research Council, one of the UK's leading research organizations, which also provided funds to support the research on which this book is based. Resources held in the digital repository will enable researchers to continue to map production histories in radically new and imaginative ways and to provide a body of evidence for women currently working in the media industries who continue to face gender discrimination and structural inequalities at work. Many women interviewees participated in the study because they were motivated by the idea of building connections between generations of women. For one interviewee, "If they [women] aren't going to talk about it, how is anyone going to know about it?" Another one said, "History is important," as we learn through "the mistakes and successes" of the past.[34] The goal of restoring women to history is also the goal of "restoring history to women" and has been a powerful drive in feminist methodology.[35] As Caroline Ramazanoğlu argues, "Feminist research is politically *for* women; feminist knowledge has some grounding in women's *experiences*, and in how it *feels* to live in unjust gendered relationships."[36] These principles have been at the heart of the study and its commitment to record and disseminate women's oral histories. The oral recordings have enabled present-day practitioners to explore their occupational heritage and understand the historical roots of current working practices in their industries, where vertical and horizontal sex segregation remain rife. As historian Joan Sangster has persuasively argued, such forms of labor history, which emphasize wage work and unions, are "far from passé, they seem all the more urgent as we witness the global degradation of human labor amidst neo-liberalism."[37] In an era when the institutional sexism and discriminatory practices of the media industries have been sharply exposed, we need histories of women's work—their skills and contributions, battles and successes—more than ever.

Scope and Structure

This study covers the period between 1930 and 1989, as it was during these years that the film trade union had the greatest influence over women's work in the industry. It ranges across features, shorts, and documentaries (both live action and animation), which reflects the union's own reach across multiple sectors of production. This approach was chosen in order to make best use of the available trade union records and to explore the extent to which different production sectors offered women different opportunities for, and experiences of, work. It also allows a more comprehensive picture to emerge than has previously been possible and brings into view points of connection between women engaged in seemingly diverse tasks—for example, placing women's paint and trace work in animated shorts alongside continuity on feature films. Given the book's broad remit and the wealth of new primary materials on which it draws, some clear organizing principles have been necessary. Different jobs and work sectors are put in the spotlight at different historical moments rather than tracking a handful of roles longitudinally. The work of the continuity girl in features is highlighted in the 1930s, for example, while the animation industry's paint and trace girls are at the forefront of the 1950s chapter. These principal foci are set in the wider context of women's film work in the respective decades. The decision to adopt a spotlight approach was shaped by a number of factors, including existing scholarship, the availability of additional evidence beyond trade union data, and a commitment to extend knowledge and understanding of women's work across the fullest possible range of roles. This method allows patterns to emerge that are sensitive to both stable and new areas of employment for women. It also provides a greater number of potential connections for present-day media practitioners whose working lives continue to be shaped by the gendered legacies of historical working practices.

Chapter 1 opens by laying out the historical emergence of the film trade union and how its organization worked to favor men's labor at the expense of women's. The characteristics of the union's membership records are then described in some detail, together with an account of the data management principles that guided the study. The chapter then analyzes the number of women granted union membership and their commonly recurring roles, tracing their patterns of employment and placing that information within the wider context of shifts in the film industry. This analysis is organized by the six main categories that comprised the film industry: Floor; Research, Development, and Publicity; Art and Effects; Camera, Sound, and Stills; Cartoon and Diagram; and Postproduction.

Chapter 2 sets women's work in the context of a production boom in the British film industry in the 1930s, a time when the sector was modernizing after the introduction of sound and film studios were keen to create a new image of themselves. I show how they achieved this by linking the modernization narrative to masculinity in fan and trade publications and sidelining women and their labor in the process. It then moves on to examine women's labor in costume, continuity, and editing/negative cutting—jobs that have come to define popular understanding of women's contribution to sound-era cinema. It recounts some of the skills required to succeed in these roles and the processes through which they were assigned secondary status in film production hierarchies.

Chapter 3 continues the theme of secondary status by examining how this played out in the 1940s, a decade dominated by the Second World War and an official address to women to join the workforce as reserve labor. In the service film units, I show how women "free[d] a man for the fleet" by taking over roles in editing, projection, photography, and animation, while their work as assistants in art departments kept the "back room" of Britain's film studios functioning. This chapter also draws on the experience of women in documentary directing to introduce the concept of the episodic-interrupted career as a defining characteristic of women's employment. I use the concept to illuminate the multifaceted nature of women's occupational profiles and, in doing so, disrupt the dominant, male-defined narrative of the continuous work history as the key indicator of career success.

In Chapter 4 the focus shifts to the 1950s and women's experiences in publicity, animation, secretarial, and editing positions (specifically for the nonfiction market). In a decade dominated by debate about women's place in the workforce, relative to the home, this chapter uses women's accounts to trace multiple instances of occupational autonomy and the performance of skilled labor, revealing not only how women sought out and secured avenues for professionally satisfying work but also how their careers bring into view forms of creativity that have been neglected in existing film histories.

Chapter 5 examines the experiences of some of the first women who broke into the male-dominated domains of makeup and special effects in the 1960s, the "pioneers" of their day. Case studies reveal how women managed to establish an initial footing in these professions in the face of entrenched sexism in the feature film industry and the hostile tactics of the trade union. This chapter also puts women's work in costume and wardrobe departments in the spotlight, opening up the idea of resourcefulness-as-creativity, and explores how the world of commercials, supporting the

rapidly expanding television sector, offered new opportunities to different groups of women, affording some of them considerable professional
autonomy.

Chapter 6 focuses on the 1970s and 1980s and continues the theme
of women in male-dominated positions, extending it by contrasting the
experiences of women in the feature film sector with those who actively
built film communities outside mainstream production. Focusing first on
women in camera and sound jobs, it explores how—in the words of one
woman—they faced the choice of either "fitting in or fighting" and the
strategies they adopted to survive in a macho working environment. It
then moves on to examine women's experiences in the workshop sector,
a unique feature of the decade's film culture, which supported cross-job
working, media education, and training. Through a focus on the themes of
child care, women-only spaces, class, and ethnicity, this chapter explores
the possibilities, and limitations, of work outside the mainstream film
industry. It also opens up the intersection of gender, ethnicity, and sexuality and argues for a wider recognition of Black women's pedagogy in film
history.

A recurring theme in this study—and feminist history more broadly—is
tracing connections across different generations of women and examining
where experiences coalesce and diverge with the goal of bringing about
change. Historian Joan Wallach Scott's argument about mobilizing the
past to imagine a different future has been a guiding principle for my
research.[38] The book closes with an account of working with oral history
in a dialogue with young women at the beginning of their careers in the
media industries. It shows not only how the present continues to be shaped
by legacies of the "past" but also how women are using the past to shape
their futures as producers of media.

1
Organizing Work
Gender and the Film Trade Union

This chapter opens with an outline of the general contours of the British film industry, providing orientation for the nonspecialist reader. I then sketch out the historical emergence of the industry's leading trade union, the Association of Cine-Technicians, before analyzing its evolution and how it favored men and their work at the expense of women in the workforce. The next section describes the chief characteristics of the ACT's membership records, which comprise one of the key data sets for this study, and outlines the methodology used to work with this material. The remainder of the chapter lays out an analysis of the women granted membership of the ACT for the six decades between 1930 and 1989. This discussion is structured into six main categories: Floor; Research, Development, and Publicity; Art and Effects; Camera, Sound and Stills; Cartoon and Diagram; and Postproduction. The analysis highlights the patterns of discrimination and opportunity for women in the context of technological and market shifts and trade union changes across the era.

The British Film Industry

In over a century of filmmaking, British film production evolved from the artisan, family-run business model of the early twentieth century to a large-scale established industry with studios, production companies, laboratories, distributors, and movie theater chains. Most commentators characterize the industry's history as turbulent, its screens dominated by Hollywood films against which domestic production would always struggle to compete, and in this respect it is no different from any other European cinema, notwithstanding local differences in state aid/investment. It survives, and intermittently flourishes, by producing a mix of low- to mid-budget films, a small number of which enjoy international success. Notable points in the British industry's history are the 1940s, when the conditions of war meant that domestic films were in high demand; the 1960s, when an influx of American money bankrolled a number of high-profile, international coproductions; and the 1970s, when an economic crisis left the film industry close to collapse. Production levels in commercial feature filmmaking varied dramatically: twenty-six in 1926, two hundred in 1933, on average sixty per year in the 1940s, to around fifty in the 1980s.[1] In addition to features, the industry has produced several thousand documentaries, shorts, and cartoons during its long history. At different points in the industry's history, large vertically integrated companies have led the market: the Gaumont-British Picture Corporation in the 1930s and, in the 1940s and 1950s, the Rank Organisation and the Associated British Picture Corporation, which owned studios, production and distribution companies, and an extensive chain of movie theaters. Along with the majors there existed a proliferation of smaller production companies or units that came and went across the twentieth century with some—Ealing Studios, Gainsborough Pictures, Two Cities Films, Hammer Film Productions—more long-standing than others. Films in Britain were made in studios at Pinewood, Shepperton, Islington, Denham, and Elstree—all located in Greater London—with film being processed at specialist laboratories in West London. The bulk of the film industry was, and remains to this day, concentrated in one geographic area of the country, which allowed for relative ease of movement between studios, companies, and indeed other creative industries, such as theater, located in London's West End district.[2]

Protecting the Workforce: The Creation of the ACT Union

The industry, while never on the scale of Hollywood, still required a substantial workforce with specialist experience in all areas of production—from props, lighting, and wardrobe to the editing, grading, and printing of film. Some crafts were specific to the film industry—lighting, photography, set construction, and directing—while other craft specialties were adapted to meet the particular needs of filmmaking such as costuming and makeup. The scale of the film production workforce was of sufficient size to attract questions about how best to organize its labor. These debates go back to the late 1920s, when the government introduced quota legislation to encourage cinemas to show British-made films after the introduction of sound. This led to a sharp increase in production, which put pressure on existing film personnel, who, by the early 1930s, were reporting a marked deterioration in working conditions. As one cameraman described it, crew were now expected to work "without proper breaks, night and day . . . often to the point of illness."[3] To meet demand, studio heads began to recruit additional personnel—some local, others from abroad—cameramen initially from America and, later, film technicians fleeing Nazi Germany, dubbed colloquially "foreign technicians." With a rapidly expanding workforce operating under poor working conditions, some in the industry called for protectionist measures, and it was these factors that led to the formation of Britain's first trade union for film production personnel.[4] The Association of Cine-Technicians was formally registered as a trade union in 1933. By 1956 it extended its reach to television technicians, renaming itself the Association of Cinematograph, Television, and Allied Technicians (ACTT). It remained the most powerful force governing labor relations in the British film industry until the 1980s, when changes to legislation, training, and technology combined to weaken its control. By 1991 the ACTT had merged with BETA (Broadcasting and Entertainment Trades Alliance) to form BECTU, the Broadcasting, Entertainment, Cinematograph and Theatre Union. While BECTU continued to represent film production personnel, it did so under increasingly difficult circumstances (freelance economy, antiunion legislation), which limited its effectiveness to negotiate pay and working conditions.[5] This study focuses on the years between 1930 and 1989, as this period of time covers the emergence, establishment, and decline of the union, which set the conditions under which women's (and men's) work took place.

Gender and the Union

The ways in which the ACT organized and represented the workforce had particular and gendered consequences for film personnel. As one of ACT's founding members, Sidney Cole, described it, the original concept behind the ACT was "not so much a trade union approach in the narrow sense, but that technicians should get together in order to establish their identity in relation to the people who employed them"—that is, film studios. Labor historian Michael Chanan rightly describes this is as "a craft or guild concept."[6] This decision led to the union developing three distinct characteristics. First, directors and producers were in the same union as the rank and file they employed; this is, as Iain Reid demonstrates, one of the "peculiarities" of the British film industry.[7] Second, the ACT was effective in establishing a "closed shop," which meant all film technicians had to be members in order to work. This included those in senior creative roles, such as director and producer, to the rank-and-file clapper loaders, production secretaries, and continuity girls. Finally, it prioritized the interests of male workers, effectively building discrimination against women into the system by putting in place structural barriers that were almost impossible to surmount. This is because craft unions operate by enforcing rules of entry, typically through commonly agreed upon definitions of skill, complex systems of grading jobs, role specialization, and requiring workers to serve an apprenticeship, often for a number of years. They do this, as sociologist Sylvia Walby argues, to "retain the scarcity of their labor, and thus the price at which it could be sold."[8] This system of craft control is not inherently biased against women but rather, as Walby explains, "it does facilitate the adoption of specifically patriarchal forms of closure to a greater extent than other workplace organizational strategies."[9] Basically, it provides traction for gender discrimination to take hold. Moreover, as economists Anne Phillips and Barbara Taylor argue, "Skill definitions are saturated with sexual bias" rather than objective assessments of training and ability, with skill "often an ideological category imposed on certain types of work by virtue of the sex and power of the workers who perform it."[10] One oft-repeated example they give is of women producing boxes being classified as unskilled labor while men assembling cartons in the same industry were considered semiskilled. Scholars like Walby and others have demonstrated how these "patriarchal forms of closure" operate across a diverse number of crafts and industries, from metal trades to engineering, and my research shows that the film industry was no different. From the beginning it set rules of entry that privileged jobs and skills held by men, downgraded those possessed by women, and set in place occupational pathways and pay scales that were gendered. It was the ACT's organizing body, all men, who set the terms of the debate and defined the figure of the film technician in their own image. Three interrelated examples serve to illustrate the point.

"Low" Skill

First, women's skills and experience in majority-female roles, such as negative cutting, wardrobe, and continuity, were afforded less status and pay than jobs in camera, lighting, and other "technical" jobs that were predominantly held by men. This systematic downgrading of women's skills is reflected in the union's journal, *The Cine-Technician*, which rarely featured examples of women's work and, when it did, described it in pejorative terms. The role of negative cutting serves as an illustrative example. An essential step in the film production process, the job required skills in accuracy and timing, the ability to confidently manipulate a film joiner, and applying the exact amount of cement or emulsion to ensure that the film ran smoothly through the projector. Torn or snagged prints were the bane of exhibitors, and skilled negative cutters saved the industry significant sums of money in replacement prints. Male commentators in the pages of *The Cine-Technician*, however, described negative cutting as merely "routine stuff, done more often than not by girls with no pride or interest in their jobs, filling in time till they get married, or married women out for a little pin-money."[11] Such assessments reveal the sexual bias of skill definitions and had real material consequences for women, as the union was responsible for negotiating pay levels with employers. Moreover, characterizing women's work as "pin-money" shows how the bargaining position of the ACT was predicated on a male breadwinning wage that designated women's work as supplementary. As this study demonstrates, there were numerous examples where skilled jobs held by men—draftsman, camera operator, property master—were better paid than broadly equivalent jobs held by women, such as wardrobe mistress and production secretary. And if the union-sanctioned definitions of skill favored men, it was harder for women to make the case for promotion into more senior positions. As one production secretary observed, her role required her to deputize for the production manager, but the men around her did not "regard the job as an integral part of film making . . . [or] know how much responsibility production secretaries take and never give them credits in films."[12] It was in ways such as these that ideologically loaded definitions of skill that favored men were embedded in the union's organizational structure and pay scales.

Grading

Second, the ACT was instrumental in introducing a grading system into the film production workforce, and this also operated in ways that favored men. As film industries evolved through the 1900s and 1910s, more highly specialized job functions were created and refined over time, with unionization formalizing the process as it sought to categorize workers in a bid to strengthen its pay negotiations. By the 1940s the process was highly developed, with the ACT formally recognizing in excess of 120 different job grades, with titles such as "second" and "third assistant director," "second assistant cutter," and "assistant miniature scale sets" becoming increasingly common. Many of these grades are still in operation to this day (see appendix A).[13] Similar processes were under way in Hollywood, with Leo Rosten's 1941 study describing an "immensely ramified division of labor" where "producers found it necessary to create lieutenants and sub-lieutenants in the growing army of movie makers."[14] Greater demarcation in work processes led to a proliferation in job levels, and a gap opened up between men and women in terms of levels of pay and seniority, with women increasingly clustered into junior positions or specific areas of work. In the mid-1930s, for example, the job levels of "editor" and "assistant editor" in the British system were supplemented by a "chief editor" position, staffed entirely by men and at a salary double that of the editor. At this point women found themselves routinely classified as assistant editors under a job-level demarcation system that widened the gap between male and female workers in the editing suite and formalized assumptions about levels of skill and expertise and how it should be recognized and remunerated.

In this respect the film industry followed established patterns for employing women that were evident in many other professions. As Walby has shown, "The introduction of women clerical workers into the [British] civil service was accomplished through the creation of new grades for these women beneath those of established men." Using the case of women clerks, her observations are equally applicable to many industries, including filmmaking: "Time after time the expansion in the use of women clerks involved the creation of even lower grades with lower wages, fewer opportunities for promotion, less job security and lower status."[15] In this way an industry can expand by recruiting cheap female labor that does not directly compete with occupational positions already monopolized by men. This helps us understand the preponderance of women in low-level jobs in the film industry and how the system institutionalized vertical and horizontal segregation. Women were segregated into certain areas of work designated "female"—paint and trace, continuity, negative cutting—or clustered into the lowest-level jobs in the production hierarchy (typically defined by the prefix "assistant").

Moreover, the complex grading system meant that women could not fully benefit from the ACT's policy of equal pay. Although this policy had been in place since the 1930s, by 1975 industry researchers found that only 25 percent of women in the unionized workforce were covered in any real sense by equal pay agreements, because most were employed in women-dominated jobs.[16] As the grading system was itself gendered—with jobs done by women systematically undervalued—the claim of equal pay rang hollow. As one woman (a union shop steward) described it in 1973: "There's nothing so wonderful about a policy that says women senior engineers will receive exactly the same money as men. . . . If there aren't any women senior engineers in the first place . . . the policy of equal pay [will have] proven to be an empty one."[17] Her point is valid, and the union throughout its history trumpeted an equal pay mantra as a way of closing down debate and sidestepping its more systemic failings around women's wages.[18]

The grading system was also linked to the formal mechanisms of union representation. The union consulted its members through elected shop stewards who represented film companies, with additional committee members representing particular job positions to try to ensure that all interests had a voice. The disadvantage of this system, as industry researchers would later identify, "is that because women are concentrated into so few grades, they are likely to get proportionally fewer committee representatives per member."[19] So while women historically constituted between one-third and one-sixth of the workforce (as discussed later in this chapter), their representation as union officers rarely topped 10 percent.[20] This made it more difficult for women to influence the very mechanisms that would bring about change.

Training

Access to training was the third mechanism through which the trade union controlled entry to the profession. It formally acknowledged the film industry's existing in-house system where skills were learned on the job, with access to senior roles possible only for those who were recognized as apprenticed with experience in lower levels.[21] From the 1920s onward, for example, camera departments had operated a system whereby a "star" cameraman built up their own team, choosing individuals within it to train up to full-fledged status.[22] Under these conditions it was impossible for anyone outside the team to gain the type of experience that would qualify them for a camera position, and because women were never seriously considered as candidates for junior camera positions, they were effectively denied access to training. Moreover, as the example of the production secretary illustrates, even where women did have a relevant body of knowledge, it was not recognized as being apprenticed, or "time served," within the union's defined grading system.

Once these rules of entry were embedded in the union's structure, they became remarkably robust, organizing the film industry's labor in ways that had a negative impact on women. The rules were further maintained and policed by workplace culture. On the studio floor, in editing suites, the plasterer's workshop, and camera departments, male homosociality prevailed. This had its own languages, practices, and behaviors from which outsiders like women could be excluded. In this respect it was no different from other male-dominated occupational sectors, which, as feminist sociologists have shown, protect themselves from female entrants through "exclusionary practices" such as banter, swearing, sexist joke telling, and patronizing statements intended to undermine women's "self-confidence and sense of competency."[23] Moreover, women who take on jobs marked as "men's work" frequently find themselves targets for harassment (often sexual) and bullying. Women's oral history interviews in this book show how men employed exclusionary practices in the film industry, which were particularly striking in the areas of special effects and camera (see chapters 5 and 6).

As with all systems of control, power is never total or evenly distributed, and women's workplace fortunes varied temporally and by sector. The conditions of World War II witnessed certain relaxations around women's employment, opening up a broader range of film trades to them, while nonfiction filmmaking and commercials (lower forms in the production hierarchy) gave women greater scope for more senior creative roles than feature films, certainly in the 1950s and 1960s. And, of course, throughout the historical sound period, a small number of individual women in senior creative roles did buck the trend and played leading roles in Britain's film culture: documentarian Mary Field in the 1920s and 1930s, writer and director Muriel Box in the 1940s and 1950s, and animator Joy Batchelor in the 1950s, among others. But their successes in no way invalidate the evidence of structural inequality. For the most part, the rules of entry were remarkably effective in instigating and shoring up the gender segregation of the workforce, especially during a historical period when women were socialized to perform a supportive role in society. It was 1975 before the union itself formally identified structural inequalities in the workplace in its report *Patterns of Discrimination against Women in the Film and Television Industries*, widely recognized as a landmark study in women's labor relations. Identifying problems is an important first step, and small, incremental changes took place in the 1970s and 1980s, aided by greater access to training, which disrupted the established apprenticeship system. But as more contemporary studies show, women's employment in the media industries continues to be marked by gender biases and segregation.[24] What is less commonly recognized—and what this study evidences—is how much of this bias and segregation stems from systems put in place historically. These types of discrimination have shaped workplace traditions, practices, and habits that have outlived the demise of the closed shop and the deregulation of the media industries.[25]

It is only through engaging with this history that we can understand and tackle contemporary issues, a point I return to in my closing chapter.

Trade Union Records: A Methodology

While union systems disadvantaged women, one of the benefits for the historian is that they led to comprehensive record keeping. As discussed in the introduction to this book, labor records are a well-recognized source of data for analyzing the workplace, and the British film union holds a complete collection of membership application records dating back to the early 1930s. Because the union operated a closed shop, the collection is particularly wide-ranging, consisting of records for above- and below-the-line roles, including directors and producers, along with the many more rank-and-file jobs that made up the bulk of the film production and processing workforce. The collection provides a unique and previously unseen look at Britain's film industry and its workers.

Given the size of the collection, I want to outline here some of its salient features, as these are integral to the historical argument. Each person applying for membership completed an individual form that recorded key information about their job title, employer, rate of pay, and demographic data including sex, age, and name (see appendix A for a sample). There are scores of job titles recorded on the forms, including camera operators and assistants, stills photographers, continuity girls, editors, scenic artists, clapper loaders, negative cutters, publicity assistants, costume designers, printers, graders, positive assembly workers, draftsmen, boom operators, clerks, secretaries, and numerous others. Just listing these positions reminds us of the many people involved in the production process and invites us to look beyond the more common focus on the director, producer, and others in the small number of senior creative roles.

There are equally impressive numbers of employing companies. These range across major studios such as Pinewood, Shepperton, Gainsborough, and Rank, to the myriad number of smaller production companies that form the footnotes of film history. Workers in the film processing laboratories were also members of the ACT union: negative cutters, printers, and graders in companies such as Rank, Kays, Olympic, Technicolor, and Humphries, which collectively employed thousands of technicians. The union's reach extended beyond the feature film sector to companies specializing in the production of documentary, instructional, promotional, and animation shorts: Halas and Batchelor, Larkins, Shell, World Wide Pictures, Common Ground, and the Crown Film Unit among others. The collection also includes the records of camera operators, photographers, editors, and librarians working for newsreel companies like Movietone News; the cameramen employed by press agencies at Odham's and Horrochs; and the staff at the National Screen Service, which produced cinema trailers on behalf of the studios. These were joined in the 1960s by clapper loaders, directors, editors, and secretaries at companies like Ewart's and Garrett's, which specialized in producing advertisements for cinema and television. The ACT also represented television technicians who joined the union from 1957 onward, after the 1955 launch of commercial television in the UK.[26]

The collection in total comprises almost sixty-six thousand individual records, making it one of the most comprehensive in British media history and of significant scholarly value. Yet the total workforce involved in film production extends beyond the reach of even this collection, and there are two important exceptions to consider. First, a small number of film production jobs were represented by a rival union, the National Association of Theatrical and Kine Employees (NATKE). While NATKE's principal concern was representing workers from the exhibitors' sector (cinema projectionists, electricians, cashiers, ushers, etc.), a handful of workers in feature film production jobs held NATKE membership under a 1947 interunion agreement.[27] These included carpenters and joiners, plasterers, riggers, propmen, makeup artists, hairdressers, and those in wardrobe departments, although it excluded costume/dress designers, who were classed as members of the ACT's art department. For the purposes of a study about women's employment, this means that data concerning some of the key functions women performed in film production, especially hair and wardrobe, are not represented in the ACT collection. Unfortunately, there are no equivalent NATKE records to consult, as these have long since been destroyed.[28] A full list of the jobs held by members of the ACT and NATKE is included in the appendixes.

Second, although the film industry was a closed shop for much of the twentieth century, production companies were permitted to employ a small number of nonunion members in minor roles: runners, mail carriers, clerks, and production assistants among others. This was itself part of the apprenticeship system where those who undertook junior functions gained invaluable on-the-job training and would hope to eventually move up into a job that was fully unionized.[29] We can see this system reflected on individual membership forms, where an applicant is able to list, for example, two years' experience when they apply for union membership. But some in junior positions would not have made it to full membership, and it is impossible to quantify the total numbers of women and men in this category. The question of who is and is not included in the data set has implications for historiography, reminding us of how those whose labor was not formally documented can become absent from history. I have tried to balance this absence where possible through data triangulation, using oral history and other sources to bring women's work into view, especially in wardrobe and makeup departments.

Notwithstanding these caveats, the key strength of the ACT collection—and the value of its records for research—is that it encompasses a far wider range of the film industry's workforce than has previously been available to media historians. Given the size of the collection, it needed careful handling to be used meaningfully, and in this next section I briefly lay out the process I used for the study. Core data pertaining to position, department, employer, salary, gender, year of application, and union membership number was first extracted from the paper records and transposed into a Microsoft Excel spreadsheet. Next, the collection of sixty-six thousand records was sorted into four broad categories; Television, Film, Laboratories, and Miscellaneous. Television was the largest category, with just over twenty-eight thousand records; followed by Film, with just under twenty thousand records; Laboratories, with sixteen thousand; and a Miscellaneous category of two thousand workers.[30] My interpretation of "Film" was deliberately broad and included providers of essential ancillary services such as the development and hire of camera, projector, and sound recording equipment operators. This allowed me to include companies such as British Acoustic Films, which employed women in inspection and assembly roles.[31]

Once the four broad categories were populated, the twenty thousand film technicians were further subdivided into seven categories: Floor; Research, Development, and Publicity; Art and Effects; Camera, Sound, and Stills; Cartoon and Diagram; Postproduction; and Office. The core data from each membership record of the film cohort was then assigned to one of the seven subcategories. These categories broadly correlate with the union's organization of the workforce into shops and branches. Art and Effects were broadly craft-based (draftsmen, costume designers, scenic artists, and matte process artists), while Research, Development, and Publicity were writing-based roles and included scenario writers, readers, researchers, and all roles in the publicity department. The category of Camera, Sound, and Stills included lighting technicians, camera operators, clapper loaders, boom operators, and darkroom assistants, while Cartoon and Diagram included paint and trace workers in animation studios; title, lettering, and background artists; colorists; and animators. In the Floor category were directing, continuity, production, and casting roles, while the Postproduction category captured a broad range of functions pertaining to the editing, archiving, and distribution of film; the manufacture, maintenance, and repair of specialist equipment for the film industry; and process jobs in studios (print examination, repair, and assembly). The Office category included more than three hundred clerical support workers such as stenographers, accountants, bookkeepers, and invoicing clerks and is not discussed in any detail in this study. Once data from the records had been sorted and assigned to a category, searches and statistical calculations were performed. The material presented in this book, through charts and the main table in appendix C, is based on this data set.

The remainder of this chapter draws on this data to lay out a summary and analysis of the workforce in each major category. My focus is exclusively on film technicians, the twenty thousand union records in this category, of which just over five thousand came from women.[32] The following analysis focuses on those five thousand records and the patterns they illuminate about women's work in the historical sound era. The material is organized by the six major categories. Each category is prefaced with an overview of the function it performs within the production process, followed by a decade-by-decade description of the patterns of roles held by women and changes over time.[33] Within these, key names and micro case studies are used to give a flavor of a broad range of women's work in the film industry.

Trade Union Records: An Analysis

Floor

The category of Floor is responsible for getting the story filmed and has financial, administrative, and creative functions. It includes the roles of producer and director (plus assistants), continuity, production secretary, and casting (see appendix B). The producer chooses the story, puts the creative team together, and manages the budget, supported by production managers, production secretaries, and specialists in casting. This team is largely office-based. The director's team is based on the studio floor or on location, supported by first, second, and third assistant directors and continuity staff. Floor is the third-largest recruiter of unionized labor after Camera and Postproduction and, as with all sectors, has the greatest volume of intake coming through the supporting roles. The hours can be long, especially for directors and continuity staff, who often continue working after the day's shooting has finished. The percentage of women in the sector's workforce has historically been one of the highest, around one-third, and rising sharply in the 1980s to just over 50 percent as women moved into producing roles. But there are clear gender distinctions in the supporting roles—men in assistant director jobs, women in continuity and production secretary jobs—which, in turn, had an impact on the individual's career progression. Charts 1 and 2 show the number and percentage of applications by decade.

1930s: In the 1930s just under seventy women were accepted for union membership, most working at the bigger film studios as continuity girls or "floor secretaries" (a commonly used term in this decade). Their application forms show that most had several years' experience and were relatively well paid. The continuity role involved working at the director's side, taking notes and supplying him with detailed information about the shoot, and employing an encyclopedic knowledge of the script (see "Continuity Girl"

Chart 1. Floor: Numbers by Gender

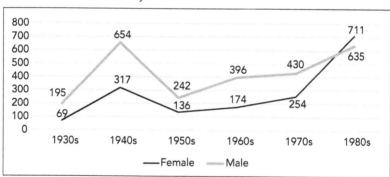

Chart 2. Floor: Percentage by Gender

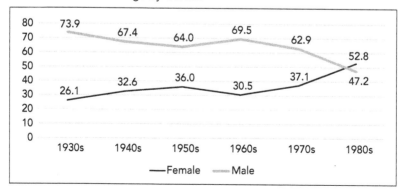

in glossary). The use of the occupational nomenclature continuity "girl" to address those in this position reflects how this was an entirely feminine domain: no men held the role in this or any other decade. Conversely, it was men, not women, who were recruited in droves as third, second, and first assistant directors. Here there was a clear progression pathway for men, who could move through these ranks, potentially into the directors' chair in due course, while no comparable career pathway existed for continuity girls, where the job was an end in itself. This is explored in more detail in chapter 2.

1940s: There was a spike in recruitment in the 1940s, in all sectors, as union membership was now compulsory as a result of the Second World War and the mass organization of labor. Almost one thousand workers joined in Floor positions, of which one-third were women, the majority of whom joined through continuity and production secretary jobs. If the continuity girl was the director's right hand on the studio floor, the production secretary performed a similar function for the production manager, who, in turn, supported the producer. Key to the role are outstanding organizational skills, as the production secretary has operational duties such as handling the unit lists and call sheets, which give order to the myriad routine functions that support a film shoot on a daily basis (see "Production Secretary" in glossary). As with continuity, this is a feminized position involving paperwork and people skills; two areas in which women were thought to excel.

Two new areas did open up for women in the 1940s—namely, casting and assistant directing. A dozen women joined as casting directors or assistants in the immediate postwar years (1946–48), most of whom were employed by big film studios like Gainsborough and British Lion. This emerging trend is discussed below. Additionally, two dozen women were employed in more senior positions in directing, or as studio/production managers, although always with the "assistant" prefix. Most had several years' experience in the film industry, suggesting they were formerly apprenticed women who were being promoted into assistant roles due to the wartime shortage of men. A few worked in features—Elizabeth Montagu at the prestigious London Film Productions, Louise Birt at the less salubrious Butcher's Film Service—but most were in documentaries. With modest budgets and small crews, it was easy to justify moving women into assistant directing roles, and they joined the ranks of established documentary directors such as Ruby and Marion Grierson.[34] The war did not set any precedents for women to be accepted into senior directing jobs in feature film production; that would have to wait until the 1980s.

1950s: In the 1950s total recruitment in the Floor sector dropped to less than half of the previous decade, but the proportion of women to men increased slightly as the demand for female labor (production secretaries) was higher than for jobs typically dominated by men. One woman joined the union as a director, the well-established Wendy Toye, whose acceptance into the ranks of British directors was exceptional. She joined Muriel Box—the only other woman directing features in Britain—whose long career is discussed by Sue Harper in her book *Women in British Cinema*. The majority of women's applications continued to be made through the production secretary role, with most employed by the larger studios, but even smaller companies and those specializing in nonfiction film were recruiting production secretaries, an essential part of the film studio workforce.

Market shifts saw further advancements in casting, an area that had first opened up for women in the 1940s. Film studios were now actively developing casting alongside publicity as part of their wider international ambitions, and several casting directors joined the union, including Peggy Smith at Twentieth Century Fox, Thelma Graves at Ealing Studios, and Jenia Reissar at Romulus Films. Women (and men) in these roles had first started to join the union in the 1946–48 period, and this trend continued in the 1950s and 1960s. Numbers are relatively modest—no more than twenty for each decade—and with equal numbers of women and men evenly spread across the casting director and assistant roles, labor in this sector was not yet vertically segregated by gender. Women's recruitment remained consistent in the 1970s and 1980s while men's all but stopped: the profession had become feminized. As the role combined "masculinised business tradition" with feminized clerical and communication work, women could be accepted into the role based on assumptions about their proficiency for typing and talking.[35] Once they had a toehold as assistants, women could move into the more senior casting positions being vacated by men who were moving into producing, a transition that was harder for women to effect. Over time, this trend became established in Britain (and Hollywood), and women gradually made the casting profession their own.

1960s: In the 1960s total recruitment went up by nearly one-third, although the proportion of women to men dropped slightly, as male labor in the assistant director position was in great demand. In this decade big studios jostled alongside smaller independents in an increasingly crowded marketplace that demanded features, commercials, and training films. This mixed economy had some benefits for women and there were interesting new developments. The majority of the union's intake were production secretary recruits, but in addition to these were thirty women joining as production managers, assistant directors, and directors, figures that are comparable to wartime levels. Here there seem to be three main routes of entry. Some women worked at small companies specializing in nonfiction and had worked their way up from production secretary roles to producer/director, a route that was possible in shorts but not features. Others were part of husband-and-wife partnerships, most notably Joyce Chittock, whose husband was a well-known producer/director and industrial films correspondent for the *Financial Times*. The husband named the company John Chittock Productions after himself, but Joyce described herself on the union form as the company's production manager and equal partner. At a time when it was difficult for women to get a bank loan in their own right, naming the family company after the male partner was the only option in the face of discriminatory business practices. The exact nature of Joyce's involvement is difficult to establish, a well-recognized problem when researching women's film histories, where their contributions are often concealed by more publicly visible male partners whose labor is easier to record.[36] Finally, women joined the union in more senior creative roles after gaining several years of experience abroad or in acting. These included Mai Zetterling and Estelle Richmond, both of whom moved into directing in the early 1960s after acting careers in British films, and director Midge Mackenzie, who learned her craft directing television commercials in New York and would later direct the drama-documentary *Shoulder to Shoulder* (1975) about British suffragettes. In sum, the profile of these and similar women illustrates a broader point about how women came to hold senior executive roles in the British film industry at this time: prior experience, gained abroad or in acting; familial relations; and, for most, employment in the documentary/nonfiction sector. Moving into directing in any capacity in the features sector was an opportunity that remained closed to women.

1970s: This pattern continued in the 1970s with steady recruitment in production secretary/assistant roles along with women elbowing their way in as producers, associate producers, and, very occasionally, directors, carrying on the fledgling trend that had started in the 1960s. Women came to these more senior roles through particular routes. Some had their own companies, often co-owned with a husband/family member, such as producer Joan Cherrill, working at Roger Cherrill Ltd., another company named after its male partner. Other women were moving into film after several years working in television; producers Elspeth Kennedy and Glynis Sanders and directors Caroline Goldie and Judith Williamson fit this pattern. In total almost fifty women joined the union as producers, associate producers, or directors during this decade, some working in features, many more in what were deemed the lower levels of the production hierarchy: shorts, documentaries, educational films, children's films, and commercials. As Harper claims, some may have been hired on a contract basis for their organizational skills rather than as producer-auteurs, but there is a sense that a broader range of jobs were opening up for women in this decade.[37]

1980s: In the 1980s Floor became the largest recruiting category of all sectors, outstripping even Camera and Postproduction in terms of union applications processed (just over 1,300 applications in total to this category). This was due, in part, to production levels and a softening of rules for admission to the union, but real growth was also taking place in women's employment in this sector. Just over seven hundred women joined through Floor positions, finally rebalancing the workforce in women's favor. The majority (approximately five hundred) were production secretaries/assistants, continuing trends that had been in place for several decades. Women continued to perform strongly in casting, with thirty joining the union this decade compared to only one man. By now this occupation was a female stronghold in terms of not only recruitment but also in company ownership, with many casting assistants joining women-owned companies such as Jill Pearce Casting, Anne Henderson Casting Ltd., and the company set up by the renowned casting director Susie Figgis. Broader changes to the position of women in society were finally being felt in the film industry.

But the biggest change was that almost two hundred women joined the union in some sort of "producing" or "directing" capacity—namely, producer, associate producer, production manager, director, second assistant, or third assistant director. In addition to the now established pathways that we have seen in earlier decades, there were three new developments. In the area of producing, union records show that some women were now able to start careers in nonunion roles such as general "assistant" and work their way up to associate producer and then producer. This was the case for Sarah Radclyffe, whose application for union membership was endorsed by director Derek Jarman, with whom she had worked on *The Tempest* (1979). While such trajectories were a long-standing feature of the shorts and documentary sector (and continued to be so in the 1980s), they had rarely figured for women in the world of feature filmmaking. The difference now was that opportunities were made available to women through figures like Jarman, who were themselves outsiders to the film establishment. Radclyffe's case highlights how existing job pathways in producing became newly available to women in the 1980s.

In the directing field, women benefited from the policies of new funders, including the British Film Institute's (BFI's) Production Board, which supported alternative, art cinema in the UK. This was the case for the Czech-born, Royal College of Art–trained animator Vera Neubauer, who was accepted for union membership as a director in 1981 when the BFI funded her animated short *The Decision* (1981). Finally, a small number of women made some headway into the notoriously closed ranks of the directing culture in the feature film industry. This pattern is exemplified by Deborah (Debbie) Vertue, who was accepted for membership as a third assistant director in 1982 after three years working as a "runner," a general "dogsbody" role to the director. Vertue went on to earn a handful of credits on feature films before moving into television as a production manager. Hers might seem a modest achievement until we remember that such roles had been practically closed to women since the Second World War. Getting a start in what were established transfer pathways for men—from runner to third assistant to second—was a new and welcome achievement in the 1980s, although Vertue's eventual shift into production management rather than film directing suggests how pathways continued to be gendered. Getting in is hard enough; getting on can be even harder.

Looked at in general, we can see that women were the linchpins of the Floor sector, especially in the continuity and production secretary roles, which supported producing and directing. These roles gave them a deep, grounded understanding of filmmaking, but they could not progress into more senior positions in the team, because the union's system of grading job levels did not recognize their professional expertise as valid training. Women were therefore stifled in terms of career advancement. In the face of those restrictions, they took what opportunities they could, and three patterns are evident. First, they took the continuity and production secretary roles and made them their own (see case studies in chapters 2 and 4). Second, they carved out an area of professional expertise in casting, blending interpersonal skills with business acumen. Third, they moved into the producer role through diverse routes and pathways that included working in nonfiction, forming creative partnerships with their husbands, and repackaging experience gained abroad or in acting/television. There is a huge amount of creativity by women in this sector who are laboring under innocuous job titles like "production secretary." The closing of the gap between women and men in the 1980s was partly due to the rise of independent filmmaking but also women's sheer tenacity; they had been doing the job under a different title for years. But even here men did not power-share the director's chair; instead women took over as producers.

Research, Development, and Publicity

Research, Development, and Publicity is a writing-based category that includes the roles of screenwriter, scenario editor, reader, researcher, publicity writer, and publicity assistant (see appendix B). Scenario and Publicity are relatively small departments for studios with less demand for workers than the more labor-intensive categories of Postproduction and Camera. These are office-based roles with relatively regular working hours, making it easier for women workers to balance their jobs with their domestic duties. While a handful of women (and rather more men) may get a screen credit for their writing, the majority of the labor is background work: reading, fact-checking, summarizing, editing, and producing copy that is accurate and engaging. It requires an attention to detail, a facility with language, and good all-around office (i.e., clerical) skills, and is some of the most invisible labor in the film industry, where a nondescript job title like "researcher" belies the skill involved and the contribution made to production. As the requirements of the job could more readily be fit to norms of femininity, the doors were open to women, especially in junior positions, and they constituted one-quarter of the union intake, rising markedly in the 1980s to approach nearer 50 percent. Charts 3 and 4 show the number and percentage of applications for those positions by decade.

1930s: In the 1930s recruitment in the Research, Development, and Publicity sector was small: only six women as opposed to twenty-four men. The low numbers can be explained by the union's strategy of focusing its energies on technical workers and the fact that scriptwriting was a relatively new profession in Britain. The women recruits were in research and development roles—writers, readers, and scenario editors—occupations that had traditionally been more open to women in film production, if

Chart 3. Research, Development, and Publicity: Numbers by Gender

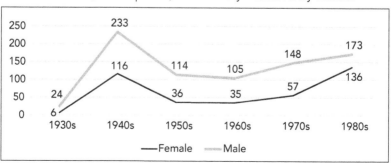

Chart 4. Research, Development, and Publicity: Percentage by Gender

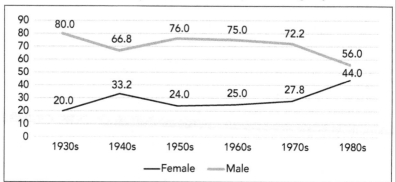

only because of their presumed expertise in addressing cinema's female audience. We know from screen credits and trade press that there were many more women active as screenwriters during this decade, including industry leaders Lydia Hayward, Marjorie Gaffney, and Alma Reville. It is likely that supporting roles in the workforce were also filled by women who spent their time systematically reading, summarizing, and occasionally polishing the writing of others with little expectation of a screen credit. The studios had to respond to the new demands for dialogue that the introduction of sound had placed on them, and women were a reliable source of labor that the union had yet to organize.[38]

1940s: There was a noticeable spike in applications by both women and men in the 1940s, brought about by the demands of World War II and the now compulsory requirement for union membership. Women now made up one-third of the union intake to the sector: 116 recruits in total. A small number of women joined through scriptwriting roles, and indeed scriptwriting continued to offer career opportunities to women, but these jobs did not reflect the majority of the sector's activity. Instead, there were two distinct patterns to the recruitment of women that set a trend for the next two decades. In the first half of the 1940s, most women were joining the union through scenario department roles, as researchers, readers, and assistants, many at Ealing and Gainsborough, two of the leading film studios of the day. In the second half of the 1940s, recruitment was driven by activity in the Publicity sector, part of a wider aspirational drive in the film industry to better promote its product and stars abroad. The Rank Organisation alone recruited sixteen women, and thirty men, to its publicity division in the 1947–48 period, and other studios and production companies were similarly active, albeit on a smaller scale. Publicity was a growth area in the film industry, and union records show both women and men being taken on in junior and senior roles.

1950s: These developments in publicity continued in the 1950s. Although the numbers of women dropped noticeably, down to only thirty-six in total, they continued to be accepted to publicity jobs as both assistants and full publicists. These included Mary Dipper, who had previously worked in Odeon's publicity division and listed her salary as "by arrangement"; clearly there was room for negotiation for those with the requisite skills and experience. The most senior women in publicity had several years of experience, which some had gained in journalism. Publicity was not a feminized domain, however; around thirty or so men also joined the union this decade in publicity roles. But the mix of men and women in the profession has its own history. The role's combination of storytelling and caretaking (especially of stars) was deemed appropriate for women, while traveling with the company as a unit publicist during shooting was thought to be better suited to men.[39] Career ladders within the profession were gendered, with men more able to use the role as a stepping-stone into other production jobs, while women were often stuck in assistant roles or moved sideways into a production secretary role. The opportunities and constraints of the publicity role are explored in more detail in chapter 4.

1960s: In the 1960s the total numbers and ratio of women to men remained consistent with the previous decade, but there were some changes to the types of jobs held by women. It was business as usual in terms of publicity assistants, with several young women joining the union, all of whom were employed by the bigger studios of MGM, Rank, and for Harry Saltzman, the coproducer of the increasingly popular James Bond films. But a new development was that ten women joined as researchers/writers, most employed by the government-funded Central Office of Information (CoI), which commissioned and distributed public information films and printed material on a range of health, education, and welfare topics. The women were time-served professionals, between the ages of twenty-eight and forty-six, who had previously held jobs in journalism, the civil service, or the BBC, and the CoI benefited from their expertise in information retrieval, fact-checking, and ability to write clear and concise copy.

In addition to researchers were half a dozen women who applied as screenwriters in the 1960s, often co-listing "director" in the job-level category. These included veteran American actress, writer, and producer Bebe Daniels, who came to Britain to work in radio in the 1960s, and the Italian Caterina Arvat, who wrote and directed a number of short promotional

films for British pop musicians in this decade. Others included writer/
director Mira Coopman Hamermesh, a graduate of the Slade School of Art
(London) and the Polish National Film School (Lodz), and Linda Moller,
who described herself as a "writer/director—and everything else too!"
What is noteworthy about these women is that they gained their experience abroad and did not work in British features; they either freelanced
(Hamermesh) or had their own companies (Daniels, Moller), albeit, in
Moller's case, small one-woman outfits. Mainstream studios of the 1960s
seemed to be stuck in the past, with little interest in developing women's
talents in writing.

1970s: Recruitment remained buoyant in the 1970s and almost sixty
women joined the union. The economic downturn in the British film
industry hit feature production hard, but it still needed readers, researchers, and publicity assistants, with women more prominent in the nonfiction field. The established patterns of recruitment of women to these
roles remained, and the Central Office of Information continued to be a
major employer of well-educated young women. Some women seemed
to have come up the hard way—one of them listed her training as "typing and making tea" before transferring to the role of reader, an example
that provides insight into the career pathways for women. Others could
circumvent the system if class privilege permitted; for instance, Lady Mary
Asquith joined the union as a research assistant for Theatre Projects Film
Productions. A member of the prominent Asquith family, her union form
reads like a veritable "who's who" of British cinema, her membership
endorsed by no less than Ken Russell, Nicholas Roeg, and Tony Richardson. Nepotism, always a feature of the British film industry, did occasionally work in women's favor.

1980s: The 1980s show a dramatic increase in recruitment; the total
number of union applications to the sector approached wartime figures,
with the numbers of women in particular increasing rapidly. More women
did not mean that men stepped aside from the plum screenwriting jobs.
Of the 136 women recruits to this sector, only a handful were scriptwriters, working for small companies or freelancing. They joined the ranks
of established directors such as Sally Potter and Zelda Barron, who were
scripting their own films as a way to retain creative control, a pattern that
could be traced back to the 1960s.[40] The majority of women—more than
100—joined the union as researchers, some working in the features sector, some for companies like Goldcrest Films, others for the independent
film cooperatives that proliferated this decade. But the biggest employer

of women as researchers was the nonfiction sector, with new specialist companies entering the market. Dragon Medical and Scientific Communications, which produced educational shorts on health topics, and Oxford Scientific Films, which specialized in natural history, were big recruiters during this decade. The records show that the women they employed were in their late twenties, some listing university degrees on their applications. This was not a feminized role, as equivalent numbers of men joined as researchers at these and similar companies, but the understanding of scientific and technical language that such positions required is something that should be more widely recognized in accounts of women's labor.

In sum, women were reliable recruits in the Research, Development, and Publicity sector, readily accepted as part of a workforce that needed skilled office labor to function effectively. Paying attention to detail, working systematically, and having a facility with language were all skills women were presumed to hold by dint of their sex, and union records show that companies were happy to employ them on a regular basis, with the proviso that they did not expect to progress to more senior roles in the creative hierarchy or receive credits for their work. For many women this may have been an acceptable trade-off for a job that could fit around domestic responsibilities. As market needs evolved and new employment areas opened up, women could be slotted into the workforce, as they were in publicity roles in the 1940s and 1950s and as researchers and writers in the nonfiction field in later years. It was this that accounted for the narrowing of the gap between men and women in the 1980s rather than any dramatic changes to the features sector.

Art and Effects

Art and Effects is a broadly craft-based category including roles such as art director, draftsman, costume/dress designer, scenic artist, matte artist, and special effects artist (see appendix B). The art department is one of the largest in the studio, and art direction (now known as production design) takes the lead in conceiving the "look" of a film world. Workers in this department have overall responsibility for designing and producing the sets in a film, including painted backdrops, costumes, and scale sets, and their work is closely connected with staff in the special effects department, particularly matte artists.[41] The hours are long and the demands of night work (setting up sets for the next day's shooting) make it a particularly difficult area for women with family commitments. Most of the time, women constituted roughly one-fifth of union intake in this category, mainly in a fairly narrow range of positions at the lower end of the pay scale, although the gap between women and men narrowed noticeably in the 1980s. Charts 5 and 6 show the number and percentage of applications for Art and Effects jobs by decade.

1930s: In the 1930s no women joined the union through Art and Effects roles; union membership in this decade was an all-male affair. The leading art directors of the day were men—Vincent Korda, Alfred Junge—as were the ranks of the art and effects departments, suggesting they recruited in their own image. The union records, however, are not the entire picture, and a small number of women did hold senior creative roles, including costume designers Gordon Conway and Doris Zinkeisen and art director Betty Langley, all sufficiently high-profile to feature in the fan and trade magazines of the day (see chapter 2). And further down the ranks were women in assistant/supporting roles, including Carmen Dillon, who

Chart 5. Art and Effects: Numbers by Gender

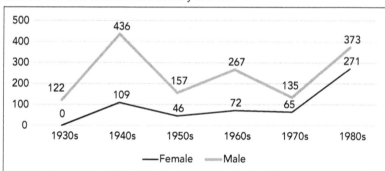

Chart 6. Art and Effects: Percentage by Gender

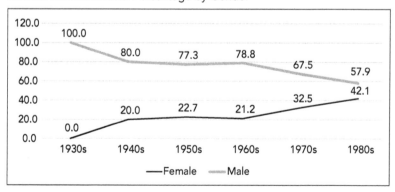

would go on to develop a substantial career as an art director. This begs the question of why these women did not sign up for union membership. For some, their work in the British film industry was short-lived (Gordon Conway, for example, returned to the United States in the mid-1930s), while others perhaps chose not to join, but that degree of optionality was to end abruptly with the arrival of the Second World War.

1940s: There was a sharp uptake in union applications in the 1940s, with just over one hundred women joining the union, alongside more than four hundred men. This major transformation was brought about by the Second World War, which had an impact on labor across all sectors of the film industry, because union membership was now compulsory. Transformation only went so far, however, as records show that the majority of women were joining in either costume or draftswomen roles, setting a pattern of recruitment that was repeated in subsequent decades. A smaller number joined as scenic artists, set dressers, and assistant art directors, including Carmen Dillon, Betty Pierce, and Peggy Gick. Draftswomen and assistants were recruited as part of a wider demand in the film industry for workers specializing in technical drawing, who were pulled into the drawing office, which was, in Pierce's words, the "real 'back-room'" of the film studio, tasked with translating the art director's vision and rough sketches into a comprehensive set of drawings from which the construction team would build sets.[42] Women remained overshadowed by male recruits, and none of the women recruits held the status of "senior" or "chief" draftsperson, roles that were entirely filled by men. Many were young women new to the industry and taken on to meet the wartime demand for instructional films. But others, like Dillon, Pierce, and Gick, who were trained as architects, held more senior roles, and it is likely that their responsibilities outstripped the "assistant" prefix attached to their job title (see chapter 3). Women's incursions into this area represent a modest breakthrough that continued in subsequent decades.

Applications by women in dress/costume jobs were significantly higher than their male counterparts, with twenty-three applications from women compared to three from men. Some of these were from designers such as Beatrice Dawson and Elizabeth Haffenden, who had well-established careers and were finally joining the union, while other women joined in assistant positions, including Phyllis Dalton, who would later establish a long career as a costume designer. All recruits through costume roles were made between 1946 and 1948, probably as a result of new union rules that brought these positions fully under the ACT's jurisdiction, but the level of experience recorded on the union forms demonstrates that all women, assistants and juniors, had been working through the war. It was the 1940s that established women's dominance of the costume field, with labor needs driven by film studios like Gainsborough, which specialized in costume dramas, one of the most popular genres of the decade.

1950s: In the 1950s the ACT's intake to Art and Effects roles dropped to around two hundred in total, although the proportion of women to men remained the same as the previous decade—roughly one-fifth. Records show that most women were taken on as background artists or painters and tracers for companies like Pearl and Dean Productions, which specialized in cinema advertising. A handful of women in costume design roles joined the union for the first time during this decade, but there was limited real growth in this area, as studios were making fewer costume genre films. Only one young woman was taken on as a costume trainee (at Pinewood Studios); the rest were established practitioners who primarily designed for opera and theater: Margaret Furse and sisters Margaret and Sophie Harris. It is likely that their union applications, now compulsory, were a consequence of one of their occasional forays into film rather than any sustained expansion in the film industry's labor needs this decade.

Other recruits to Art and Effects jobs included half a dozen women joining as draftswomen and a couple of puppeteers employed to work on children's adventure programs. They were the earliest recruits to what would become a significant employment area for women in the next decade. The draftswomen had just a few weeks of experience when they joined the union, but since they were in their mid-twenties, it suggests they had been in employment or training elsewhere before coming into the film industry. It is plausible that they were graduates of Britain's expanding art school sector, which offered a socially sanctioned route to young women with ambitions for further education at this time. There was certainly plenty of work in Art and Effects, with records showing draftsmen, matte and scenic artists, and title and lettering artists all signing up for union membership, but the sector was recruiting only men to these roles and seemed to have largely closed its doors to women. It was not alone, with sociologists of the day commenting that the "talent, experience and skill" of British women was being wasted across many areas of employment.[43] The union applications reflect this broader social trend, showing how women were being accepted into a narrow range of filmmaking positions now that the wartime exigencies had passed.

1960s: In the 1960s Art and Effects experienced growth in demand for its labor with nearly 350 new recruits joining the union, although the proportion of women to men—one-fifth—remained the same. Recruitment was driven by expansion in companies such as AP Films (later Century 21), which made the well-known series *Thunderbirds* (1964–66) and *Stingray* (1964–65). The demand for technicians with specialist skills in animatronics and special effects was a defining characteristic of 1960s filmmaking, with recruitment driven by the needs of big studios such as MGM and Eon Productions (which produced James Bond), as well as smaller companies including Hawk Films and Bowie Films. In terms of craft labor, it was once again men who benefited most from these developments. Scores of men were taken on across an ever widening variety of roles ranging from draftsman, graphic artist, assistant art director, matte artist, and costume designer to puppeteer, special effects assistant, model maker, and lip sync operator. As usual, the range of roles for women was rather narrower and clustered in three main areas: puppeteers, costume designers, and draftswomen. The recruitment of women as puppeteers continued a trend that had started the previous decade, but the 1960s saw a step up in the numbers of women, with sixteen joining as puppeteers or trainees. Most women were young, in their mid-twenties, with one exception, Geraldine Granger, who was taken on at a senior level. Granger had ten years' experience in the role and previous membership of both Australian and American Equity. Her union application highlights how experience gained abroad had currency with British film companies, mitigating gender discrimination when certain key craft skills were in demand (see chapter 5).

The area of costume design enjoyed a boost in this decade, with nineteen women joining the union, a mix of experienced personnel and juniors/assistants. Experienced practitioners included Doris Langley Moore and Jocelyn Herbert, women who primarily designed for the stage with occasional forays into film production as freelancers. But there were newer recruits, including Jocelyn Rickards, designing for the James Bond films, and Yvonne Blake, working on low-budget horror films. The upturn in costume recruits reflects genuine growth in the sector as production trends in the British film industry for historical fare (both fantasy and realist) put craft skills in costume in high demand, a trend that continued in subsequent decades.

The rest of the women recruits were either draftswomen or in relatively junior roles in art departments, including lettering artist, assistant, and set designer. But there was one new development in this decade: half a dozen women were employed as matte artists at either the big studios of Shepperton and MGM or the smaller companies of Hawk and Bowie. This role involved painting landscapes and settings onto glass, which were then integrated into live-action footage (see "Matte Artist/Painter" in glossary). Recruits included Joy Seddon (who became Joy Cuff upon marriage), who was art school trained and highly skilled, and that, combined with family connections, enabled her to break into a role that had been closed to women in the 1950s. Seddon and her peers were pioneers, breaking new ground on the studio floor, although, as chapter 5 discusses, this led to dire repercussions from sections of the male workforce.

1970s: The 1970s saw a marked drop in the total number of union applications to Art and Effects as the film industry experienced an economic downturn, with production levels in British studios shrinking. But, paradoxically, women accounted for a noticeably larger proportion of the Art and Effects workforce; now women made up almost one-third of the union intake. Despite the squeeze on production, women were still needed in the established areas of costume design and puppeteering (both makers and operators), and there were some important new developments in art design, with twenty or so women listed as assistant art directors or in similar roles. While the 1970s have been categorized as "a bleak period for women art directors," which witnessed the end of Carmen Dillon's long career, the union records point to some interesting emergent trends.[44] Assistant art director Margaret Ann Mollo (wife of costume designer John Mollo) joined the film industry in 1972, where she dressed the sets of iconic British films including *Theatre of Blood* (1973), and Katherina Kubrick (stepdaughter of Stanley) joined in 1976 as an art department assistant, most famously designing the iconic steel teeth for the character "Jaws" in James Bond's *The Spy Who Loved Me* (1977). Other notable recruits were Valerie Charlton, wife of Julian Charlton, whose production company made *Monty Python and the Holy Grail* (1975). Art school trained, she specialized in model making and visual effects, and her career—and on-set experience—is typical of many women of her generation. By her own account, she assisted in making props for films while simultaneously looking after the couple's children and making tea and sandwiches for the crew. She helped director Terry Gilliam with initial designs and prototype models for *Jabberwocky* (1977), only to lose the commission when the film's special effects supervisor, John Brown, insisted the work be undertaken by his men.[45] The model work was eventually returned to Charlton, but her experience is significant in that it reminds us how much of women's work takes place in the teeth of entrenched opposition and almost always in conjunction with domestic responsibilities. So there were small pockets of opportunity for women to be involved in art design in the 1970s, although the fact that these were achieved through creative partnerships between spouses and family links suggests there would be some way to go before parity of access was a reality for all women.

1980s: It was the 1980s that saw the highest number of women in Art and Effects: 270 in total, representing 42 percent of the total intake into this sector. The gap between women and men narrowed significantly in this decade as changes to union and labor laws in the UK ushered in a more casual freelance economy around film production. Eighty of the new recruits were in costume jobs, either designers or assistants, working freelance or attached to independent production companies. Many women (and men) were being accepted for union membership now on the basis of short-term contracts often lasting no more than a few months. Some of the costume women in this cohort transferred to ACTT from partner union NATKE, which represented wardrobe staff, while others had their form stamped "9c to grade," indicating their status as workers who already held union membership in what was designated a lower job level or grade. The growth in raw numbers hides the fact that there was much movement of labor in the costume field during this decade; many costume designers and assistants operated in a precarious working landscape, where a few months' work could be followed by periods of unemployment. This had further ramifications, leaving them with the decision of whether to continue paying membership fees or letting their registration lapse and hoping the ACTT would readmit them if and when film production work became available.

Women in art direction and design roles faced similar challenges, where short-term contracts were the norm. Several joined as full art directors in this decade, the best known being Gemma Jackson, whose one-month contract with Working Title Films in 1984 led to a number of important British features, including *Mona Lisa* (1986). She worked across film and television for the remainder of her long career (including multiple episodes of *Game of Thrones*, 2011–13) and indeed her application suggests how she and other women were hedging their bets when it came to work, listing "promos," "commercials," "video," and "shorts" on her union form alongside "features" as suitable areas for employment. Women, perhaps more than men, knew the value of adaptability at work. This was also evident in the role of "stylist," a new position that entered the lexicon in the 1980s. These were dual roles, with about two dozen women listing "stylist/set dressing," "stylist/assistant art director," or "stylist/costume" on their forms. All were self-employed, earning daily rates of pay, and it was mainly women's work; only four men listed some variation of stylist as their job during this decade. This suggests that some women responded to increasing casualization by reinventing themselves professionally, adapting their persona to suit the dictates of the market. And with the union's bargaining power weakened, it was in no position to police the traditional rigid job demarcations that previously would have made this initiative impossible.

In general, women performed two distinct functions in this sector: (1) as reservists in supporting roles such as draftswoman and assistant, and (2) as leaders in costume, both design and production. When new production areas opened up and created pressure for labor, such as animatronics in the 1960s, women took the opportunity to move into the workforce, populating the lower-level positions of matte artist and puppeteer. Readiness met opportunity again in the 1980s when rigid job demarcations seemed to soften in Art and Effects, and women, who had less invested in established creative hierarchies, were able to position themselves favorably in the marketplace. This, along with equal opportunity legislation, accounts for a narrowing of the gender gap in this sector; women moved from 20 to 40 percent of the workforce over the course of fifty years.

Camera, Sound, and Stills

Camera, Sound, and Stills is a technical category and includes the roles of lighting cameraman, camera operator, clapper and loader, sound recordist, boom operator, stills cameraman, and retoucher (see appendix B). The camera department is responsible for lighting a scene; camera placing and movement (including tracking, panning, and crane shots); choice of lens, filters, and film stock; and general maintenance. The sound department has three divisions—production, dubbing and scoring, and maintenance—with sound camera and boom operators recording dialogue and sound during shooting, while dubbing mixers post-sync additional dialogue, music, and special effects. The stills department produces specialist photographic images to be reproduced in publicity materials, including portraits of stars and action pictures of key scenes in films. The percentage of women in the sector's workforce has historically been the lowest in film production, usually between 1 and 5 percent, with no significant change until the 1980s. The only women permitted entry in this area were those in supporting/assisting jobs, often doing postproduction work on film stills. This sector, more than any other, is a boys' world predicated on sexist assumptions about men's natural aptitude with technology at the expense of women. Even the junior roles of camera assistant or clapper loader were jealously guarded from women, as these were seen as trainee positions for young men, and camera work in particular operated under a rigid apprenticeship system that denied women access to training. Recruitment blatantly targeted men through job notices that promised "Top salary for the right man" as rostrum camera operator.[46] Charts 7 and 8 show the number and percentage of union applications for Camera, Sound, and Stills by decade.

1930s: In the 1930s the ranks of the Camera, Sound, and Stills sector were largely closed to women. This was the single largest recruiting sector for men during this decade, with over eight hundred joining the union in some form of camera, sound, or stills job. By comparison, only a handful of women are present in the records, and all are employed in the stills department. Here they retouched film stills, and most worked at Gaumont-British, the leading studio of the day. Women "retouchers"—the occupational term used on their application forms—supported the work of a team of stills photographers and printers, all men. The job of

Chart 7. Camera, Sound, and Stills: Numbers by Gender

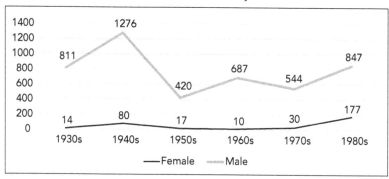

Chart 8. Camera, Sound, and Stills: Percentage by Gender

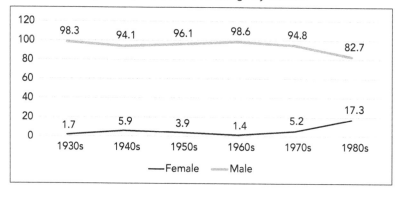

retoucher involves cleaning up the images and removing any flaws and blemishes; to succeed in this position, the retoucher needs a good eye for detail and familiarity with pictorial styles and the aesthetic sensibilities of a film studio. Only one man was taken on as a retoucher, which suggests the job was a female domain and was paid accordingly: typically, between one-quarter and a third of the salary of a stills photographer. The job of retoucher remained the most commonly held role for women in this sector for the next three decades.

1940s: In the 1940s there was a spike in recruitment, with union applications by women up to eighty in total, which represented just under 6 percent of all recruitment in the Camera, Sound, and Stills sector. This increase was entirely due to the Second World War putting pressure on male labor, and, as a consequence, the range of film jobs open to women did broaden this decade. Thirty union applications were from women working in stills photography as spotters, trimmers, and retouchers, while a small number joined in the more senior positions of photographer and photographic assistant, the most experienced being Ellen Sheridan, a stills photographer at Publicity Pictures. The remainder of the women—approximately two dozen—were employed in the camera or sound departments of British studios. This was a new development, with most British studios (Crown, Shell, Verity, Halas and Batchelor, Ealing, Gaumont-British, and others) taking on women as camera assistants or trainees. Some, like Sarah Erulkar and Rachel Judah (both at Shell), were part of a small cohort of Indian-born film technicians (men as well as women) who worked in the British film industry, with Erulkar going on to forge a long career in film production. However, these two dozen recruits were thinly spread, as individual film studios hired no more than one or two women into camera or sound positions in the 1940s. Even under the extreme circumstances of war, these remained jobs for men. Women's modest gains in this sector need to be understood in this context.

1950s: This change was not sustained in the 1950s, though, when applications by women dropped to their prewar levels. Only a handful were accepted for union membership, the majority employed in the feminine role of stills retoucher. However, applications by men to the stills department were similarly low during this decade, suggesting that overall recruitment in the Camera, Sound, and Stills sector had flatlined. There were four women taken on in junior sound jobs as boom operators and assistants, which represents some sort of progress, if only compared to their total absence from camera positions. But these were the lowest jobs in the creative hierarchy, where a "pleasing personality" was highlighted in trade accounts as more important than theoretical knowledge of sound technology, which goes some way to explain why women were tolerated in these roles.[47]

1960s: Things were even worse in the 1960s, when only ten women secured union membership despite the Camera, Sound, and Stills sector enjoying a spike in recruitment. This came on the back of American finance bankrolling British studios, which stimulated production growth, but it was men who benefited, leaving the politics of gender discrimination unchallenged. Women represented barely 1.5 percent of all applications to the sector this decade, an abysmally low figure even for an area that had a long history of shunning women's skills. Of these, seven were retouchers; one was a camera loader at a small company, Athos (Deirdre Tollemache); and another was a camera trainee at Rank Advertising (Karen Sully). Why these companies employed solo women alongside the majority-male workforce is unknown, and I have been unable to establish how their careers developed. The third applicant was the well-known fashion and documentary photographer Marilyn Stafford. American born, mentored by Henri Cartier-Bresson, and married to a British foreign correspondent, Stafford moved to London in the mid-1960s. Here she worked freelance for the *Observer* and as a stills photographer for feature films and commercials.[48] At the point she applied for union membership, Stafford was forty years old with an established reputation, so her appointment should not be seen as foreshadowing radical change in the British film industry. Indeed, it would be almost twenty years before the numbers of women photographers with union membership would reach double figures.

1970s: Things picked up in the 1970s, when the rate of women in the film industry increased to a figure comparable to that of the 1940s. This was a welcome move in the right direction but hardly groundbreaking given that it amounted to only thirty women compared to the more than five hundred men joining the sector. Five women were taken on as stills photographers, including the Finnish-born, British-trained Sirkka-Liisa Konttinen, who would go on to sensitively document working-class women's lives as part of the Amber Film Collective. Three women joined as rostrum camera operators and six as sound recordists or assistants, the most notable being Rosemary Eastman, who, with her partner, Ronald, specialized in wildlife sound and produced films for the BBC's Natural History Unit. And a dozen or so women were accepted as camera assistants and clapper loaders, the latter responsible for loading the correct film stock into the camera magazine (see "Clapper Loader" in glossary). Finally, a tiny number of women were getting their feet on the very bottom rung of the camera department ladder. This cohort included Diane Tammes, one of the first women to graduate from the camera course at the newly opened National Film School (1971) and who worked with Laura Mulvey on *Riddles of the Sphinx* (1977). Women like Tammes were early adopters of specialist national training schemes, which offered some form of alternative pathway to the established apprenticeship systems that excluded them. The experiences of Tammes and Konttinen are explored further in chapter 6. Looking at the cohort as a whole, what stands out is how varied are their backgrounds. Some were young, in their late teens, others in their early thirties, some with formal training (the National Film and Television School, or NFTS, and the Scottish Film Council), others describing themselves as "self-taught." There were clearly no easy routes for women into commercial camera or sound jobs in this or indeed any other decade.

1980s: The 1980s witnessed some modest advances for women. One hundred and seventy-seven joined the union through jobs in Camera, Sound, and Stills, representing 17 percent of the total intake to this sector and the highest proportion of women since records began. Thirty came through sound jobs, mainly sound recordists, boom operators, and assistants, either working at commercial companies specializing in shorts and documentaries or at the new state-supported film cooperatives that flourished in the 1980s. Another fifteen women joined as stills photographers, many of them freelance, but there were no new recruits to the retoucher role, a function that at this point was probably either outsourced by small production companies or undertaken by the photographer herself. Of the remaining 130 applications, a handful came through the lowest camera positions of clapper loader, rostrum camera operator, and camera assistant at companies producing feature films. These included women like Sue Gibson, another graduate from the National Film School, and Chyna Thomson, whose father was a leading cinematographer. There is little evidence of real change to the gender composition of the camera workforce in commercial cinema. Where change did take place was through the film cooperatives, which produced documentaries, campaigning, and training films. They created the new role of "cross-grade technician" to reflect collective working practices that, in theory, gave women access to camera roles.[49] The increase that we see in women's participation in camera jobs in this decade is through film cooperatives such as Sheffield Film Co-op, Black Audio Film Collective (BAFC), Sankofa, and Amber. Data from the union records indicate that working outside the mainstream—in cooperatives or documentary/training contexts—remained the best way for women to work in camera and sound jobs during this decade.

In general, women were rank outsiders in technical roles like camera and sound, barely tolerated even during the dire emergency of World War II, and only grudgingly accepted for consideration in the 1970s–'80s, when it became impossible to ignore them, not least because external training went some way toward challenging the established apprenticeship system. It was only the stills department that threw work their way, probably because the requirements of the "retoucher" role—attention to detail, "cleaning up"—fitted a skill set that was deemed feminine. And once this function became unnecessary, women lost out. The stark absence of women from this, more than any other sector in film production, highlights how the union and employers hid behind a smokescreen of equal pay while practicing the active exclusion of women from this workforce.

Cartoon and Diagram

Cartoon and Diagram is a visual-based sector requiring specialist skills in drawing, painting, graphics, photography, and storytelling. "Cartoon" and "diagram" are industry terms for functions that use animation for different effects: diagram films are educational, using animation to show how something works; cartoon films are entertainment. Key roles in this category include animator, artist, in-betweener, layout, colorist, and paint and tracer (see appendix B). Cartoon and diagram functions are performed either in distinct departments within existing film studios or in specialist companies, of which Halas and Batchelor and Larkins were the largest and operated alongside a plethora of much smaller animation studios. Historically, the sector has had close links with the advertising industry and commercial television, which, in the British context, account for much of its work, but it also did steady business producing special titles and animated inserts for films, as well as the occasional feature. Such work is labor intensive, requiring celluloid frames to be hand-drawn and -painted, a process that continued until the 1980s. Union records show that women were well represented in this workforce, typically around 40 percent of all recruits, but these figures mask gender divisions. Women were clustered in the lower-level jobs in the creative hierarchy, typically paint and trace, while men most often entered the industry as "in-betweeners." This is a type of junior animator's role; an in-betweener is responsible for the drawings that come in between the key drawings. From this job, the male recruits could progress to the higher and better-paid positions in the workforce (background artist, animator). Charts 9 and 10 show the number and percentage of applications in the Cartoon and Diagram sector by decade.

1930s: Recruitment to the union from the Cartoon and Diagram sector was on a very small scale in the 1930s; only ten applications were accepted, all men, who worked at Publicity Pictures, a company that produced cartoon advertisements for the cinema program. All were employed as film cartoonists, animators, or artists, and while there are no union records for women this decade, it is likely that Publicity Pictures and competitor companies like Anson Dyer used women's labor in some capacity. As we have seen in sectors such as Art and Effects, an absence of union records does not mean an absence of labor. It is more likely that women were either working on a freelance basis or, if they were company employees, their roles were not yet recognized by the union.

Chart 9. Cartoon and Diagram: Numbers by Gender

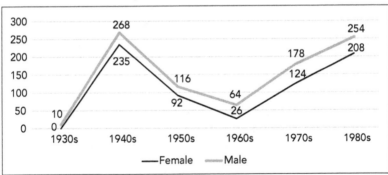

Chart 10. Cartoon and Diagram: Percentage by Gender

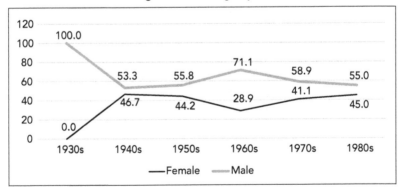

1940s: The absence of women in the Cartoon and Diagram sector changed dramatically in the 1940s when the Second World War created a significant demand for instructional and propaganda shorts, which, in turn, put pressure on labor, pulling many more women into the industry. Just over five hundred workers joined the union in Cartoon and Diagram this decade, with women accounting for almost 50 percent of the intake. The majority of the women were employed in the lower-level positions, typically as paint and tracers or colorists, jobs that involved hand-painting the innumerable cels that were used in the animation process (see "Paint and Trace" in glossary). This was painstaking and detailed work that required good brush skills, an eye for detail, and the ability to work quickly and accurately, as the "look" of each cel had to be consistent. This role segregation established a trend for women's employment that continued until the function of paint and trace in the animation process was replaced by new technologies through the 1990s. Frequently ignored in critical discourse or dismissed as merely routine work, painting and tracing was in fact a job that required highly skilled workers (see chapter 4).

Alongside paint and tracers were a smaller number of women holding senior creative positions in the workforce, chiefly as artists and animators, roles that would later become more difficult for women to occupy. Many were employed at Halas and Batchelor, the company cofounded by Joy Batchelor, which had Vera Linnecar, Kathleen Murphy, and Stella Harvey on the team. Collectively, these women contributed much to the studio's well-respected output during the war. The union records show that all companies had some women as experienced animators on their payroll, including Cynthia Whitby at the Shell Film Unit, Rosalie Crook at Anson Dyer, and Katherine Marshall at Publicity Pictures. Generally speaking, women were better represented in senior-level positions in the animation industry than any other sector of production at this time.

1950s: This situation changed in the 1950s. While the total intake of recruits dropped to just over two hundred, the proportion of women to men stayed roughly the same. The difference now was that women were almost exclusively taken on in paint and trace functions. There were some exceptions to this rule, with a handful of women recruited to more senior jobs, mainly background artists and assistant animators. The most notable was Alison de Vere, who would later win critical acclaim for her work. But the overwhelming majority of senior positions were being filled by men. There was plenty of work in the sector as commercial television, introduced in 1955, needed cartoon advertisements, but it was distributed in the industry along gendered lines, which worked in men's favor. The distinctions in the workforce were so sharp that by 1957 the British trade press was referring to paint and trace as "an entirely feminine process."[50] There was no reflection on why this should be the case, nor was there acknowledgment of the difficulties that women with aspirations faced in moving up to higher positions. There were plenty of well-qualified women looking for work during this decade—Britain's art schools were turning out scores of design graduates—but the Cartoon and Diagram sector channeled them into its most junior jobs, content to draw on their skills while holding out less chance of progression than previously.

1960s: If the job outlook for women in the film industry was bad in the 1950s, it became worse in the 1960s when even paint and trace jobs dried up. There was a dramatic decline in recruitment in this decade, with only ninety workers in total joining the union, of which a mere twenty-six were women. It is likely that work in the Cartoon and Diagram sector was being diverted to the many new, specialist advertising companies opening up in Britain whose employees were not yet under the union's jurisdiction. The only recruitment of women to more senior roles were at the Halas and Batchelor company, where Yvonne Pearsall and Anne Jolliffe joined as animators. Both were Australian-born and had trained professionally in that country before moving to Britain, part of a long-standing migration wave in which many Australians, especially women, traveled for work.[51] Pearsall went on to work in American television while Jolliffe most famously animated the character "Boob" in *Yellow Submarine* (1967–68) and later won an Academy Award (shared with Bob Godfrey) for her work on *Great!* (1976). Jolliffe provides an interesting case study that illuminates how gender discrimination operated in the Cartoon and Diagram sector at this time. She reputedly left Halas and Batchelor when she discovered that her male coworkers were better paid than she, and indeed records from the union database verify this: Jolliffe earned five pounds less per week than the men in the same position who were recruited at the same time.[52] So much for equal pay. Companies that were not prepared to invest in training women were nevertheless happy to take those with valuable professional experience and skills gained abroad while paying them less for their labor. It would be another ten years before Britain's much-needed equal pay legislation would take effect and provide women with some official redress.

1970s: Women's prospects improved in the 1970s, which saw a noticeable upturn in the total numbers accepted for union membership, with women once again making up 40 percent of the recruits. Increased production in the sector created the demand for labor, and Britain's animation studios were kept busy in the 1970s making a wide range of public service films, commercials, children's programs for television (*Danger Mouse* [1981–92]; *Count Duckula* [1988–93]), and films for cinema and television, such as *Watership Down* (1978) and *The Wind in the Willows* (1983). Women continued to keep the paint and trace departments going through their skilled brushwork, and at the same time were some modest signs of progress for women into more senior roles. Almost two dozen listed their position as assistant animator or animator during this decade, and their demographic profile is illuminating. Many were highly educated or graduates from Britain's leading art schools, including the Royal College of Art (Gillian Holton) and Central St. Martins, London (Penelope Grant). Others had experience gained abroad, including Joan Swanson at Walt Disney and Sheila Rock at the Boston Film School. Given the difficulties women faced, where moving up from paint and trace to more senior jobs was nearly impossible, women with aspirations had to create alternative pathways into the industry, and here they mirrored the experience of women in camera, directing, and producing. The most senior creative roles in the Cartoon and Diagram sector (chief or key animator) continued to be dominated by men, but this decade saw a small number of women employed as animators, including Marie Szmichowska, Rosemary Welch, and others who were part of the team who contributed to flagship films such as *Watership Down*. As these new recruits joined the union, they took their place next to established animators such as Kathleen "Spud" Houston and Alison de Vere, whose solo careers flourished during this decade, with de Vere winning the Grand Prix at the Annecy Festival for her seven-minute short, *Mr. Pascal* (1979). Thus, there were small pockets of opportunity for women in the sector at this time, although, once again, they had to take more circuitous routes than men to find them.

1980s: These welcome developments continued in the 1980s. Recruitment levels in Cartoon and Diagram were back to those last seen in the 1940s, with almost five hundred new recruits, of which over two hundred were women. In addition to the stalwarts in paint and trace, there were three other areas where women were now visible in the workforce. First, it became more common to see women in the grade of in-betweener, the role that had been the traditional entry point for men into the industry (see "In-Betweener" in glossary). This generation of women had higher expectations and were perhaps more prepared to insist on equal opportunities at work, supported now by legislation. Second, there was a small but steady stream of women joining as animators and assistants—almost forty in total—building on developments of the 1970s. Some were freelancing or self-employed, and those with strong creative ambitions may have turned to animation as a way to sidestep the more intractable gendered hierarchies that characterized live-action features. Some of these women would go on to build high-profile careers, including Emma Calder, who joined the industry in 1988 and made award-winning films and music videos, and Joanna Quinn, who created the famous "Beryl" character in *Girls Night Out* (1986). Finally, developments in the independent film sector led to the emergence of new cooperatives making campaigning films, and some of these specialized in animation. The most notable was the Leeds Animation Workshop, which produced a number of iconic campaigning shorts on women's issues, including *Give Us a Smile* (1983) about sexual harassment. As a film cooperative, the women worked collectively and, like the cross-job-level technicians in Camera and Sound, took a hand in all stages of the production process, thereby bypassing the rigid job demarcations that characterized the commercial sector (see chapter 6). The 1980s bore witness to greater opportunities for women in animation, with movement within established job hierarchies and scope in the independent sector making a difference.

In general, women were the backbone of the Cartoon and Diagram sector, which was one of the biggest recruiters of women's labor. It relied on the women whose skills in brushwork turned out the thousands of hand-painted cels that were the building blocks of the animation process. Like continuity and production secretary, this was a role that women made their own in the face of restrictions to career progression within the sector. Alongside them was a small but significant number of women in more senior creative roles. Typically, they were highly educated and trained, often with experience gained abroad, which employers were happy to draw on when it suited the needs of business. For most of the sixty-year period, women represented 40 percent of the union intake, but within that there was change to the proportions of women in senior positions. They lost out to men in the 1950s and 1960s when opportunities for progression were closed down, but they narrowed the gap in the 1970s and 1980s, taking advantage of changes in funding regimes to carve out a more favorable position for themselves in the industry.

Postproduction

The Postproduction category covers a broad range of functions pertaining to the editing, archiving, and distribution of film; the manufacture and maintenance of specialist equipment for the film industry; and process jobs in studios (print examination, repair, and assembly). Key roles are supervising editor, editor, assistant editor, dubbing editor (sound), negative cutter, librarian, and assistants (see appendix B). Editing is responsible for assembling the film through cutting and joining sections of film, and there are a number of stages in the process as the film moves from initial assembly (where scenes are put together in script order), to rough cut (where rhythm and pace are added), to fine cut (the version with sound and music that is signed off on by the director/producer).[53] The number of staff on the editing team depends on the prestige of the production. A big-budget "A" feature would have several staff members with different levels of skill and responsibility, while smaller features, including documentaries and shorts, would have one editor and possibly an assistant. Career progression is achieved by moving through job levels, from second and first assistant to editor. The role has historically been more open to women, who have cut and joined film since the early years of cinema, and this trend is reflected in the Postproduction figures. This sector is one of the largest recruiters of labor, including both men and women, but the percentage of women applicants varies noticeably—sometimes as high as one-third, other times dropping to a sixth. There are clear gender distinctions, with men over-represented in senior positions and women clustered in junior/assistant roles, from which it took them longer to progress. All of the major film studios employed editors, but there were also companies offering editing services in and around London and self-employed editors taking short-term contracts, especially for the documentary, shorts, and commercials sector. This meant it was one of the few areas in film production where people could work part-time or more flexibly, and for this reason it has been an attractive occupation for women. Charts 11 and 12 show the number and percentage of applications in the Postproduction sector by decade.

Chart 11. Postproduction: Numbers by Gender

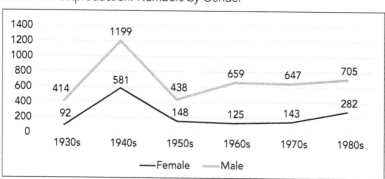

Chart 12. Postproduction: Percentage by Gender

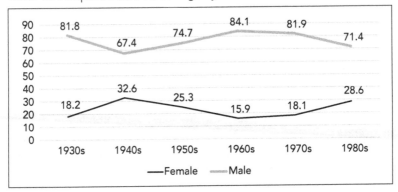

1930s: In the 1930s just over ninety women joined the union through postproduction roles, and there are two distinct profiles. The majority were in relatively junior-level positions with variations on the "cutting room assistant"/"assistant cutter" title. Some of these were new recruits to the role; others had a few years' experience. The assistant was the organizer of the cutting room, responsible for the cleaning and maintenance of machinery, marking up rolls of film, labeling shelves, and cataloging "trims" (film frames discarded by the editor in the cutting process that were retained as a contingency). It was the assistant's job to put in place a system to enable the editor to perform their role. As assistants progressed, they would be allowed to cut film and handle some of the routine aspects of the process to build up experience. In addition to assistants was a smaller cohort of experienced editors with ten or more years in the business. Their wages were double those of assistants and on par with continuity girls; these were well-paid jobs for women in 1930s Britain and worth hanging on to if personal circumstances permitted. With work histories stretching back into the 1920s, these women (and the new recruits) were part of the long tradition of women "cutters" that had started in the silent era. By comparison, men's roles in Postproduction were more varied and ranged across projection, equipment maintenance, printing, and grading, as well as editing. Over four hundred men joined the union in Postproduction roles, making this the second-largest recruiting sector after Camera. Due to the volume of workers in the industry, the union was keen to ensure that this labor was organized, and they put efforts into doing so, but the downside of that attention was the creation of finer job distinctions, which had negative repercussions for women. Toward the end of the 1930s, a new job title, "chief editor," appears in the records, populated entirely by men and commanding a higher salary. This was either a supervisor's role, with responsibility for overseeing the work in the cutting room, or a way to pay a higher wage to those working on prestige features. This was the beginning of the formal process—along the lines outlined earlier by Sylvia Walby (see the introduction to this book)—by which women would be clustered into jobs designated as "junior." The subject of editing is explored in more detail in chapter 2.

1940s: Such gender discrimination was temporarily halted in the 1940s by the Second World War. As demand for films increased (documentaries, features, and training), so did the need for labor, and seventeen hundred workers joined the union through Postproduction roles, of which one-third were women. The majority were in jobs deemed semiskilled and included repairing and quality-checking film prints before dispatch, testing the electrical components of cameras and projectors, camera mechanics, and film librarians and negative cutters for newsreel companies and film studios. Scores of women also joined as editing assistants at companies specializing in documentary (Shell, Crown) and film trailers (National Screen Service), and all the major film studios took on women in their editing suites. By the end of the war, it was common to see female-only cutting-room crews, and some of these women would go on to forge long careers, most notably Anne V. Coates. Along with these new recruits were women already established in the industry who could now more readily move up through the ranks, as men were in short supply. These included Vera Campbell, Noreen Ackland, and Thelma Connell, with Connell participating in a symposium in 1944 about women's contribution to the nation's film studios (see chapter 3). Women were a highly visible presence in editing roles in the 1940s.

1950s: The job situation for women changed dramatically in the 1950s. Not surprisingly, recruitment dropped after the war, with just under 150 women joining the union, representing one-quarter of all applications during this decade. But now women were overwhelmingly clustered into lower-level positions, continuing a pattern that had started toward the end of the 1930s. One of the biggest employers of women's labor was British Acoustic Films Ltd. (part of the Rank Organisation), which specialized in the manufacture of sound recording, camera, and projection equipment. Almost 50 women joined the union this decade through their employment in electrical assembly jobs, where they assembled and tested the electrical control units in the equipment. Within the company there was a clear division of labor by gender, with men in higher-paying jobs as packers, drivers, storekeepers, and instrument makers, roles that had been filled by both women and men in the 1940s. By drawing clear distinctions between jobs by gender, British Acoustic (along with many other companies) was able to operate within the union's equal pay regulations while systemically excluding women from better-paid areas of employment. A small number of women joined the union as negative cutters and editing assistants, but the union records show that most of the editing positions in British companies were now being filled by men. This was especially the case in the bigger, more prestigious film studios and production companies such as Ealing, MGM, and Rank. While women with established careers continued to secure work in the film industry during this decade—notably Vera Campbell and Thelma Connell, the latter combining work with pregnancy and parenting—the pattern of union recruitment suggests that openings into the field were narrowing for women. Other sources indicate that the nonfiction sector, commercials, and budget second features were particularly important in providing women with work (see chapter 4).

Where women did get some professional responsibility was in managing the film libraries of the companies that produced nonfiction film. These include Elizabeth Wallis, chief librarian at British Transport Films, and Anne Plowden at the prolific Rayant Pictures Limited, among others. These were highly responsible positions in which the librarian developed a specialist, encyclopedic knowledge of film through cataloging, serving the growing audience appetite for sponsored films across schools, universities, motoring clubs, women's institutes, and holiday camps. This was not a feminized work role—the union records also show men in these jobs—but women secured good positions in this area of employment, most probably because of the role's association with education.

1960s: Women's fortunes in the 1960s were mixed in terms of editing and other postproduction roles. While their recruitment dropped to one-sixth of the sector's intake—the lowest point of the sixty-year period—the careers of established women editors were flourishing. Anne V. Coates worked on *Lawrence of Arabia* (1962)—a major coup, as it was one of the most prestigious features of the decade—and Noreen Ackland earned her first solo editing credit for *Peeping Tom* (1960), an important film in British cinema history. In this respect, Harper is correct to argue that women's editing careers "peaked in the 1950s and 1960s."[54] But this is only half the story, and such successes mask what was a pattern of declining opportunity for women. Those who were hired found themselves in the lowest-level jobs of negative cutter or trainee editor, but, increasingly, these trainee and assistant editor positions were being filled by men, who were being recruited in ever increasing numbers. At this point in history, British film production was booming, bankrolled by American finance, with British studios equipped with modern editing technology. And editing styles were changing across Britain, Europe, and America, with a snappy style and shorter shot length the new, preferred norm. Editing was at the vanguard of technological and aesthetic change, and, given its enhanced status, it is likely that a power grab took place whereby women were deliberately excluded from opportunities by men in positions of authority vis-à-vis recruitment. Certainly there is evidence of blatant discrimination; for example, one of the leading editors of the day, Jim Clark, claimed that "a man who spoke tolerable English would be preferable to a woman," and director Ronald Neame did his best to avoid employing women editors because he thought they "were too into their homes and their boyfriends."[55] By the end of the decade, the withdrawal of American finance saw many technicians—especially freelance editors—facing unemployment, and under these conditions men were even more likely to jealously guard what employment opportunities remained. But although it was becoming harder for women to get their foot in the door as trainee editors, the union records show they were at least still being recruited to positions in film libraries for companies such as British Movietone News and the Commonwealth News Film Agency. Numbers were modest, however—only a dozen across the entire decade—and certainly not sufficient to offset the loss of opportunity in editing. We know from other sources that in the face of these restrictions, women editors found the commercials sector a more hospitable place to work (see chapter 5).

1970s: In the 1970s women's fortunes in Postproduction were consistent with the previous decade. A slight increase in numbers masked the reality that women in editing were largely confined to the most junior jobs of negative cutter, second assistant editor, and trainee, and that even these were becoming more difficult for them to access. Overall growth in the sector, albeit modest, is accounted for by men's continued movement into editing jobs. And once in, men would progress more quickly through the ranks than their female counterparts. Feminist researchers working on a report for the union in 1975 found clear gender differences in men's and women's experiences as assistant editors. Men were moved more rapidly through the system than women, who, generally speaking, were more likely to have educational qualifications and to have spent longer working in the industry in other roles before moving into editing.[56] The career of Lesley Walker is a case in point: she worked as a runner, receptionist, secretary, and assistant editor for different employers, including film laboratories, a company producing commercials, and in children's films, before finally moving into editing features at the end of the decade.[57] The union's own report confirmed how the occupational odds were stacked in men's favor and how women had to work harder either in school or on the job to get to the same positions as men.

1980s: The 1980s saw a sharp increase in the numbers of women in Postproduction jobs, nearly three hundred, which represented almost 30 percent, a welcome improvement from the previous two decades. Some of the growth came through companies providing film library services and national and regional film archives that employed women as librarians and archivists. The other major development of this decade was the growth of film cooperatives, which provided an effective training ground for women who had been otherwise marginalized from film production. They were especially important in starting the editing careers of women like Nadine Marsh-Edwards, who would go on to become a leading figure in independent Black cinema. And those with established careers like Lesley Walker were now well placed to make the transition into features, which she did by first editing low-budget independent films (Derek Jarman's *The Tempest*), and, from there, stepping into main features, which included epics like *Cry Freedom* (1987). But we should be careful of overstating the case, as the 1980s did not represent a halcyon time for women in editing. In the increasingly freelance marketplace, adaptability was a necessity, and everyone—women and men—had to be prepared to take on promotional films, corporate films, and similar fare to gain experience. However, this does not mean there was a level playing field, and residual gender prejudices survived. Editor Alex Anderson was firmly convinced that she was accepted into the ACTT union's editorial section in the early 1980s because the committee assumed she was a man, an observation that suggests there may well have been women whose applications were unsuccessful. Certainly, in Anderson's estimation, women went through a more rigorous screening process than their male counterparts, with reports of them "get[ting] all sorts of queries about their experience and how they got the job and so on."[58] Women still had to deal with skepticism about their professional skills and abilities, openly expressed by men in positions of power.

In general, women were the stalwarts of the Postproduction sector, assistants who could be relied upon to bring order to the cutting room and organization to the film library. While there is a long tradition of women cutting film, what stands out from the union records is the mixed fortunes they faced in Britain. The history of the female-run cutting rooms of the Second World War was swept aside by the misogyny of the 1960s, which made it increasingly difficult for women to access even entry-level positions. Many of those in the industry were kept going by work in the lower rung of the production hierarchy: commercials, nonfiction, and second features. There was significant improvement in the 1980s as new independent forms of filmmaking emerged, but in the face of prejudicial attitudes that were resistant to change, women had to be resilient in order to survive.

Conclusion

The film industry relied on women's labor even while it discriminated against them as a social group, channeling them into a narrow range of jobs that official bodies undervalued and categorized at the lower end of the skill hierarchy. Gender discrimination was written into the union's job-level systems, which, in turn, shaped the reward and recognition mechanisms of the industry. This had an impact on women's pay, their promotional chances, and the levels of responsibility they could reasonably expect to hold. These factors constrained opportunities for women, and patterns of employment must be understood within this context.

The union records reveal the fluctuating conditions of women's employment as the film industry itself came under pressure to change. Across the sixty-year period, three key elements emerge as factors shaping women's employment. The first of these is market shifts and production trends. As these evolved over time, demand for labor in areas where it was socially acceptable for women to work waxed and waned. This was especially the case for roles in costume and paint and trace work in Britain's animation studios. And as new areas opened up that demanded specialist labor, women were more readily accepted into roles that did not drastically challenge normative femininity; publicity and casting jobs, for example, were socially acceptable, as they relied on the job holder to exercise "caretaking" skills. The second element, an extension of the first, is the funding supporting the film industry. In the 1960s Hollywood majors bankrolled British studios, which resulted in the industry becoming more international in scope and outlook, which in turn extended to production personnel. Several important women joined the workforce at that time—as animators, directors, and writers—typically with a wealth of experience gained abroad. Although this did not lead to significant structural change in the industry—indeed chapter 5 shows the extent to which many male unionists perceived women's labor as a threat—their presence is evidence of the extent to which financial imperatives could soften ideological beliefs. A further development of this trend was evident in the 1980s when women found a space in the grant-aided film cooperative sector, whose ideologies were broadly in step with the goals of second-wave feminism and equal opportunities. And, of course, in both cases, women in more senior creative roles were disproportionally working on the margins of mainstream feature production—in shorts, documentaries, training, and lower-budget films. Finally, external training gave women some opportunity to circumvent the internal apprenticeship system, which prioritized men, with art schools in the 1950s and 1960s and film schools in the 1970s important as places where women could learn the types of craft skills required by film production. But they invariably started in the film industry at the lowest rung of the production hierarchy and took longer to progress than their male peers, who, of course, had been earning a wage as apprentices or juniors. The experience of women during the Second World War gives a sense of what was possible, but that this took place under such extreme circumstances shows how inhospitable the film industry had become to the idea of women's labor in anything other than roles it could designate as "supporting." Although opportunities for women were constrained in terms of work, responsibility, and pay, many were determined to seize what was available for as long as their own contingent personal lives made doing so a reasonable course of action. The following chapters show in depth how this played out in practice.

2
The 1930s

Modernizing Production

The 1930s was one of the most prolific and volatile decades for feature film production in Britain. In 1927 a total of 53 feature films were produced by British studios; by 1933 this had risen dramatically to 152 features.[1] This transformation in fortunes was brought about by a combination of new sound technology and the 1927 Cinematograph Films Act (CFA), a protectionist measure to ensure that British screens showed a quota of British-produced films. This stimulated production and led to the establishment of new film companies and a construction boom, with new studios being built and existing ones modernized to meet quota demands and to adapt to the new sound technology.[2] Three new floors were built for Gaumont-British studios at Shepherd's Bush, British Lion had new studios at Beaconsfield, and the revamped facilities at Denham and Pinewood were proclaimed "state of the art."[3] More films meant greater demand for labor, and as the production workforce expanded, concerns were voiced about poorly trained technicians and quota films with shoddy production values. Not only was studio space modernized, but the working practices of technicians were brought up to date as well, with changes made to internal organization in order to bring "more streamlined modes of production" into Britain's film studios.[4] Also circulating was a wider debate about training and "filmcraft," which I will return to shortly, and as the industry rushed to modernize, some professions enhanced their status. Art direction in particular benefited from improved facilities, and the status of the art director was raised through the pioneering work of Alfred Junge and the studies published by Edward Carrick.[5] It was under these conditions that

Britain's first trade union for film production personnel was established. As discussed in the previous chapter, the Association of Cine-Technicians was formed in 1933 and not only organized the expanding workforce but also negotiated pay and working conditions with film studios.

However, the industry still faced a number of challenges in this decade. After the initial investment boom, some companies were struggling to survive; one estimate suggests that fifty companies went into liquidation in 1930 alone, many as a result of general mismanagement and the cost of purchasing the new sound recording equipment.[6] Developments were further hampered when the film industry suffered a financial crash in 1937. But production received a boost in 1938 in the form of the second Cinematograph Films Act, and, notwithstanding the volatility in the sector, it is widely accepted by historians that by the end of the decade "an infrastructure has been established that facilitated the industry's expansion and ability to survive crises in the 1940s and beyond."[7] This chapter opens by laying out how the key features of the British film industry impacted women's labor and then presents an overview of their presence in the workforce using union membership application data. I go on to examine how fan publications like *Picturegoer* represented women filmmakers and women's work in the industry during this time of expansion and modernization. Three case studies follow that examine in detail women's work in costume, continuity, and editing—areas that have come to define popular understanding of women's contribution to sound-era cinema.

The Film Industry and Women's Labor

The increase in film production levels created a demand for "feminine" labor, and as we will see, women were actively recruited to secretarial, continuity, and editing roles. Here the film industry, with its studios and processing laboratories based in and around London, was in competition with many other businesses providing employment for women in the 1930s. Social historians have shown how expansions in clerical, retail, and leisure industry jobs in the 1910s led to a "white blouse" revolution that drew single, educated young women into the workforce.[8] They were joined in the interwar years by the one and a half million unmarried women over thirty-five whose chances of marriage had been drastically curtailed by the heavy population losses of World War I.[9] Spinsters, as they were pejoratively termed, were not only dependent on their own wages, but many were also supporting elderly parents and in this respect needed a "breadwinner" wage. Film production was one of the many expanding industries in the interwar years that looked to women as a necessary part of its workforce. *Picturegoer* held it up as an attractive employment destination for women, with features titled "Meet the Script Girl," "Women behind the Camera," and "Lady with Scissors" published in the early 1930s.

But industry expansion also had some negative consequences for women. Greater job opportunities led to closer scrutiny of pay, working conditions, and the organization of labor, which, in turn, triggered interventions by the union that ultimately disadvantaged women workers (see chapter 1). Grades were more tightly demarcated and defined, and, as the editing case study will illustrate, women were increasingly restricted to more junior-/assistant-type roles. Wider legislative frameworks also had an impact on employment opportunities for women in the film industry; for example, the 1937 Factories Act limited the number of overtime hours women could work in any one day or week.[10] Although film studios did not fall within the act's remit, film processing laboratories did, and protective legislation effectively barred women from the more senior/skilled roles such as printing and grading, because overtime work was expected from employees in these roles. Thus, the emergence and strengthening of the union, seemingly a good thing, worked to demarcate roles along gendered lines that, in turn, operated systematically to marginalize women's roles. Opportunities for women in the film industry were therefore mixed; high levels of production created a demand for skilled labor while the organization and management of labor increasingly placed new female recruits in junior/supportive roles.

Women and Union Records: An Overview

How did women fare as film technicians in the light of these mixed fortunes? Just under two hundred women applied for union membership, which represents 10 percent of all applications received by the ACT in the 1930s. Most of these were in either postproduction roles (negative cutting, editing, stills retouching) or secretarial positions on the studio floor, and a handful were employed as script readers or writers (see appendix C). Within this relatively narrow range of roles, however, there was some diversity, with women employed across a range of senior and more junior positions. Those at the top end included continuity girls and floor secretaries at some of Britain's biggest studios, such as British Lion, Elstree, and Gaumont-British. Those with several years' experience included the well-respected Tilly Day, who was earning eight pounds per week when she joined the union in 1935. This was a good wage for a woman in the 1930s, comparable to that of a female teacher and rather more than the wages of waitresses and shop assistants, who were paid around one or two pounds per week, respectively, at this time.[11] Women in senior editing roles earned a similar rate of pay, including Winifred Cooper at the Granville Picture Corporation and Mary Mansell at ATP Studios. And some production companies employed women as scriptwriters, including Evelyn Barrie at Rock Studios and Lola Harvey and Marjorie Deans at British International Pictures (BIP).[12] These and other women were evidently experienced professionals with well-established careers and were perhaps part of the first wave of "white blouse" recruits who had entered Britain's workforce in the 1910s. Union records show that some were single while others were married, complicating any simplistic narrative that women either worked for pin money or gave up work entirely when they married. Indeed marriage itself was no barrier to the employment of women in film production roles, unlike teaching, nursing, the civil service, or the BBC, which barred the employment of married women until the end of the decade.[13] At a time when British society was actively encouraging women to see themselves as housewives, some women in the film industry were clearly not leaving their jobs to fulfill a state-sanctioned domestic destiny.

The bulk of the applications came from women who held more junior positions, typically cutting room assistants, negative cutters, less experienced floor secretaries, and scenario readers and writers. These included women who would go on to establish long careers in the British film industry, such as Vera Campbell, who eventually became assistant editor to David Lean, and Katherine "Kay" Mander, continuity assistant and documentary director. Many more women in the early film industry had career profiles that are as yet unknown, including Caroline Johnstone, cutting room assistant at Joe Rock Productions; Edith White, film librarian at the Strand Film Company; and Brigid Maas, employed as a reader at London Film Productions. Wages for women in these lower-level positions were a more modest two to three pounds per week, less than their peers in continuity but still better paid than waitressing and with more prospects for career progression. Equally revealing is where women are absent from early ACT records. There are no union applications from women for the roles of art director, model maker, or draftsperson—although dozens of men were being recruited to the union through these roles—and, with the exception of a handful of stills retouchers, no women were employed in the camera or sound departments of Britain's film studios. As far as union data is concerned, these departments were bastions of male power, their ranks well stocked with hundreds of young men earning a pound or so a week as clapper boys but who could reasonably expect to earn significantly more when they progressed to more senior-level jobs; a chief cameraman, for example, earned upward of thirty pounds per week in the mid-1930s.

But trade union data presents a particular picture that, certainly for this decade, is not wholly representative of the full range of women's work in the British film industry. The ACT union had yet to fully establish a closed shop and some film studios were slow to sign up. Indeed one of the industry's biggest employers, British International Pictures, reputedly refused entry to a union representative in 1937 and threatened members of its workforce with dismissal if they joined the ACT.[14] Women's initial low membership rates were compounded by the fact that the union put its energies into organizing in camera, lighting, and sound, roles that were dominated by men, and only later turned its attention to the rest of the workforce in any systematic way. Other sources point to women in a broader range of positions. In 1933 *Picturegoer* published a *Who's Who and Encyclopaedia of the Screen To-Day*,[15] which listed women working in the film industry as directors and assistant directors (Mary Field, Marjorie Gaffney, Alma Reville), writers and scenarists, or screenwriters, (Ethel Dell, Elinor Glyn, Lydia Hayward, Margaret Kennedy), publicity managers (Billie Bristow, Sybil Sutherland), casting managers (Leila Stewart), dress designers (Gordon Conway), art directors (Betty Langley), wardrobe supervisors (Ann Morgan), and a floor secretary (Mildred E. Cox). This gives a snapshot of women who, through senior, creative roles, were shaping film production through casting and directorial decisions, script choices, design aspects of mise-en-scène, and promotional work. And we know from existing histories that a new generation of women was already coming up through the ranks at this time; documentary directors Ruby and Marion Grierson, Evelyn Spice, and Margaret Thomson; art director Carmen Dillon; and animator Joy Batchelor were all beginning their careers in the 1930s. Without overstating the case—the pages of *Picturegoer's* "Encyclopaedia" were resoundingly dominated by men—there is concrete evidence of women's presence in the film industry across a broad range of jobs, and at senior as well as junior levels. Certainly, as far as *Picturegoer* was concerned, the topic of women in the film industry was of interest to the magazine's readership. The next section examines this in more detail and illustrates some of the ways the expansion of the British film economy was perceived through a gendered lens.

Picturegoer and the British Film Industry: "Women rule the screens"?

As Britain's leading fan magazine, *Picturegoer* satisfied the interests of its readership for a regular diet of star profiles, industry gossip, fashion, and news about the movie business. Although much of its focus was on Hollywood stars and films, it also covered domestic production and developments in the British film industry. Its regular "Round British Studios" feature offered a digest of films currently in production, and it supplemented this with occasional in-depth pieces. At a time when the domestic film industry was going through a period of rapid change, the magazine offered different and often contradictory pictures of women in the workforce. In the early 1930s, it published a number of "successful women" profiles and polemics about women's role in the business of film-making, many of these penned by women filmmakers. These included features of well-known women such as American editor Margaret Booth ("Lady With Scissors," 1932), reflections on women's qualities as film-makers ("Why Women Should Make Films," 1931), how-to descriptions of jobs ("Meet the Script Girl," 1931), and advice on how to break into the industry ("The Place for Women in the Film Studios," 1935). These built on established traditions in fan magazine discourse, which had been profil-ing the film industry as an employment destination for women from the 1910s onward. As Antonia Lant has demonstrated, features about directors such as Alice Blaché and Lois Weber appeared regularly in American and British magazines, along with debates about their skills and competencies as women, and by the 1920s there was a vibrant industry in the publica-tion of how-to manuals for the film trade, with one publication listing twenty-nine jobs open to women, including fan-mail reader, plasterer, script holder, cutter, and director.[16] Women as film workers were, in Lant's terms, considered "well worth a story" by the fan and trade magazines of the day.[17]

In the pages of *Picturegoer* in the 1930s, scenario writer was one of the most frequently mentioned roles for women, with Britain's Mary Murillo and Lydia Hayward profiled alongside Hollywood's Jeannie MacPherson and Frances Marion. Britain's first film censor, Mrs. George A. Redford, was mentioned as were Gainsborough's continuity writer Ann Newnham and the secretary of Britain's Film Society, Josephine Harvey, leaving the author of one article, Isadore Silverman, to proclaim triumphantly that, in 1931 at least, women "rule the screens of the world."[18] British director Mary Field sought to encourage other women to follow in her footsteps, reflecting on the many socially sanctioned "feminine" attributes women could bring to directing (empathy, patience, attention to detail, persis-tence), as long as they were prepared to "begin from the bottom rung of the ladder."[19] Actress and theatrical producer Auriol Lee similarly sought to entice women into the film business in her 1932 piece "Women Are Needed in British Films." For Lee, Hollywood set the benchmark, its stu-dios being "filled with women," including department heads, and she called for women to get involved in British production and "take the raw edge off men's work."[20]

There was a change of focus, however, in the magazine's output around 1934. As the studio construction boom got into full swing, there was a renewed interest in filmmaking in the country. Studio visits by high-profile dignitaries were arranged to boost the industry's profile, with the Japanese ambassador and the Prince of Wales visiting Elstree Studios in 1931 and 1932, respectively.[21] New studios and sound technology required appropriately trained staff, and a number of book-length studies giving "instruction in filmcraft" were published. These included *Filmcraft* (1933) and *Film Production* (1936), both written by director/screenwriter Adrian Brunel, which gave detailed information about the different elements of a production unit (including continuity, set construction, makeup) and how to ensure they worked together for maximum efficiency. And the drive to modernize the British workforce and its practices led leading producers like Michael Balcon to bring international experts into the country to share ideas about filmcraft. American editor Margaret Booth, for example, was part of a cosmopolitan team Balcon built at Gaumont-British to deliver on his ambition to produce quality British sound films.

Picturegoer was an ideal platform to showcase the new developments taking place in British studios. It published an eight-page special in 1934 that laid out extensive photographs of the major British film studios, including external shots of physical buildings and grounds and internal "behind-the-scenes" photos of departments such as art and props and the carpentry and plasterers' workshops. Aerial panoramas were used to convey a studio's size, and technicians at work were shown through a mix of actuality and staged imagery. These photographs, supplied by the studios, were intended to display material assets (studio buildings, cameras, personnel, etc.) and thereby construct a narrative of the British film industry as strong and vigorous. Erin Hill has categorized similar images in her study of Hollywood promotional tours as types of "self-portraits ... [which are] revealing in both what they display and what they withhold from view."[22] What is striking about the images in *Picture-goer* is that women are largely absent, even though the expansion of the British film industry was made possible by their labor. The *Picturegoer* article maps the production process by singling out departments that are dominated by men: art, carpentry, props, camera, lighting, and editing. In particular, it gives priority to set design, which can be read as a reflection of the growing professional power this department wielded in British studios. Women as members of the workforce are present only as stars (Anna Neagle on set with director Herbert Wilcox), extras (in a communal dressing room), or as editors depicted working with men in the studios' cutting rooms. Despite *Picturegoer*'s *Who's Who* listing women working as directors, costume designers, and scenarists, none of this labor is recorded through these self-portraits. It seems that alongside the usual male self-aggrandizement was a gendered narrative that explicitly linked men and masculinity with the new modes of professionalization. This became even more transparent in the advertising for editing suites that appeared toward the end of the decade, which, as we will see later in this chapter, explicitly associated women with outdated practices and equipment.

This change of tone vis-à-vis women's work was reflected in a piece published in *Picturegoer* in 1935. Titled "The Place for Women in the Film Studios" and penned by M. Haworth-Booth (billed as "the first British woman producer"), the article recommended that women aim for the trades of script girl or cutter, while those with ambitions to direct were advised to "lie low" and take every opportunity to "learn, learn, learn" on the job.[23] If they could make themselves indispensable to the director, they might become an assistant within two years, but Haworth-Booth warned aspiring women they would face the obstacle of "male tradition," as difficult (as she described it) as trying to "move the Albert Hall," and counseled that women may find producing more welcoming. Her piece suggests that by the mid-1930s, women still had a place in the British film studios, but it was being imagined in increasingly narrow terms.

Becoming "Dress Conscious": Costume Departments in Britain's Film Studios

It seems that the representation of women technicians was contradictory, certainly as it was played out in the pages of *Picturegoer* in the late 1920s and early 1930s. On the one hand, women were depicted as central to the expanding film economy, with the industry held up as an attractive employment destination for them. On the other hand, it was principally men's labor that was emphasized in studio self-portraits intended to showcase the new, modern film industry. Nowhere was this contradiction more evident than in the portrayal of costume design. At this time fan magazines were publishing numerous articles calling for film directors to be more "dress conscious," arguing the importance of costume to the new film economy and reporting enthusiastically on the work of women designers, including Gordon Conway and Doris Zinkeisen, who had been recruited by British film producers as fashion experts.[24] But at the same time, evidence from other sources suggests that costume design lacked adequate workspace in the newly revamped British studios, its under-resourcing indicative of its value in screen culture relative to other areas of production such as cinematography and art direction.

This next section examines in more detail women's labor in this area of film production, through a case study of Gordon Conway (1894–1956), one of the most prolific women costume designers in Britain's film studios during the 1930s. Conway's diaries and personal correspondence provide a unique insight into her working methods and are especially valuable because there are no equivalent firsthand accounts of costume design from the perspective of wardrobe staff during this time, nor are there any records of costume designers or wardrobe staff—male or female—present in the ACT archive, which means we lack data on salaries and workforce demographics. That the nearest equivalent roles of art director, draftsman, buyer, and set dresser are well represented in the trade union records—roles that were all filled by men at this time—points to one of the ways in which women's labor in spheres commonly designated as "feminine" has been elided in official records. Extracts from Conway's personal papers have been published in her biography, penned by cultural historian Raye Virginia Allen, and these, along with Conway's articles in film fan magazines, help us draw a map of costume labor practices at a time of significant change in the British film industry.

Costume design has never been a role exclusively held by women; indeed many of the industry's leading designers have been men. In the context of Britain's film industry in the 1930s, John Armstrong and Joe Strassner were considered the top designers of the day, alongside fashion designer Norman Hartnell and stage designer Oliver Messell, who worked on some of the biggest British films of the decade. This led some historians to conclude that the profession at this time was almost entirely male dominated, but a number of women were of sufficient standing to receive individual screen credits.[25] In addition to Gordon Conway were Doris Zinkeisen (*Nell Gywn*, 1934; *Victoria the Great*, 1937), Cathleen Mann (*Chu Chin Chow*, 1934; *Things to Come*, 1936), and Italian fashion designer Elsa Schiaparelli, who designed costumes for Nova Pilbeam in *Little Friend* (1934) and Maurice Chevalier in *The Beloved Vagabond* (1936).[26] Credited together with Joe Strassner was Marion Horn, who earned over twenty screen credits as a wardrobe supervisor between 1935 and 1937 (listed as "Marianne"), and wardrobe supervisors Ann Morgan and Joyce Auberon, who were sufficiently noteworthy to be singled out for mention in the pages of *Picturegoer*. And there were women like Lily Payne, whose screen credits start only in 1947, when she was listed as Ealing's wardrobe supervisor, but whose career actually stretched back to the mid-1930s, when she had worked with the star Gracie Fields at Ealing's studios.[27]

But notwithstanding women's visibility in the profession, there were, and still are, gendered hierarchies within costume departments; construction and maintenance functions (cutting, sewing, repairing, ironing, etc.) disproportionately fall to women, and design and supervision roles are more likely to be held by men.[28] Feminized job titles such as "wardrobe mistress" were widely used in the industry at this time, with Adrian Brunel and other commentators likening the role to a "female property master" whose key attribute was being "handy with her needle."[29] It was these feminine associations with sewing and the world of domesticity that meant costume design and maintenance was a more likely employment destination for women, and it was women who led the debate about designing for films that appeared in fan magazines like *Picturegoer* in the 1930s. Through this debate we can see women's struggle to formulate the costume designer's job and the role of costume in the total look of the film, a struggle that, as I will show, was only partially successful.

At this time Britain had yet to establish the type of specialist in-house costume departments that had been a feature of Hollywood studios for several years. The usual practice for costuming British films relied on a combination of hiring outside design talent, renting stock from theatrical costumers, and actors wearing their own clothes. This led to what was perceived as a catalog of errors reported in the pages of *Picturegoer*, which bemoaned "badly groomed stars in dowdy clothes," a leading lady who arrived on set to find no costume for her to wear, and film producers who were content to put a girl in a frock and "take up the slack with a couple of safety pins and pray it wouldn't show in the close-ups."[30] The magazine was lukewarm in its assessment of how British studios were shaping up, claiming that while screen clothes "have certainly shown improvement in 1931 . . . too little vision is yet displayed."[31] Film director Adrian Brunel included costume in his "filmcraft" series, cautioning against clothes that were either too "fussy" or "undistinguished," or designs that failed to register on the screen, and recommending that greater attention be paid to "costuming in pictures."[32] In Brunel's assessment, the problem of costume could be resolved by women, who, he thought, were "particularly suited" to dress designing because they had "an eye to composition and detail."[33] They were also more prepared than men to tolerate the modest wages and poor working conditions that the profession attracted relative to other sectors of the industry.

Brunel's comments, however, do point to wider industry recognition at this time, certainly among the more ambitious British studios, that costumes needed to be cinematic—that is, designed with the camera in mind. Gordon Conway was at the vanguard of these debates and was forthright in the pages of film fan magazines about the need for what she called "better dressed pictures."[34] Her career presents an illuminating case study because of her central position in Britain's film studios. Her background was in illustration and design, and in the 1910s and 1920s she was producing artwork for *Vanity Fair*, designing theater posters, sketching for couturiers, and designing costumes for cabaret and theatrical performers. By the late 1920s, Conway was designing for British films and, in a remarkably productive phase, designed costumes for more than thirty features between 1929 and 1935 before retiring from the profession on the grounds of ill health. Her work included many of the industry's biggest features, such as *High Treason* (1929), *Sunshine Susie* (1931), and *The Good Companions* (1933), which demonstrated her skill across historical and modern design and received high praise by both critics and audiences alike (see figs. 1 and 2). *Sunshine Susie* won *Film Weekly* readers' poll for best British film, *The Good Companions* received a Royal Gala Premiere, and *High Treason* showcased a dazzling array of both glamorous and practical daywear for women, the costumes being the key selling point in the film's publicity and press books.[35]

Figure 1. Gordon Conway's sketch for the "Three Wishes" dress worn by Jessie Matthews in *The Good Companions* (1933). Source: Harry Ransom Center, Gordon Conway Collections.

Figure 2. Studio photograph of Jessie Matthews wearing Conway's designs in *The Good Companions* (1933). Source: Harry Ransom Center, Gordon Conway Collections.

Conway was a leading voice in the industry and laid out her design philosophy and ambition for "dressing the pictures" in a number of astute articles that illustrate a highly attuned cinematic sensibility. In "Dressing the Talkies" (1929), she argued that "the story's the thing" and put forward "my theory that clothes can and do tell the story" and that the designer should strive "by means of line and drapery and materials to express that story in terms of clothes."[36] Elsewhere she asserted the designer's responsibility to ensure that "the frock does not quarrel in colour or in line with the sets" and that "a properly designed frock should belong as distinctively to the film for which it is designed as do the sub-titles."[37] Here she proposed that a film should have a coherent approach to production design, with costume a crucial element of that film's overall look, a position that departs radically from the practice of carelessly adapting off-the-peg clothes in a haphazard manner. In this respect Conway was in step with the concept of "total design" that was reshaping art direction in Britain's film studios at this time, with proponents like Alfred Junge advocating for a film's "look" to be carefully planned before shooting and in consultation with all relevant designers.[38] The extent to which Conway herself was involved in such discussions remains to be seen. She was certainly mindful of, in her words, "the effect properly designed clothes can have on an artiste's performance," and had made a study of new color systems like "panchromatic films" to better understand how the color, tone, and hue of fabrics would photograph.[39] She called for a full understanding of the photographic properties of fabric, arguing that "one material is not exactly like another in the camera's eye," and that using cheap materials would only result in costumes that looked cheap on the screen.[40] That her designs were singled out by critics who described them, approvingly, as "striking" and Conway as a "star" is further evidence of how far her thinking and execution had advanced the possibilities of costume design for film.

Achieving Conway's vision for "dressing the pictures" required proper resourcing, and as early as 1928 she was calling for studios to set up autonomous film wardrobe departments, saying that every British studio should employ "its own designer and dressmaking staff as they have in Hollywood."[41] But she frequently expressed her frustration that, in her words, "so few people amongst makers of movies take it [costume design] seriously."[42] Her diaries for the years between 1927 and 1933 provide a unique insight into her working practices as a designer and the uphill struggle she faced in attempting to realize her professional ambitions. For much of this time she was working freelance on a picture-by-picture basis, seemingly without dedicated studio space and with only a minimal team to support her. That she designed for films made at different studios (including Gainsborough's Islington studios, British Lion's Beaconsfield studios, and Gaumont-British's revamped facilities at Shepherd's Bush) makes her contemporary descriptions of both work process and conditions broadly representative of British film production culture of the period.

Conway's diary entries indicate that it was more common for her to liaise directly with producers, directors, and cameramen rather than art directors, and this suggests that costume and wardrobe were operating on the periphery of the art department rather than being fully integrated into the team.[43] This seems to have had implications for accessing resources, facilities, and, as we will see, wider recognition within the industry. In terms of workflow, she would receive a commission and production budget from the producer, draw up sketches and agree on designs for the film's principal characters, and, after that, work directly with couturiers, costumers, and department stores. Allen's accounts show how Conway directly supervised the "measurements, fabric and accessory selection, pattern approval, draping, and fittings," all of which took place away from the studios.[44] She liaised with all the major theater costume businesses in

London (B. J. Simmons, Nathan's, Berman's et al.) and shopped for accessories (stockings, gloves, costume jewelry, parasols, handbags, shoes) in
the capital's department stores and markets. During the course of her
career in British studios, Conway performed other duties, including buying props, set dressing, and assisting with the casting of extras. She also
undertook private commissions from screen actresses to provide them
with costumes, some of which they later wore in their film roles, although
these designs were never acknowledged in screen credits.[45] This suggests
that her contribution to British film culture is more extensive than has
been recognized previously. Her role demanded extensive knowledge of
local specialist suppliers, acute business acumen to negotiate prices, a
talent for research and specialist shopping, skills in original design and
alterations, and a high level of emotional intelligence to massage egos and
manage expectations.

Conway's diary entries and other correspondence suggest that she did
not have ready access to the type of centralized workspace in a film studio
that characterized the well-established Hollywood system, complete with
its team of assistants and a well-stocked wardrobe department on which
to draw. Allen estimates that Conway carried out most of her film work
with never more than "four helpers" at any one time, despite working on
some of the highest-profile films of the day.[46] Lacking studio workspace,
Conway spent much of her time moving between different geographical
locations, and given the size of Central London alone, this was a heavy
drain on her time and energy.[47] Her pocket calendars from 1932 when she
was preparing designs for both *Marry Me* and *There Goes the Bride* (star-
ring Jessie Matthews) record multiple appointments scheduled into small
time slots across an extended working day, revealing the conditions under
which she labored as a freelance designer, even one operating at the top
of the professional ladder.[48] Working freelance—and with ambitions to
see British studios develop specialized costume departments—also meant
establishing and maintaining professional networks, and in addition to her
day job, she regularly hosted social events for what she described as "film
men" at her Bryanstone Court apartment in Marylebone, London, which
also served as an office and studio space for fittings. Around this time
she was given a contract by Michael Balcon, then head of production for
Gainsborough/Gaumont-British, who appointed her head of the studio's
newly formed dress department. Her appointment was widely trumpeted
in the British press, with Gaumont-British lauded for opening the "First
Studio Dress Department" in the country, and her working conditions
briefly improved; she was assigned a car and driver and, in 1932, a full-time
assistant, Margaret Watts.[49] Reflecting on her new role, Conway stated

that her ambition was to develop the department to "employ about thirty girls in my workroom. Not including designers and assistants" and to grow to "at least fifty before long."[50] This would have brought the costume department in line with Gaumont-British's art department, which by that time was well staffed with a team of art directors (including the renowned Alfred Junge) ably supported by scores of draftsmen and scenic artists, who, as the union records show, were all men. Conway's ambitions for a fully functioning costume department along the lines of those in Hollywood were short-lived. Her assistant lost her job after six months due to budget cuts at the studio, and Conway's own ill health (brought about through overwork) cut short her career, and she effectively retired from film work around 1934–35.

What can be concluded from Conway's accounts about the broader picture of gender and costume departments in the 1930s? Costume was simultaneously visible and absent in contemporary debates. It was acknowledged as an important part of the "filmcraft" narrative, and practitioners like Conway were given space in the pages of *Picturegoer* to lay out a design philosophy. But costume was modestly resourced in terms of staff and facilities compared to art direction and other areas of production. This ambivalence is made further evident in the conspicuous absence of costume from the studio self-portraits that were published in the *Picturegoer* special of 1934. Either specialist workspace was not available to be photographed or, if it was, it was not considered "worth a story" by the studio. And when *Picturegoer* published its *Who's Who and Encyclopaedia of the Screen To-day* in 1933, it was Hollywood's costume department that was featured, with an article "Dressing the Stars" penned by MGM's leading designer, "Adrian." When it came to showcasing new advances in the film industry, it's hard not to conclude that the male-dominated studios were blind to women's significant contribution in costume design and afforded it little status in the narratives of modernization that circulated at the time.[51] This absence has been replicated in film historiography, where there is little scholarship on costume design from this period, certainly compared to set design and art direction. Despite Conway making a number of astute pronouncements about design principles, she did not publish the kind of studies that consolidated art director Edward Carrick's reputation. While she certainly had the talent and professional knowledge to be able to do so, she was presumably too busy making up for the shortfall that accrued from the slender resources with which she and her team had to work.

And what of the other women working in costume at this time? Of Conway's assistants, Margaret Watts later became a costume designer in her own right under her married name, Margaret Furse (her husband was production designer Roger Furse), and won an Academy Award for costume design for her work on *Anne of the Thousand Days* (1969). Marion Horn would later become wardrobe supervisor at Ealing Studios until her retirement around 1947, but she also earned a co-credit for costume design for the Jessie Matthews film *Gangway* (1937). To what extent occupational mobility, from wardrobe to design, was possible for women at this time is unknown; there is currently insufficient evidence from which to draw firm conclusions. I return to the story of women in wardrobe and costume roles in more detail in chapter 5, but I turn now to women's experience in secretarial and continuity roles, two of the biggest recruiters of women labor in the 1930s.

Continuity Girls

If women's work in costume and wardrobe is absent from the ACT records, their work in secretarial and continuity roles is, by contrast, highly visible. Women in these roles form one of the largest cohorts of female applications to the union in the 1930s, second only to editors and negative cutters in the size of the workforce and scale of contribution they made to the industry's production boom. Forty women categorized themselves as continuity girls or assistants, a further fourteen as floor secretaries, six as secretaries, and three as script secretaries, with two women holding dual roles (combining floor secretary with continuity). Those with several years of experience earned between seven and eight pounds per week, which was effectively two-thirds of the wage earned by a first assistant director, a position held by men. These were broadly equivalent roles in terms of skill and responsibility, the wage differential showing how value was attributed to the role on the basis of the job holder's gender. It was these types of pay discrepancies between jobs that would later be challenged by women. The chair of the Continuity and Production Secretary Section, Teresa Bolland, used the pages of the ACT's journal in 1953 to highlight the issue of pay inequality between jobs of equal value, arguing: "The pay of Continuity girls should be higher—the work is just as responsible as a 1st Assistant's, and pay should be on a level with his."[52] These comments, coming twenty years after continuity girls first joined the union, show how difficult it would be for women to achieve pay parity. Many of the continuity girls who joined the union in the 1930s were in their late twenties, often single, with some form of secretarial training or further education, and financially self-supporting. Their expectations for interesting and financially rewarding work were not always met in full, but continuity work was a responsible job with a degree of status. To understand it more fully, this case study draws on women's descriptions of their work in continuity, both contemporary and retrospective, to outline the chief characteristics of the role, its place in the production hierarchy and how that served the interests of male workers, and the technical and interpersonal skills women needed to perform successfully in the role. It draws on interviews and written accounts by several women (Kay Mander, Meg Bennett, Toni Roe, Tilly Day, Alma Reville, Phyl Ross, Phyllis Crocker, and Ann Skinner) whose working lives span a number of decades (from the 1920s through to the 1960s), giving a commonality of experience from which to build a representative picture of continuity work in Britain's film studios.[53]

Continuity in Britain's film studios was an entirely feminine domain—no men applied for the role through the trade union—and in the 1930s the position was in a state of transition.[54] As women's descriptions on their union records illustrate, continuity remained closely linked to roles such as floor secretary and script secretary. This was a legacy of the more informal production system of the previous decade, where the floor secretary role could combine aspects of script editing and continuity.[55] By the 1930s and the establishment of the ACT union, the role was the subject of increasing attention. Job flexibility was anathema for the union, which described their motivation in 1938 as trying to "work out a clear-cut definition of . . . each particular branch of work" and finding continuity particularly frustrating, as "there is no hard and fast rule of what the job includes."[56] This frustration may have been behind the number of female-authored descriptions of the job that appeared in print at the time, circulating as part of the wider filmcraft debates in the film industry. Continuity girl Martha Robinson published a well-received memoir in 1937, while Meg Bennett and Toni Roe penned detailed descriptions of their workdays, published, respectively, in Adrian Brunel's book *Film Production* (1936) and the industry journal *The Cine-Technician* (1936).[57] In a manner similar to costume workers, continuity girls were also struggling to express, concisely and systematically, what their job involved and how the multitasking nature of the role functioned on a scale comparable to that of assistant director.

These and other accounts went some way toward laying down the essential elements of the role, highlighting its specialist skills and challenging common misconceptions about the job. Documentarian Kay Mander initially characterized continuity as "an entirely non-technical job, one that can be done by any reasonably efficient secretary with good shorthand and typing and a cast-iron memory," but she radically revised her opinion when she herself moved into continuity work in 1937.[58] Mander, a leading voice in the union in the 1930s and 1940s, used the pages of the union's journal, *The Cine-Technician*, to mount a defense of the role and to lay claims for the job holder as "indeed a technician," with all the status that implied, but her comments suggest how the case had still to be made as late as 1940. Indeed, Mander concedes that "many other technicians" hold the view that continuity is merely secretarial and that it is these associations that have contributed to how the role has been recognized and remunerated. Wider recognition was to be welcomed because, as Toni Roe found, "the post of script girl is the only one open to women on the actual floor," indicating how production roles were narrowing for women in British studios by the time her article was published in 1936.[59]

The parallel Teresa Bolland drew between the roles of continuity and first assistant director highlights how continuity is at the center of film production. An oft-repeated description by women of the role is that of the "director's right hand," their function to "supply him with any detail he may desire to know" about the shoot (see "Continuity Girl" in glossary and fig. 3).[60] This is no mean feat and required the job holder to be fully versed in what Phyllis Crocker (continuity, 1930s–1970s) described as a "hundred and one technicalities."[61] Kay Mander's description of the continuity girl's "encyclopaedic knowledge of the script" is particularly apt here.[62] As the director's right hand, the continuity girl was on set throughout rehearsal and shooting and was, in Crocker's words, "at hand to prompt both director and artists on dialogue, movement, position and

Figure 3. Connie Willis, continuity girl, working beside Alfred Hitchcock on *The Man Who Knew Too Much* (1956). Source: The Cinema Museum.

effects."[63] Through copious note taking, she recorded detailed information about scene setups and relayed this information to relevant parties, the purpose being to ensure that, in Toni Roe's description, "action or clothing . . . match[es] up from one shot to another . . . [ensuring] the ultimate smoothness and polish of a good film."[64] More than just a conduit for relaying information, the continuity girl was responsible for, in the words of Ann Skinner (continuity, 1950s–1970s), making "directors' work *work*, you know."[65]

Achieving "smoothness" was hard work, and the continuity girl was an extremely important part of production, working not only with the director but also with several members of the production crew. Meg Bennett's description of her working day in 1936 name-checks a dozen different crew members. These include artists, whose clothes and accessories were verified by her; the clapper boy, to ensure the scene numbers on his board were accurate; the cameraman or assistant, to record total footage and lens for each scene; the stills photographer, to produce a "set still"; and the propman for any set dressing.[66] She had to respond to questions being "fired at her from every member of the studio staff, the cameraman, the sound recordist, the director, the producer, and the artists," and success in the role demanded skills in quick thinking as well as extensive knowledge of the script. Bennett also wrote continuity reports for the heads of production and editors (recording footage shot, artists and sets used, etc.), prepared call sheets for the following day's shooting, and viewed rushes with the director and editor (see fig. 4).[67] Indeed the relationship with the editor was key; Phyllis Crocker described her role as "liaison between the director and the editor" and commented how the time she had spent in the cutting room in a previous job had "benefit[ed] me enormously" as she learned how footage was assembled into narrative chronology.[68] Being well versed in filmmaking's "hundred and one technicalities" meant continuity girls were, in Mander's assessment, "the director's technical assistant," and some directors leaned heavily on them.[69] Angela Allen (continuity, 1940s–2002) made fourteen films with director John Houston and recounted being in charge of the second unit, shooting scenes on *Roots of Heaven* (1958), as she "knew his style."[70] Although Allen's experience may have been unusual, her description attests to the significance of the continuity role and provides context to Teresa Bolland's calls for pay parity with the first assistant director role.[71]

Meg Bennett characterized the continuity job as requiring "excellent powers of observation, a very good memory and endless patience"—something for which women were assumed to have a natural aptitude—but her description also hints at the significant interpersonal skills the job

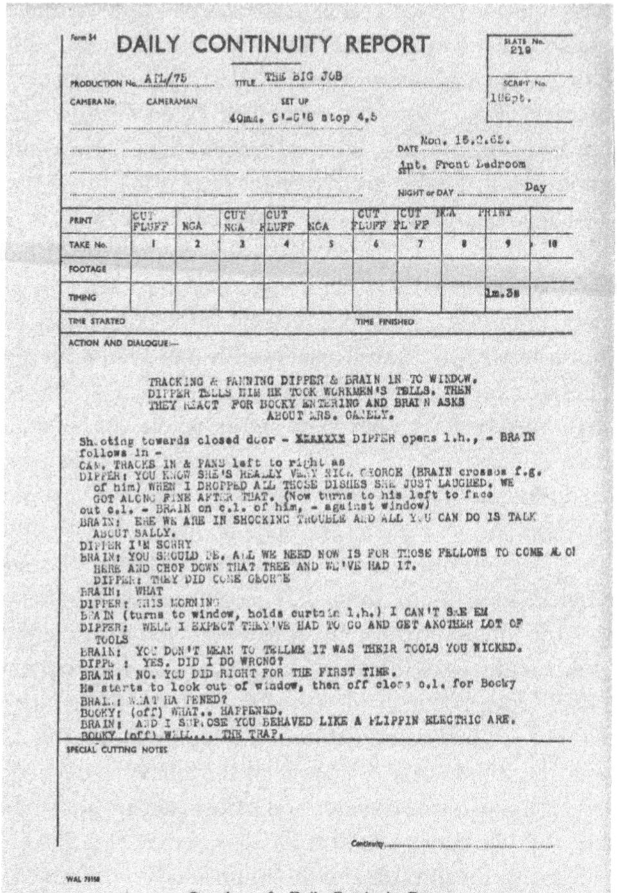

One sheet of a Daily Continuity Report

Figure 4. Sample of a daily continuity report, prepared by the continuity girl, to record the type of film and camera lens used, setting, lighting, number and type of shots, takes printed, and any instructions for the editor. Source: Elizabeth Grey, *Behind the Scenes in a Film Studio* (London: Phoenix House, 1967), 46.

demanded. Alma Young characterized the role as that of "professional fault finder," which often put the continuity girl in an invidious position on set.[72] It was the role of the continuity girl to tell other crew members when something was wrong, which had to be done tactfully while ensuring the mistake was corrected. Continuity girls also soothed egos on set and acted as intermediaries between cast, crew, and director, as witnessed by Alfred Hitchcock's reliance on the diplomatic skills of Alma Reville and Peggy Robertson, who both provided continuity on several films he directed.[73] The "smoothness and polish of a good film" relied as much on interpersonal skills as it did on camera work, and it was continuity girls that carried out the emotional labor that glued the production team together. But as professional fault finders and emotional laborers, much of their work was visible only in absentia, something of which continuity girls themselves were acutely aware. Meg Bennett vividly captures this in her description, which compares the job to "the elastic of an undergarment. . . . If they are doing their job as they should, no one notices them, but if they fail they cause unwelcome attention and extreme panic!"[74]

Bennett's quip about not being noticed is lighthearted—and many below-the-line practitioners rightly complain how their labor goes unrecognized—but for continuity girls in particular their invisibility could have dire consequences, especially during location shooting. When filming in Italy in 1965, Ann Skinner was almost left behind when the production crew moved location because she had not been listed on the movement order. Because the continuity girl is "a person on their own, they don't have a department . . . unlike the camera boys . . ., no arrangements had been made for me. . . . Camera crew, everybody else, had arrangements but there were no arrangements for me."[75] This threw her into a blind panic when she found out at the last minute that she had to catch a night train to Naples. Her experience shows how information circulates in production teams through channels that serve the needs of their male workers. Continuity may well have been at the center of production, but as Skinner consequently found, that did not necessarily translate to the role being fully integrated into a crew's consciousness and therefore planning schedule.[76] Continuity was brought under the union's framework in the early 1930s, but as Skinner's experience shows, the lack of a departmental structure made it difficult for women to speak with a collective voice that had bargaining power. Women could exercise individual agency—as Tilly Day (continuity, 1920–1970s) famously did during the shooting of *Toilers of the Sea* (1936) when she withheld her continuity sheets during a pay dispute—but the scope to make a collective argument based on issues like job parity did not come until after the Second World War when a continuity section was set up in the union.[77]

Notwithstanding these challenges, the job was popular with women, as it offered interesting work with scope for autonomy, relatively high wages, and occasional perks such as foreign travel at a time when this was restricted to the upper-middle classes in Britain. Phyllis Crocker described continuity work as "extremely interesting . . . a job which is out of the ordinary and calls for initiative," while for Kay Mander it was a way of "earning a living in an enjoyable way."[78] Within the modernization debates taking place in the British film industry in the 1930s, women in continuity were keen to stress how training was needed to succeed in the role. Phyl Ross estimated that two years of working as a continuity assistant was necessary to develop "instinctive knowledge of photography, angles, lighting and lenses."[79] Toni Roe argued for "two girls on the job," one matching and assisting the director, the other typing reports and doing more routine work.[80] By the 1940s this two-person method had been adopted as standard practice on all but the cheapest of British features. Roe's statement shows how a firm division of labor was now established, one that built on gendered assumptions that women's function on the studio floor was to support men.

The role may have been interesting, but it had its limitations. Phyllis Crocker may have had the type of "all round knowledge of the business" that made directing "the logical line of advancement," but few women made the transition. After almost ten years in the role (1935–1944), Phyl Ross found the work "automatic" and, wanting something "more creative," was frustrated to find directing closed because of a "decided prejudice . . . from the men in the industry."[81] She moved into scriptwriting instead. Crocker's suggestion that women might "branch out into the cutting-rooms" stemmed from her firm conviction that acting as "liaison between the director and the editor" made them well qualified for the role. Crocker was not alone in drawing connections between continuity and editing. In 1923 Alma Reville had published an article titled "Cutting and Continuity" in the trade press, which called for "the art of both" to be "thoroughly mastered" to avoid the tedium of the "long-drawn-out film."[82] Reville argued that it was only through the "continuity writer" having a "working knowledge of cutting" that "smooth continuity of action" could be achieved. Women like Reville, Crocker, and the many others who worked in continuity knew what made a good film and through their knowledge and skills helped bring it to fruition. For that reason alone, they were almost certainly too valuable to promote to the director's chair.

In this final case study, I examine the position of women in cutting rooms in the 1930s. Women in postproduction roles formed the largest single cohort of applications to the union that decade—just over ninety in total, of which one-third were from editors or assistant editors, and two-thirds were negative cutters, positive joiners, or similar grades. Women in these roles were mainly employed by the bigger studios, such as Gaumont-British, Fox British, and British International Pictures. I bring the voices of women editors and negative cutters into the story here as they shed new light on notions of creativity.[83] Often categorized as routine or low-skilled work, especially negative cutting, women's accounts reveal how they saw their roles as requiring a high degree of skill and themselves as custodians of the craft. This case study looks first at women in editing, and how the industry's modernization agenda worked in men's favor, before examining the skills and pedagogic labor performed by women in negative-cutting roles.

Editing

There are long-standing associations between women and cutting that go back to the early days of cinema. Editing, like continuity, is commonly perceived as a supporting role, the editor acting as a sounding board for the director in the pursuit of his (occasionally her) creative vision. Director Jean-Luc Godard famously described this as "*tourner est masculine, monter féminin*" (shooting is masculine, editing is feminine), with the former role being the more creative of the two.[84] In her 1923 article "Cutting and Continuity," filmmaker Alma Reville described the editor's role as looking after the "small technical details too numerous to mention" while making sure that your work did not "remind your audience they are viewing a picture made by a mechanical machine."[85] It is this combination of detail work and invisible labor that has made editing more open to women workers and the role appear as feminized, even though men worked in the field. Editor Colin Crisp's description of the job as "that of the little woman" is an apt summation of the gendered associations of the role.[86] Practitioners' descriptions of the work often conjure up feminine imagery, with editing connected to domestic labor through descriptions that liken it to sewing or patching.[87] British editor Thelma Dunaway/Myers/Connell (hereafter Myers) described her role as "rather like a weaver, who is provided with the various coloured threads which form the warp and woof and from them has to design and execute the finished pattern" (see "Editor" in glossary).[88]

Historically, all forms of cutting were seen as variants of manual processing, for which women, with their "natural" aptitude for patience and dexterity, were well qualified. As Kirsten Hatch has shown, "Assembling reels and cutting negatives was tedious work that often fell to young working-class women" in the early years of cinema.[89] A typical career pathway for many women was to move from the ranks of negative cutting into higher-level editing jobs. Siân Reynolds has shown how women in France came into editing after years as "manual process workers, developing, printing or hand-colouring film," and a similar pattern is evident in Hollywood and other national cinemas.[90] Alma Reville's early career in Britain mirrors this trend of occupational mobility; she moved into script supervision and cutting after time spent as a rewind girl at Twickenham

Studios. At this point editing was not seen as a specialist occupation and was "a common point of entry for many newcomers to the film industry, particularly women."[91] But the introduction of sound in the 1920s raised the profile and status of editing, and this had negative repercussions for women, as men were increasingly positioned as authorities on editing and paid accordingly. These emerging hierarchies are evident through union applications, trade advertising, and firsthand accounts, and I will examine each of these in turn.

The union processed 30 applications from women in the 1930s who listed their job title as editor or assistant editor/cutter, compared to 130 applications from men in corresponding roles. Women therefore comprised just under 20 percent of all applications in the industry's editing jobs, making them a small but significant proportion of the intake. Average wages for women and men were roughly comparable where they held the same position. Assistant editors earned between three and four pounds per week in the mid-1930s, editors between six and eight pounds, although there was some variation depending on experience in the role. These levels of pay indicate that the role was comparable to continuity in terms of occupational value. By the second half of the 1930s, the records show that a broader range of salaries was being paid to men, with some wages as high as twelve to fifteen pounds per week. These were for men in chief editor roles at British Lion and British and Dominion Films Ltd. This variation can be explained, in part, by differential pay rates for editors (and other technicians) on prestige features compared to "quota quickies," but there were other, wider shifts taking place in the industry that were driving this agenda.[92]

As the decade progressed and the film industry responded to the introduction of sound, cutting rooms underwent changes in technology and work processes, many of which were imported from the United States. Britain's leading editor, Thorold Dickinson, went to Hollywood in 1929 to study sound techniques and on his return introduced new approaches to editing in British studios. Elstree revamped their cutting rooms, equipping them with new technology in the form of synchronizers and sound-and-action-head Moviolas, and new work practices were also imported.[93] In Hollywood a combination of bigger departments and the complexities of cutting sound led to what Erin Hill has described as "a more rigid hierarchy of apprentices and masters," with new classifications like "assistant cutter" being introduced into the workforce. These processes of specialization, she argues, aided men, as many department heads assumed women would struggle with the new technology.[94] Union records show similar changes taking place in the British workforce, with the ACT drawing increasingly strict demarcations between jobs as new crew positions of "chief editor," "editor," and "assistant" were formalized.[95] By the middle of the decade, it was becoming standard practice for British studios to use one editor and one assistant on most feature films, and around this time the title of "chief editor" began to appear on union application forms.[96] This newly created role was occupied solely by men; women increasingly joined the union as assistant editors rather than full editors. By the end of the decade, the union set wages for a top-level editor at twenty pounds per week and lower for assistants, a move that effectively widened the gap between male and female workers in the editing suite and formalized assumptions about levels of skill and expertise.[97] In this respect, editing follows the pattern identified by sociologist Sylvia Walby (discussed in chapter 1) where industries expand by creating new junior-level jobs with lower wages and status, which are then filled by women.

Trade advertising in the union's journal shows how women were being sidelined in Britain's cutting rooms, purposefully associated with industry traditions that were now deemed outmoded. One of the industry's leading editing companies, Normans, based in Central London with private bays for rent, drew an explicit, gendered contrast between the old, outdated cutting rooms of 1900—filled with women—and the up-to-date editing bay of 1937, where men took the lead in handling the "modern equipment" (see fig. 5). As with the studio self-portraits discussed earlier in this chapter, it is the figure of the male professional who signposts the film industry's modernization narrative. And it is men who colonized the debate on the new technology, claiming an authoritative voice on the art of editing. Innumerable articles were published on the subject of editing in Britain in the 1930s, including Dan Birt's "The Principles of Film Recording," Ian Dalrymple's "Commercial Cutting," Sidney Cole's "From the Cutting Room," and Thorold Dickinson's "On Cutting." Women were not entirely absent from this debate, with fan magazines profiling the visit of leading American editor Margaret Booth to British studios in 1932. Booth's visit to Britain was at the invitation of Gaumont-British's head of production, Michael Balcon, who brought her over "to see that MGM's British cutting-room is organised according to MGM's Hollywood standards."[98] Despite Balcon's professional respect for Booth, whom he recognized as "one of the best in the business," her presence did not engender a wider acceptance of women in higher-level editing jobs in British cutting rooms.[99] Indeed there is a wider irony here that while women were being relegated to the sidelines by men, the industry simultaneously looked to experts like Booth to bring their male workforce up to speed. I will return to the question of women's pedagogic labor shortly.

Figure 5. Advertisement for Normans editing bays. Source: *The Cine-Technician* (April–May 1937).

Firsthand accounts by women editors working in British studios in the 1930s also reveal the gender prejudice and hierarchical cultures they faced in the industry. Thelma Myers joined the union in 1936 as an assistant continuity girl with eighteen months' experience to her name. From continuity she worked her way into editing, serving first as an assistant editor to David Lean before earning her first screen credit as an editor for *In Which We Serve* (1942). This seemingly smooth professional trajectory belies the prejudice she faced as a woman, and her recollections of British cutting rooms, written in 1944, make for sober reading:

> When I first started I came up against a great deal of prejudice from the male members. It was felt that the cutting-room was one department which it was exclusively the boys' prerogative to staff. . . . I was actually told that women would never make good editors by reason of their sex. . . . They would, for instance, favour cutting to the handsome hero at the expense of the heroine.[100]

Myers went on to forge a long career as an editor in the British film industry, most notably through a professional partnership with the director/producer team of Frank Launder and Sidney Gilliat, who famously enjoyed success with the St. Trinian's films. She was BAFTA-nominated for her editing work on *Alfie* (1966), earned a reputation in the industry for her fast cutting technique and no-nonsense style, and was highly respected by those she trained. Editor Peter Honess remembered her as "quite an extraordinary woman."[101]

In fact, it was her extraordinary talents that placed her in high demand, but behind the platitudes lies a story of a lack of generosity within the industry. Accounts by Myers's colleagues reveal how the male culture of the studios stifled female ambition. Production secretary Mary Harvey recalled how Myers was "very knowledgeable, she always wanted to direct" but was never given the opportunity or encouragement to pursue this pathway.[102] Fellow editor Teddy Darvas's recollection of Myers "working out every shot" for Launder and Gilliat, who, he claims, "relied on her" to resolve "difficult sequence[s]," points to Myers being too valuable to promote.[103] There were similar parallels in Hollywood's studios, where Erin Hill finds women editors being "put back as assistants" by men in supervisory positions who were presumably happy to have talented women around as long as men ultimately wielded the power in the cutting room.[104] Myers's own description of the editor's role is revealing: "Their job is elastic; they have more freedom than the unit on the floor . . . [and] the editor's job . . . is more creative than anyone else's, except, perhaps, the writer's and the director's."[105] This was certainly true in her hands, where, faced with a working environment in which the odds were stacked against her, she took what opportunities she could to exercise her creative autonomy in the role. Chapter 4 returns to this theme in more detail when I look at the creative work performed by production secretaries and documentary editors in less than auspicious circumstances.

Even though British studios had little interest in fostering the professional talents of women in editing, they nevertheless were content for women to be organized as workers, and the union in particular singled out those in cutting rooms. In 1938 the union's journal published an article by Alison Selby-Lowndes, a continuity girl active in union politics, that directly addressed the women cutters working in small firms in Soho, imploring them to join the union.[106] Describing them as a "numerically powerful . . . section of the trade . . . who work for well below the average rates," the union was keen to ensure that these women "who can be got on the cheap" were brought under their control, not least because they could undercut the wages of men.[107] These "numerically powerful" women were the short-term cutters, the rank-and-file workers who turned over the volume of film that drove the production boom and who swelled the ranks of the film laboratories and studios. Selby-Lowndes disparaged them as "more or less of a dead weight in the struggle for a satisfactory standard of wages and conditions," but examining their working lives and experiences suggests an altogether more fascinating picture.

Negative Cutting

Applications to the union show that women in postproduction roles typically joined the industry at age fifteen or sixteen, starting out as positive examiners and film joiners, where they earned about a pound per week in 1935. From there they could expect to progress to negative cutter within three or four years, with weekly wages between two and three pounds. A small number of women held more senior roles, including Mary Baker, chief negative cutter at Fox Film Studios, and Alice Hogger, head of negative cutting at Elstree's Film Laboratories. These women were older and had a wealth of experience cutting and joining negatives, training others, and quality-checking their work (see "Negative Cutter" in glossary). Baker was thirty-seven when she joined the union in 1935 with over twenty years' experience, while Hogger, age forty and married, had worked in the industry since 1912. These supervisory positions earned them a wage of between four and five pounds per week, comparable to assistant editors but far from the weekly income earned by experienced continuity girls. By contrast, union records show that men had access to a wider range of roles, including the developing, printing, and grading of film; film drying; and chemical mixing. Here wages were higher—printers and developers earned between three and four pounds per week in the mid-1930s—while negative cutters working a nightshift were all men and, in 1938, earned an extra ten to fifteen shillings per week than their counterparts (male and female) on the day shift.[108]

Union records show that by the 1930s all film printing and grading jobs were held by men, but there is evidence that women had previously worked in these better-paid roles. In 1940 the union published an article in its journal that profiled "The Johnstone Sisters" and their work as printers and graders in the British film industry.[109] Bizarrely, the women are referred to in coded terms as "Miss CK" and "Miss EH," but union records suggest the latter was almost certainly Emily Hilda Johnstone, who joined the union in 1937 when she was working as a charge hand (supervisor) in the positive room at Denham Film Laboratories. Then earning five pounds per week, she was single, age thirty-five, and had fifteen years of experience in the industry. Whatever the journal's motivation for concealing the women's full names, the article nevertheless provides a fascinating glimpse into the history of women's work in this area of production and how the range of jobs available to them narrowed through the 1920s and into the 1930s. Emily and other women like her moved into printing roles vacated by men during the First World War. These "hand-turn sight printing" jobs also included grading and were extremely well paid at between three and three and one-half pounds per week in approximately 1916.[110] Emily, her sister, and other women continued to find work as film printers for some time after the First World War but were eventually replaced in this role by men, at which point they took what employment was open to them in either negative or positive film work.

The journal's profile of Emily shows her working as a negative cutter at British International Pictures on a number of prestige productions, including *Moulin Rouge* (1928), *Piccadilly* (1929), and *Blackmail* (1929), the first British feature in sound. This film presented cutters with a challenge, as negatives did not have edge numbers in the early days of sound, and it was the negative cutter's job "to cut by matching frequencies."[111] This was no mean feat, as director David Lean recalled of his time as a junior editor at Gaumont-British, where, he claims, many directors "hadn't the foggiest idea how to synchronise sound and picture." As Lean explains, "You had to hold the film together tightly in your hand, and move it laboriously, sprocket by sprocket, foot by foot, through your fingers and make marks with a grease pencil every so often. . . . It *was* very difficult."[112] Lean's description opens up to view the skilled work that women like Emily Johnstone must have performed as negative cutters, her wealth of experience making her an invaluable asset to the film studio, especially crucial at a time of radical technological change.

Nevertheless, the journal's profile of "The Johnstone Sisters" concludes that while they are "competent women . . . [m]ost of the work is routine stuff, done more often than not by girls with no pride or interest in their jobs, filling in time till they get married, or married women out for a little pin-money."[113] This patronizing assessment shows how women and their work were viewed by some sections of the industry, and it bears no resemblance to how women themselves described their work. There are few surviving records from the period of women's employment in this sector, especially from a woman's perspective, which makes an oral history interview with negative cutter Alice May (Queenie) Turner, recorded in 1993, all the more valuable. Turner joined Pathé Labs in 1934 at the age of fourteen and started "at the bottom . . . stripping cans (of films)" and putting perforation holes in film.[114] From there she progressed to positive

joining, which she described as "very precise" work, before moving to negative cutting, where she handled newsreels, commercials, and a number
of key films, including *Ice Cold in Alex* (1958). She also worked on Second
World War color footage of warships, shot by the famous amateur filmmaker Rosie Newman. The last phase of her professional career was spent
as a librarian at the Imperial War Museum's film archives in the 1970s.
Her firsthand account gives an invaluable glimpse into the work world
of women in the laboratories. Trained by a female supervisor, Blanche
Harborough, Turner remembers a community of women at Pathé Labs
comprised of young trainees and older "ladies" with overall supervision
by a man, revealing how remunerative employment opportunities were
gendered. She recounts in detail the process of hand joining in ways that
communicate the pleasure she derived from her work:

> I had a Bell and Howell foot joiner. . . . It was lovely . . . joining and scrape
> it, pull it down, pull it down. . . . We used to have these little brass presses,
> there was a "B" on the hinge . . . and you used to have a scraper and a straight
> edge. And you had to do it perfectly . . . to make sure it didn't get a line
> coming down with a big space in it. . . . It was an art.[115]

The union's assessment of the work as "routine stuff," done by girls "with
no pride or interest in their jobs," is undermined by Turner's description,
which shows the precision, timing, and judgment the role demanded.
Hollywood film director Edward Dmytryk—who credits the female cutting staff at Paramount with introducing him to the basics—was closer
to the mark when he described "hand splicing as a skill. . . . Splicers had
to learn just how much of a frame to cut, how to . . . soften the emulsion
that had to be removed . . . how to apply the right amount of cement and
then fit the pieces together so precisely that the doubled film would ride
smoothly through the sprockets of the projection machine."[116] Moreover,
women like Queenie Turner, the Johnstone sisters, and Dmytryk's mentors
trained hundreds of men who came into the industry through negative
cutting before moving on to other roles. Turner recalled, "I had a whole
load of trainee boys. . . . They always used to call me 'Mum,'" a statement
that suggests Turner's position as a well-respected, experienced custo-
dian of a set of craft skills.[117] Turner, like Margaret Booth and presumably
countless other women, performed pedagogic labor, effectively helping
men into positions that were rapidly being closed off to women. It is for
these reasons that these women are remembered as a powerful force in
the film industry by those who crossed their path. For documentary film
director Margaret Thomson, recalling her time spent at the Gaumont-
British Instructional film library in 1936, her abiding memory is of the

"redoubtable neg cutters . . . women who were fierce and powerful."[118] The accounts of Turner, Thomson, and others show how work categorized by male commentators as feminized, of low status, and routine—done by women for pin money—emerges through women's own words as pedagogy and a form of skill-as-art (in the sense described by Raymond Williams in the introduction). Clearly some women, like men, did mark time in their jobs, and, unlike Queenie Turner, most did not end up as archivists at a national institution like the Imperial War Museum, but many did take pride in their work, the skills they developed to execute it successfully, and the training they gave to others. It was their labor—as much as that of the David Leans and Michael Balcons of the film world—that underpinned the film industry's rapid expansion in the 1930s.

Conclusion

The film production market was exceptionally volatile in the 1930s, shaped by the forces of rapid expansion and contraction. This led to a demand for "feminine" labor, in continuity/secretarial roles and cutting jobs, which meant there was plenty of work for women in the film industries of London. But unionization, with its particular forms of institutional organization and thinking, also meant greater job demarcation, and this had gendered consequences as male domination of employment opportunities took hold. Women increasingly found themselves in jobs that now attracted less status and pay, even though much of the work they performed in those roles required high levels of skill. And women found that their work became less visible, especially in the self-portraits that the studios produced to showcase how the film industry was modernizing. Implicit in these narratives—which showcased men's work—was a skepticism about women's technical capacities. This invisibility was particularly ironic in the case of costume design, where women like Gordon Conway did so much to develop professional practices and design philosophies specific to "dressing the pictures." The film industry did modernize, but it did so in ways that disadvantaged women and fostered male domination of employment opportunities. The next chapter examines how, in the light of these conditions, women film technicians fared under the particular circumstances of war.

3

The 1940s

Wartime Opportunities

The Second World War had a significant impact on the British film industry. Many film studios were requisitioned, leading to a dramatic reduction of available studio space; there was a shortage of raw film stock; and clothing and other key commodities were rationed, changing how the studio's wardrobe departments operated. The production of feature films decreased markedly, from an all-time high of 225 in 1937 to around 60 features per year, but the shorts and documentary sector grew significantly during the war to meet increased demand for newsreels and instructional material, much of which was commissioned by the government.[1] Indeed the state was heavily involved in film production and took a keen interest in the film industry, recognizing the propagandist and patriotic capabilities of the medium. British audiences flocked to the cinema—weekly attendance reached an impressive 30 million by 1945—and while Hollywood films remained popular, there was an appetite for homegrown products, including features, newsreels, and documentaries, that could connect with the special circumstances of a nation at war.[2] This chapter focuses first on key developments that affected women in the film industry—notably, the conscription of men and the active recruitment of women as replacement labor—before drawing an overview of women's work in film production. I then move on to three case studies that illustrate the scale and quality of women's achievements during the 1940s: documentary directing, the service film units, and women in the art departments of British studios.

Women as Reservists in the Film Industry

The conscription of men, the active recruitment of women, and the union's organization of the workforce were the key factors shaping the experience of women in the film industry during this decade. Many male film technicians initially enlisted in the armed forces, but the country's introduction of conscription in 1940 triggered a debate in the film industry about whether technicians might better serve the national interest by fulfilling the government's mass communications agenda. When the war broke out in 1939, it was initially only men over the age of thirty, working as camera operators, sound recordists, editors, film librarians, or in photographic processing, who qualified for reserved occupation status, thus making them exempt from military service.[3] This policy was revised at the end of 1940 when the government's Ministry of Labour granted exemption to all "legitimate film technicians," with the ACT given the responsibility to decide who qualified as "legitimate."[4] In a strategic move, the ACT tied legitimacy to union membership. The result was that "technicians now queued up to join ACT, the only body with the authority to categorise them as a reserved occupation."[5] This strengthened the union's power, and membership increased dramatically—just over five and a half thousand applications were received during the 1940s, a threefold increase over the previous decade—and the union made significant progress toward becoming a closed shop. There was further consolidation in the postwar years (1947–48) when the union drew up new agreements that saw in excess of one hundred jobs come under its purview. Despite their reserved occupation status, however, many male film technicians elected to join the armed forces while others moved into the military service film units. One estimate suggests that three-quarters of the film industry's male workforce were in the armed forces during the war.[6] With fewer men available to the film studios, opportunities for women did open up during the war, although it would be remiss to suggest they moved en masse into senior creative roles. It is more the case that, as historian Jo Fox has argued, "the war extended opportunities for women, accelerated their progress and diversified the nature of their assignments."[7] Evidence from the union database supports this assessment.

With more women coming into the workforce, the union was keen to ensure their labor was organized, albeit in ways that conformed to expectations about gendered pathways and women as a reserve army of labor. The early 1940s saw a number of debates take place in the pages of the union's journal about women technicians, and these capture the ambivalent lens through which the union viewed its female workforce.

On the one hand, it subscribed to the wider patriotic narrative that British industries, including the film trade, should "supply all the man-power we can for the Fighting Forces" and recognized that women were indispensable for the "release [of] manpower."[8] One indicator of this is how the film union fell in line with wider, albeit tentative, steps taken by the wartime government to help women into industry by providing support services related to shopping and child care. For instance, the union helped some film processing laboratories negotiate "priority shopping tickets" for women in their employ. These enabled women to preorder food goods from the grocer and sidestep waiting in long lines, thus demonstrating how women's labor was valued.[9] Through the pages of the union's journal, it is also evident that women were becoming increasingly visible in the union as shop stewards, including editors Kitty Wood at Gaumont-British Instructional and Kitty Marshall at Basic Films, and directors Margaret Thomson and Rosanne Hunter at the Realist Film Unit.

But these developments also need to be viewed alongside other sources, some of which suggest how the union viewed women as second-tier technicians whom it treated with suspicion. The ACT protected the rights of its established workforce by creating a new category of "war emergency membership" for new recruits. This gave workers temporary union membership that could later be rescinded, requiring the technician to reapply for full membership. Although records in the database show both men and women recruited as war emergency members, it was disproportionately applied to women. In April 1940 the first "For Women Technicians" column was published in *The Cine-Technician*, edited by documentary director Kay Mander. The topics and tone give a flavor of how the union regarded its female workforce. In the laboratories, for instance, women were to be recruited only when all other avenues had been exhausted, including unemployed male workers in any other position, relatives of laboratory workers serving in the forces, and unemployed studio technicians wanting to transfer into laboratory work. Women were reminded that their participation as replacement labor was contingent on their ensuring that "when the war is over the full rights of employees have been preserved"—that is, women were caretakers, with responsibility to look after male privilege.[10] And although the union supported equal pay and what it termed the "rate for the job," the principal motivation behind this was less social justice and more a commitment to ensuring that women did not undercut male workers. In a 1946 article published in its journal, the union categorized its women film technicians as "a danger to their male colleagues unless they are paid the rate for the job."[11] The publication date of 1946 is significant, as it coincides with the report of the Royal Commission on Equal Pay.

Although the report's modest recommendations were ultimately rejected by the postwar Labour government, it is likely that the ACT would be keen to ensure that pay in the film industry did not attract any wider attention.

Women and Union Records: An Overview

Given these ambivalences—recruiting women into the workforce but in ways that did not significantly disrupt gendered norms—how did women fare as film technicians during the 1940s? Women's applications increased from 10 percent of all ACT applications in the 1930s to just under 28 percent of all applications in the 1940s. Just over five and a half thousand technicians applied for ACT membership, of which just over fifteen hundred were women (see appendix C).[12] Women continued to work in significant numbers in continuity, as production secretaries, production assistants, and in general secretarial roles in studios, film companies, and film laboratories. Editing remained a key employment field for women, with many joining the union as trainees or assistant cutters. They swelled the ranks of the existing editing workforce to such an extent that by the end of the war some technicians observed that "cutting room crews . . . generally were 100% female."[13]

In addition to these traditionally feminized labor sectors, the range of film trades open to women does seem to have broadened during the decade, and some interesting patterns emerge. There were greater opportunities for women in animation studios, which recruited women in droves, as artists, animators, model makers, colorists, painters, tracers, and in-betweeners. Women worked in the film libraries of the Crown Film Unit, the RAF Film Production Unit, and at production companies such as Gainsborough and Two Cities. The ranks of the art department were swelled by women, who joined the industry as draftswomen, scenic artists, set dressers, dress designers, art directors, and assistants/apprentices. Women worked in the scenario department as readers, researchers, and writers; they joined as publicists, casting directors, production managers, and studio managers. They made modest inroads into camera roles, as film loaders, assistant directors, sound camera and production trainees, and in the stills department, where they were recruited as stills photographers, retouchers, and assistants. Some of these applications came from women who were already well established in the industry and were finally applying for union membership—documentary director Mary Field and animator Joy Batchelor, for example—while those in the more junior/assistant roles were, not surprisingly, relatively new to the film industry and recruited to meet the demand for labor. Other appointments were the direct consequence of changes taking place within the film industry and the postwar ambitions of key studios. Rank, for example, set up a "Charm School" to groom British stars in 1947, and the studio recruited women as fashion writers (Joyce Stannage) and publicity directors (Catherine O'Brien) supported by several assistants as part of its ambition to produce and promote quality films that could compete with Hollywood.[14] The trade press provides a further snapshot of women in production, which is broadly consistent with the patterns of the trade union data. The *British Film Yearbook, 1947–48* lists prominent personnel in key above-the-line roles, and women have a modest but notable presence in its pages as documentary directors, screenwriters, art directors, costume and production designers, editors, casting directors, and publicists. Indeed, the contribution of women to the wartime film economy was of sufficiently high profile to be showcased at a symposium in 1944 organized by the Royal Photographic Society of Great Britain. Titled "Women Talking," the symposium offered a platform for women to talk about their work in production and included contributions from writer Marjorie Deans, art director Carmen Dillon, and continuity girl Phyl Ross, among others.[15] The audience for and full significance of the event are not known, although it was reviewed in the film trade press suggesting it had made a wider impression; however, this may have been partly due to what was assumed to be women's "unusual" status in filmmaking.[16] So although the war may not have overturned established gendered pathways—men continued to dominate the directing and producing of feature films, as well as cinematography, sound engineering, and musical composition—it is clear from the trade union applications and other sources that opportunities for women technicians did expand during the decade.[17]

Instructing the Nation: Women's Documentary Filmmaking

Documentary filmmaking was one of the key features of British cinema's wartime landscape. It is also important as one of the areas to feature a number of high-profile women. In the 1940s the wartime government's Ministry of Information sponsored hundreds of short films on innumerable topics ranging from food rationing to home defense and air-raid precautions, made by companies such as the Crown Film Unit, Realist, Basic, and many others. The armed forces also set up service film units to produce shorts and feature-length documentaries for publicity and training purposes. As James Chapman has demonstrated, "Millions of feet of actuality footage were shot . . . by service cameramen," which was then compiled into films, some for general release, others for use solely within the services.[18] One source estimated that in excess of seven hundred documentary shorts were made during the war, although the figure is likely to be higher.[19] Crew requirements were minimal for live-action documentary shorts—a director, assistant, editor, and camera operator—and it was common practice for the director to be involved in all stages of production, including scriptwriting, liaising with specialist advisers, budget management, and postproduction.[20] This system evolved from the community/collective ethos of documentary filmmaking of the 1930s, which supported the development of an artisan model where everyone in the unit took a turn at performing different production roles. Such a system of production explains the relatively higher proportion of women in the field, as it favored them in two key ways: first, it gave them access to a type of training from which they were excluded in features, and, second, minimal crewing meant they did not have to supervise large groups of men, one of the factors often put forward to disqualify women from features work.

While the majority of these films were directed by men—certainly those that have passed into the film history canon, such as *Listen to Britain* (1942)—women were a notable presence in shorts and documentary filmmaking. Directors including Kay Mander, Evelyn Spice Cherry, Marion and Ruby Grierson, Margaret Thomson, Brigid "Budge" Cooper, and Joy Batchelor came into the industry in the 1930s and continued to work in documentary film production during the war. To their names we can add Louise Birt, Yvonne Fletcher, Jill Craigie, Rosanne Hunter, Mary Francis, Mary Beales, Muriel Baker, and Jane Massy, whose film careers started in the early 1940s, often as assistants or in continuity, before graduating to solo directorial credits.

Naming these women and listing them next to their peers is an important part of feminist scholarship. It is common for women in senior production roles to be framed discursively as "extraordinary"—that is, exceptions to the male norm—and nowhere is this more evident than in media coverage. Jill Craigie complained that publicity for her 1944 film *Out of Chaos* presented her as a "freak," while after the war the trade press was at pains to present Margaret Thomson in ways that emphasized her work with children and reassured its readership that she was "the antithesis of a blue stocking."[21] Such quotes illustrate how the figure of the woman director unsettled gender norms at this time. This "exceptionalist" discourse is part of a wider "forgetting" of women directors, itself a long-standing feature of the popular and trade press, which typically writes about women in ways that disconnect them from their predecessors, rendering any sense of a longer history invisible.[22] Moreover, the conventional practice for only minimal screen credits to be attributed in documentary filmmaking works against women, who were often in assistant/supportive roles. Many women did not object to the practice—Margaret Thomson, for example, saw it as part of documentary filmmaking's collective ethos—but others perhaps did, with Rosanne Hunter tabling a motion at the union in 1943 for assistants to have special representation on the ACT General Council.[23] Certainly making women visible matters to feminist history.

This case study examines the careers of two women documentarians: Margaret Thomson and Mary Beales. Although both worked in the above-the-line role of director, their career trajectories are quite different and, looked at in parallel, serve to illuminate the production culture of the 1940s and how women participated in and shaped that culture. Thomson's long career spanned over thirty years between 1937 and 1972, during which time she directed almost seventy shorts, while Beales and others like her had the type of episodic careers that I discussed in the introduction—working intensely for shorter periods of time before taking career breaks, often to look after children. Women documentarians have been the subject of recent reclamation, with nonfiction curators at the BFI playing an important role in making their films more visible.[24] Here I build on that research, examining in more detail Thomson's and Beales's extant films, critical reception, and the working relationships between groups of women and the informal support systems they fostered. I also mobilize these two women as illustrative examples of women's work in the sector, connecting them with their peers Rosanne Hunter, Yvonne Fletcher, Budge Cooper, and others. Their careers have been partially elided by the greater attention paid to their more high-profile husbands who also worked in documentary filmmaking, and this process of overshadowing is recognized by feminist historians as one of the frequent ways in which women are written out of history.[25] This section asks, What picture of documentary filmmaking might emerge if we put women in the center of the frame?

Margaret Thomson's long filmmaking career began in 1936 when she directed a series of ecology films for Gaumont-British Instructional (GBI). She was raised and educated in New Zealand, and a master's degree in zoology was her passport into filmmaking, as it gave her the highly specialized knowledge that GBI needed to make the series. This was followed by a few years of working in a variety of jobs, including editing, film librarianship, and foreign language teaching, before she was offered regular work at the Realist Film Unit in 1941. She worked steadily as a documentary director for the rest of the decade and quickly gained a reputation in the industry for the quality of her work. Her output was broad, ranging from horticulture (*Making a Compost Heap*, 1941; *Save Your Own Seeds*, 1943) and agriculture (*Clean Milk*, 1943; *Silage*, 1943; *Making Good Hay*, 1949) to medicine (*Open Drop Ether*, 1944; *Spinal Anaesthesia*, 1944) and general public health, especially of children (*Your Children's Teeth*, 1946; *Children Learning by Experience*, 1946).[26] Reviews of her films in the trade press frequently singled her out for praise, using terms familiar with notions of male authorship. *Clean Milk* is "made with the lucidity and technical mastery which characterises Miss Thomson's work"; *Save Your Own Seeds* evidences Thomson's "masterly touch," making its points "by purely cinematic means"; and *Sileage* is "technically interesting . . . [and] makes you want to go out and do it immediately [e]ven if you haven't got any cattle to feed in the winter."[27] So striking was Thomson's work that four of her shorts were included in a "digging for victory"–themed program of ten British documentaries, curated by Iris Barry for New York's Museum of Modern Art in 1943. Barry was unequivocal in her praise, describing the series as "the best instructional films I have seen, well-made and entirely practical yet full of human interest."[28] Indeed it was Thomson's ability to, in her own words, marry teaching with "the wider field of emotion and creativity" that elevated her work beyond the didactic.[29]

Children Learning by Experience is generally accepted as one of Thomson's most accomplished films. Sponsored by the Ministry of Education, it was intended for use in teacher training. Thomson, who herself had teaching experience, was keen to shoot it in as naturalistic manner as possible, eschewing staging in favor of extended sequences of the children "enjoying themselves and doing their own thing."[30] Her approach puzzled her cameraman Ron Craigen, who admitted, "I could never quite understand her way of working. . . . She had the idea we'll just turn the camera on and we'll see what happens."[31] The finished film uses narration and sound sparingly, with the extended silent scenes intended to encourage viewers to fully engage with the children's behavior and actions on screen. As Thomson noted, the film's pedagogical principle was that "teachers must, must take notice of that" if they were to be effective educators.[32] The film has since been credited as an early example of the cinema verité style, but nowhere was Thomson's commitment to realism more evident than in the series of medical films she made with Rosanne Hunter and Yvonne Fletcher.[33] Sponsored by Imperial Chemical Industries, the three women made eleven half-hour films on different anesthesia techniques, including *The Signs and Stages of Anaesthesia* (1944), *Intravenous Anaesthesia* (1944), and *Open Drop Ether* (1944). Intended as training tools for medical students, the films were made in the operating theaters of Westminster Hospital (London) with the support of the hospital's anesthetic team, although support only went so far. Thomson recalled that because the hospital would not let them use medical students or patients in the films for ethical reasons, the women filmmakers themselves volunteered to be anesthetized. At various points they took turns to be, in Thomson's words, "flat out on the operation table . . . [while] we filmed it." It was, she reflected dryly, "very dangerous, but there you are."[34] Notwithstanding the perils of wartime filmmaking, Thomson was enthusiastic about the working relationships she shared with Fletcher and Hunter at Realist, recalling that they worked closely together for two years to make the medical films, taking turns at directing and producing, something that would have been more difficult to enact in the features sector. Mutual support was important, especially among women filmmakers, some of whom experienced gender discrimination. Marion Grierson felt there was "prejudice against women in practically every activity," and for this reason she supported using what she described as "a little influence to swing things in the way of women."[35] Thomson was a recipient of this influence, with Grierson finding her work in the cutting room of the Travel and Industrial Development Association in 1937 and giving her copies of the journal *World Film News*, as she knew Thomson was an avid collector.[36]

If Margaret Thomson's career is more consistent with a male-defined norm of longevity and high output, that of Mary Beales can be characterized as episodic, and in that respect, it fits a more femininized pattern of working. Beales, the daughter of renowned economist H. L. Beales, was employed as a production trainee at Paul Rotha's Films of Fact company in 1943. Then seventeen, and with three months' experience under her belt, she was accepted as a war emergency worker. By 1944 Beales had gained her first screen credit, as an assistant director to Kay Mander on an instructional film about the building trade, and for the next four years she worked steadily, earning codirecting, solo directing, and editing credits for a number of documentaries, including the well-received *Fair Rent* (1946), *Dover, Spring 1947* (1947), and shorts for the National Coal Board's cine-magazine, *Mining Review*, between 1948 and 1949, a short news film program produced on a regular basis that reported on coal-mining issues. With the end of the decade, however, her screen credits petered out.

In order to make sense of Beales's career trajectory, it is illuminating to place it adjacent to that of one of her male contemporaries, Peter Pickering. The pair worked together in 1948 directing the short "Coal on Ice" for *Mining Review*'s film *1st Year No. 7* (1948), with each directing a separate unit on the film. Pickering, like Beales, came into the film industry in 1942 as a teenager (then age eighteen), although their career trajectories quickly diverged. Pickering was granted full membership, not war emergency like Beales, and was almost immediately given his first solo directing job. Called up in 1943 and demobilized in 1947, he came back into documentary film work, where, despite being, in his words, a "timid newcomer," he was given work as a director on *1st Year No. 7*. From there he went on to have a long career in documentary film production, directing 150 shorts between 1947 and 1983.[37]

In Patrick Russell's assessment, "Directing opportunities came quickly to keen twentysomethings" in the new, buoyant postwar documentary economy, but this statement fails to recognize how these postwar opportunities were gendered. If *1st Year No. 7* marks the start of Pickering's directing career, it conversely signals the end of Beales's. A combination of marriage, children, and the priority afforded demobilized men put a brake on her directing ambitions, and it is hard not to see Beales and others like her as reserve workers brought into the industry to release manpower and perform a caretaker role for men like Pickering. On the one hand, this evidences one of the most oft-repeated assessments of women's wartime employment: that it transformed opportunities for women before a return to gender norms. But women's experiences and preferences were often, as Penny Summerfield argues, "more ambiguous and contingent" than this picture allows.[38] Beales did carry on working, although her postwar career was typical of women with children for her generation and class. Directing was replaced by occasional freelance editing; behind-the-scenes work for her second husband, documentary director Michael Orrom; and working as a sculptor, the discipline in which she had originally trained.[39] Other female documentary makers had similar profiles. Kay Mander "opted out" of directing after the war, choosing continuity work for feature films because she knew it would be easier to get employment, while Marion Grierson, who did "a bit of script writing" when her children were evacuated away from the family home during the war, eventually retrained as a youth service worker.[40] I have not been able to trace the postwar career of Rosanne Hunter, whom the trade press described in 1943 as "ably following in the experienced footsteps of Miss Thomson," but perhaps she followed her contemporary Budge Cooper into directing for the National Coal Board's *Mining Review*, which flourished from 1947 onward and provided employment opportunities for many women, especially editors. I return to *Mining Review* in the next chapter.

Why did women succeed, relatively speaking, as directors of wartime shorts and documentaries? Women like Thomson and Grierson were part of established networks and were well placed to support new recruits like Rosanne Hunter and Mary Beales. More generally, the more artisan model of production in documentary was a key factor, giving women access to training, while the smaller budgets and crews worked in their favor. And prolonged location work, always a challenge for women with domestic commitments, was not a requirement for small-scale documentary filmmaking. Thomson, Grierson, and others were the most high-profile women who left a clear archival footprint, but their "pioneering" status needs to be placed within the wider context of the hundreds of other women working in documentary, instructional, and factual filmmaking in below-the-line roles. Many of them worked in the Cartoon and Diagram sector, which expanded rapidly in the 1940s, employed as paint and tracers, animators, draftswomen, in-betweeners, and lettering artists. They helped produce the innumerable diagrams, filmstrips, models, and animation backgrounds for short films and also worked as projectionists, maintenance engineers, librarians, and dispatch clerks, an integral part of the workforce that ensured those films reached their audiences. I discuss women's work in animation in some detail in chapter 4, focusing on the highly feminized work sector of paint and trace, but now I turn to focus on women's work in the service film units, as this little-known history brings into view some remarkable achievements by women.

Serving the Nation: Women in the Naval Film Section

The UK had three service film units active during World War II—the Army Film and Photographic Unit (AFPU), the Royal Air Force Film Production Unit, and the Royal Navy Film Section—plus the Army Kinematographic Service (AKS), which was responsible for producing and exhibiting films within the army.[41] The naval film unit had its headquarters and studio at Portsmouth on Britain's southwest coast, with negative cutting done by the Women's Royal Naval Service, based in London, while the army and RAF film units were based at the requisitioned Pinewood Studios near London. While the service film units themselves have been the subject of scholarship—especially the AFPU, which produced a number of celebrated feature-length documentaries—little attention has been paid to the role of women in these units.[42] Records are sketchy, but evidence from the union database and some extant firsthand accounts offer a glimpse into the work of a group of highly trained women film technicians in these units. I want to focus in particular on the naval film unit, as descriptions of the unit's operations written by women, alongside recollections of the men who served under them, suggest how women played a wider role in the unit's operations than has previously been understood in film history.

The role of women in communications during wartime, as wireless operators and radar plotters, has long been recognized, but women also worked in the service film units as editors, negative cutters and film repairers, clerks and packers, secretaries, diagram artists, librarians, projectionists, and in continuity. Records from the ACT union membership database show upward of fifty women applying for union membership through one of the three main service film units, with 1943–44 and 1946–47 being peak years for applications. Most of the women were unmarried and under thirty (as might be expected under conscription legislation) with prior experience in the film industry. These included Peggy Rignold, who had previously worked as a makeup assistant at Elstree in the 1930s and joined the cutting department of the AKS in 1942, and assistant editor Noreen Ackland, who joined the same year and would later edit Michael Powell's *Peeping Tom*. The RAF employed women as negative cutters, librarians, and in continuity, and women transferred to the ACT from other unions and allied professions. Daphne Timewell transferred from NATKE to continuity with the Navy Film Section; Peggy Joan Warrington moved from a career in radio to the scenario department of the AKS's Film Production Group.

One of the most extended accounts of women's work in these sectors comes from Hazel Wilkinson, second officer in the Women's Royal Naval Service (WRNS, officially known as the Wrens) and officer in charge of the editing department of the Navy Film Section in 1944. The Navy Film Section specialized in producing short instructional films on technical and general subjects for training naval personnel. These ranged from boat drills and firing a torpedo to teaching officers how to guard a convoy under enemy attack.[43] The section specialized in animated diagrams, finding that such diagrams, combined with live action, slow motion, and edited commentary, created films that worked effectively in training situations. Principal jobs in the unit (camera, art direction) were filled by men, many of whom had been professional filmmakers in civilian life, but Wilkinson's account provides invaluable detail on the roles filled by women in the section. In this account, published as part of the "Women Talking" symposium held in 1944, Wilkinson estimates that a third of the workforce in the section's animation department were women, as were half of the artists in the filmstrip section. The section's film library was, in Wilkinson's words, "'womanned' entirely by wrens," and they were well represented in art department roles and in editing and negative cutting. There was also "a wren projectionist," "a 'chippy's mate'" (carpenter), typists, a "wren 'assistant sparks'" (electrician), production assistant, and dispatch clerks.[44] Moreover, the influx of women photographers into the section was of sufficient number to release in excess of two hundred male photographers for "more hazardous duties at sea."[45]

Wilkinson's account reveals that women held a much broader range of roles than even those recorded in the union database. To be sure, they were prohibited from camera and sound roles as part of a broader feature of service life that barred women from frontline roles and operational warships. The navy's recruitment slogan of "free a man for the fleet" only went so far. But even here there was some gradual change, with the navy softening its policies on women's service roles and, by 1943, permitting continuity girls to accompany camera units at sea during daytime location shooting, a move that put them closer to the shooting of actuality footage than has previously been recognized. Through a combination of union records and Wilkinson's description, a picture of women's broad and multifaceted war service work emerges, with women's contributions ranging across editing, photography, continuity, the preparation of lantern slides for teaching, cataloging and dispatching film, researching and preparing technical drawings, and constructing and painting sets.[46]

The high proportion of women in the section's animation department (one-third in Wilkinson's account) demands some critical reflection on their achievements. The animation department was held in high regard. Wilkinson thought it "equal to, if not better than" any comparable unit "on either side of the Atlantic," a view echoed by Roly Stafford, who served as a sound technician in the Navy Film Section during the war. In Stafford's estimation, it was "a unit of great distinction . . . absolutely brilliant . . . with about 30 wrens and sailors . . . mak[ing] wonderful animation films."[47] These films were highly technical and invaluable as instructional tools and had the ability, in Wilkinson's words, "to show accurately and simply all the incredibly complicated moving parts of a gun's mechanism and their relation to each other," in a way that was superior to actual photography.[48] And the department's work went beyond animated diagrams. Editor Joe Mendoza worked under Hazel Wilkinson's command in the film unit's editing section and recalls how the entire animation department disappeared in April–May 1944, along with two camera crews, to go on location work. This was unusual; it was normal practice for only camera to go on location. In 2004 Mendoza reported that the animation department had been co-opted to work with the army in the design and construction of a three-dimensional model of a stretch of the Normandy coast (three miles long and one mile deep) where the Dunkirk invasion was to take place, including buildings, streets, and all landscape features, which was to be used for training purposes prior to the invasion.[49] While I have not yet been able to corroborate Mendoza's claim, the anecdote is tantalizing, and it is plausible to assume that if women comprised one-third of the department's workforce, it would not have been possible to construct the model without their technical skills and creative input. It certainly opens a window onto women's wartime work, where their labor as carpenters, painters, draftswomen, and model makers was essential to the success of the creative team.

Perhaps better known but equally impressive is women's collective contribution as projectionists and photographers. Wren projectionists were members of the Forces Kinema projectionists section, and, with responsibility for projecting films at naval establishments, this branch of the service had, in Wilkinson's words, "been almost entirely taken over by wrens, who run every type of projector and are working in all four quarters of the globe."[50] Here women's dominance mirrors the experience of those in the commercial/civilian exhibition sector, where, as Rebecca Harrison has shown, hundreds of women "projectionettes" kept British cinemas going during the Second World War while grappling with inadequate training and misogynist attitudes from the male-authored trade press.[51] Women in the forces fared better than their civilian counterparts in terms of training—one estimate suggests that the Ministry of Information trained almost five hundred women as projectionists during the war—and were responsible for a wide range of tasks. These included not only showing 16 mm and 35 mm films on portable projectors at a number of exhibition spaces, including barracks and dockyard cinemas, but also film cutting and servicing, as depicted in Lee Miller's famous series of photographs "Wrens in Camera" (see fig. 6).

Wrens were also heavily involved in forces photography and were, in Wilkinson's account, "interchangeable with men photographers on shore stations . . . ranging from Cornwall to the Orkneys." Wren photographers

Figure 6. Woman repairing projection equipment during World War II.
Source: Lee Miller, *Wrens in Camera* (London: Hollis and Carter, 1945), 50.

were given a three-month course at the Royal Naval School of Photography, where they received the following training:

> the use of press and stand cameras for photographing naval equipment . . .
> the photographic copying of charts and diagrams . . . the making of lantern
> slides, printing and enlarging to scale . . . [and to] load, fit and use cameras
> in the air . . . [including] the F.24 air reconnaissance camera . . . the F.46
> torpedo aiming camera . . . and the G.42 and G.45 cine-gun cameras.[52]

Wrens were also trained to process the film from these shoots. Although Wrens were not recruited to the unit's camera and sound departments, their work in the unit's photography section gave them significant technical experience with cameras, certainly to a level that was virtually impossible in the feature film sector during the war or in peacetime. While the service film units have, quite rightly, been recognized for the central role they played in documenting the war and instructing the nation's workforce (both civilian and service personnel), the achievements of these units would not have been possible without the technical skills and proficiency of women.

How many of these women carried on working as film professionals after the war is uncertain. Certainly, in Wilkinson's account, many did not see their work as for the duration only but were "very anxious to enter the film industry after the war and make it their permanent career," although the chances of continued success in technical jobs were slender. What we do know is that about twenty women were accepted by the ACT union in the period 1946–47, two-thirds in secretarial/clerical roles and the remainder accepted as film repairers and projectionists, who may have subsequently transferred to NATKE under the 1947 interunion agreement and carried on working. Recent research has suggested that certainly some women projectionists working in commercial cinema did continue their careers in peacetime.[53]

More research is needed to extend understanding of the role of women in the British armed service film units during the Second World War. How comparable were the three units (army, navy, and air force) in terms of their employment of women? To what extent did the Navy Film Section offer opportunities for women precisely because its output focused solely on instructional shorts rather than the higher-profile feature-length documentaries intended for general release that characterized the army unit's output? What this research has shown is not only that women were a highly trained and visible sector of the workforce employed across an exceptionally diverse range of roles but also that a history is missing from established accounts of the decade. Film histories prioritize the Army Film and Photographic Unit, probably because its production of feature-length documentaries, made by "star" directors and cameramen makes it easier to fit into established methods of doing film history. The history of women in the naval film unit demands a different historiography.

Designing for the Nation: Women in the Art Department

If the wartime economy benefited women technicians, drawing them into the workforce to meet the demand for shorts and documentary films, the features sector also offered them enhanced employment opportunities, and nowhere was this more evident than in the art department. The ranks of Britain's film studios (Gainsborough, Two Cities, British Lion, Ealing) were swelled by women who joined the industry as draftswomen, scenic artists, set dressers, dress designers, artists, and assistants/apprentices. A total of 550 union applications were received from art department personnel in the 1940s, of which one-fifth came from women. This was one of the largest departments in film production, with a high number of jobs that ran across the creative, supervisory, and assistant spectrum. In fact, the "assistant" category was devised to regulate the flow of labor in what was a very hierarchical department. Increasing role demarcation had been supported by the newly created Society of British Film Art Directors and Designers (SBFAD) in 1946, which sought to enshrine institutional hierarchies in British art direction.[54]

Under these conditions, and perhaps not surprisingly, entry into the art department took place along gendered lines. Men had sole possession of the art director role; women came into the industry through the more junior ranks of draftswoman, assistant, and the other roles listed above, and their labor is the focus of this case study. There were some notable exceptions to this pattern in terms of women who were already working in art department roles when the war broke out progressing to more senior levels. The most high-profile of these was Carmen Dillon, who had been in the industry since the 1930s as an assistant to art director Ralph Brinton. During this time she had built up a solid body of professional experience working on "quota quickies," and when Brinton was called up for naval work during the war, she was well positioned to "take over more or less" and assume the more senior creative role of assistant art director in the face of widespread personnel shortages.[55] A handful of women also joined the union through what were relatively well-remunerated senior creative roles: Isabel Alexander, set designer at Paul Rotha's Films of Fact; Olga Lehmann, scenic artist and mural painter at British National; and Joan Suttie, special effects and matte artist at D&P Studios.[56] But most women were new to the industry and, responding to wartime personnel shortages, came in as draftswomen, assistants, or other more junior grades. These included Colleen Browning, Freda Pearson, Sheila Graham, and Betty Pierce, who joined the union through jobs at the production company Two Cities, which was producing prestige British films like *Henry V* (1944), *The Way to the Stars* (1945), and *Hamlet* (1947). Pierce, as we will see, was noteworthy for her contributions to debates within the industry about the practice and craft of the art department.

What did women's jobs in the art department entail, and what challenges did those employed in them face as women? My interest here is not in the aesthetic style of individuals like Carmen Dillon—scholars such as Sue Harper (2000) and Laurie Ede (2007) have discussed this elsewhere—but in the gendered workings of the art department and women's collective contributions to British art direction in the 1940s. More specifically, this case study examines the operational logistics of the art department and how, despite its hierarchical structure, the "assistant" role complicates any simple distinction between creative and supporting labor.

As the spread of roles above indicates, the responsibility of the art department is to design, construct, and decorate the sets on which a film's action takes place. These three interrelated activities require a team with different yet complementary technical skills and the aesthetic sensibility to deploy them. Art director Carmen Dillon's description of her job gives an insight into how the department functions:

> First of all I would read the "treatment"—a rough outline of the story—and then try to imagine the kind of settings and do some rough sketches. . . . You always had lots of talks with the director to be sure you both had the same ideas about the look and mood of the film. Then the draughtsman would make the working drawings and the sets would be based on these.[57]

Sets were built by a construction team of carpenters, plasterers, and painters—working from the diagrams and plans produced by the draftsperson—and the set was finished by the set dresser, who instructed the drapery and property departments, in consultation with the director, art director, and chief camera operator to check the sets' overall look. In Betty Pierce's assessment, the role of the art director required "knowledge of technical drawing, sketching, ability to organise work and to control expenditure, and to 'see the job as a whole.'" Pierce, who worked in the art department of Two Cities after the war, thought those with architectural training were ideally suited for the role, a view echoed by Carmen Dillon and Peggy Gick, both of whom had also trained as architects.[58]

Despite Pierce's professional qualifications—she was an associate of the Royal Institute of British Architects—she worked in the British film

industry not as an art director (AD) but as an assistant AD and draftswoman, a common profile for women in the film industry at this time.
She joined the union in 1944 at age thirty-nine and was presumably very
experienced professionally. Certainly by 1950 she was in a position to
have an authoritative voice on the subject of art direction for film and
published a series of articles in the journal *Official Architect* that provide
an extensive and invaluable insight into the working habits and practices
of an art department in a film studio. These were based on her 1940s
experience at Two Cities, a company producing medium- to high-budget
productions intended for international distribution. The articles, along
with oral histories, illuminate the professional responsibilities of women
like Betty Pierce and Peggy Gick in what were deemed supportive roles,
by virtue of the "assistant" prefix, a title that belies the level of technical
skill and creative contribution the person in that position brought to the
finished film. They are worth examining in some detail to bring women's
work in this area into view.[59]

Draftswomen like Pierce worked in the art department's drawing office,
which she described as "a real 'back room,'" under the supervision of the
assistant art director. In Pierce's account, the assistant would often step
in for the art director and was the point of contact for the construction
team, scenic artists, and set dresser. Assistants supervised the work of
draftspersons who produced the working drawings for the construction
department, complete with "full notes of all finishes required, and . . . the
amount of wear, aged, or broken effects required."[60] Further, "Drawings
must also show which pieces of wall are to move easily in and out of the set,
to allow room for the camera; which doors and windows are to be 'practical'; where painted backings or cut-out or model views from windows are
required, and these must be calculated for correct scale and drawn out."
Draftspersons also had to be aware of budgetary constraints and produce
drawings that used "as much 'stock' as possible . . . var[ying] his design"
where necessary. In addition, they had to be highly adaptable, able to
produce drawings not only for buildings but for "ships, trains, gardens . . .
flags, furniture, weapons . . . [and] mechanical devices . . . worked out in
collaboration with the construction department, such as rocking devices
for ships and trains, working drawbridges, etc."[61] Pierce's description is
extensive, not only revealing her intimate working knowledge of both
the design process and filmmaking but also illustrating the level of skill
required by those in the roles of draftsperson and assistant art director

In Pierce's words, "Draughtsmen work from the Art Director's sketch
and verbal instructions, or . . . from photographs," but these were often
highly impressionistic or idiosyncratic, depending on the individual art

director.[62] Examining the work process in more detail undermines any strict division between "the creative" and "the technical." One of Britain's leading art directors, Edward Carrick, recalled his mentor Vincent Korda giving his assistants little more than "a vague scribble on whatever was lying around," a practice that drove some of them to distraction.[63] Carrick, in turn, imposed this vagueness on his assistant Peggy Gick, whose working relationship with Carrick started in the 1930s. She joined Carrick at the Crown Film Unit during the war and recalled the challenge of building a submarine interior for the naval drama *Close Quarters* (1943) with little more than a photograph to guide her: "Edward just gave me the photograph and said 'this is passed to you, I'm going on holiday.' I thought, oh God, it looks like a plate of spaghetti!"[64] From this inauspicious start, Gick produced quality drawings and supervised the construction team, creating a full-size and detailed submarine interior complete with chronometers and other necessary technical equipment. The end result was, in the words of Ian Dalrymple, head of the Crown Film Unit, "so well-made that, on completion of the filming, the Admiralty took it over and re-erected it elsewhere for training use."[65] Gick's only complaint was "If they'd come to me I could have given them the drawings which would have helped them also, but they didn't ask me . . . the stupid idiots!"[66] As an assistant Gick would not have been approached for the drawings, because in the production hierarchy, their creative ownership would have rested with the art director. But as we have seen, being able to interpret the vague drawings relied on Gick's ability to successfully marry her technical skills and aesthetic sensibility. This is a form of resourcefulness-as-creativity as discussed in the introduction.

Getting working drawings from art directors could be a permanent headache for draftspersons and assistant ADs, but the operational logistics of how film studios functioned added another layer of complexity that had particularly negative repercussions for women with domestic commitments. Gick complained of Carrick's infuriating habit of not "draw[ing] anything until he'd got it totally fixed in his head. . . . I was desperate for the working drawings and . . . he'd be walking around the garden thinking about it. . . . He knew it was going to take me four hours to do these drawings."[67] This often led to working into the evening, a frustrating situation compounded by the studio practice of set preparation for the following day's shooting taking place late at night. Assistants like Gick were responsible for ensuring that when the night gangs clocked in, the component parts of the set were ready for them to assemble. This often meant working until eight or ten o'clock at night.[68] Although Gick's examples stem from her time at the studio British International Pictures in the mid-to-late 1930s—and not all studios had such chaotic working habits—the culture of long hours and evening work was common practice. This meant that women like Gick and others could best function in art department roles only if they were single and without children or other domestic responsibilities. Indeed, Gick stepped back from the role when her children were born in the mid-1940s.

Other aspects of the job also worked against women, especially where they clashed with gender expectations about women in senior supervisory roles. As Betty Pierce's account demonstrates, art directors and assistants were the point of contact for the construction team: the carpenters, plasterers, and painters who built the sets. Photographs from the popular and trade press of the time show these as male domains, populated by "brickies," "chippies," and "curtain men" dressed in the ubiquitous white overalls of the tradesman. On large, prestige productions, the construction team would easily comprise one hundred men, with supervision of that team (i.e., relaying orders through the construction manager and various heads of "shops") difficult to reconcile with norms of conventional femininity and prejudice concerning women's technical and managerial capacities. That Carmen Dillon succeeded in taking on such a role for *Hamlet* was met with breathless surprise by the fan magazine *Picturegoer*, which reassured its readers that the "slight" and "chic" Dillon found *Hamlet* a "formidable task" and was ably supported as the "production was designed by Roger Furse according to Laurence Olivier's ideas."[69] Comments like these undermine women's authority, and the tone of the article makes it clear that the job was not for women.

In fact, Dillon's experience demonstrates how difficult it was for women to be accepted into a male-dominated domain. When she entered the British film industry in the mid-1930s, she was not allowed to wear trousers, give orders, or "mix with the workmen," restrictions that did her professional development no favors.[70] She remembers the film studio at Wembley being run by "a nasty little chap . . . [who] didn't like having women there at all," and her fellow art director Edward Carrick's description of Dillon as "like a really efficient secretary" detracts from her skills and gives a flavor of what women were up against in a man's world.[71] Indeed, film companies were among those businesses singled out for criticism by the Royal Institute of British Architects (RIBA) in the 1930s for discriminatory hiring practices. RIBA's Women's Committee was established in 1932 with a remit to support women's job hunting and record discrimination, with the Gaumont-British Film Corporation falling foul of its board when the architect Jean McIntosh reported the film company for refusing to hire her based on her sex.[72] Things may have improved slightly in the following decade—if only because men were lost through being called up for military service—but these issues bring into relief how difficult it was for women to work in the film industry as full art directors.

More typical was the type of career where women moved between roles at the mid to lower end of the art direction team. Betty Pierce earned half a dozen or more screen credits in the 1940s as a draftswoman, assistant art director, and, in 1951, a set decorator, and her frequent work with established art directors Paul Sheriff and Carmen Dillon demonstrates that she was a well-respected freelancer. Certainly, the quality and detail of her writing for *Official Architect* suggests a professional who was intimately connected with the working practices of an art department and had a clear understanding of how to shape traditional architectural practice to meet the unique demands of film production. By the late 1950s, her screen credits are patchy and include working as a set designer in television.

Peggy Gick's experience perhaps best exemplifies women's career profile, especially her work in the mid-1940s, which is shaped by when her children arrived. Her wartime profile was remarkably diverse. Working for the Crown Film Unit, she designed for popular and critically successful films such as *Coastal Command, Close Quarters*, and *Western Approaches*. But she also took a number of commissions in between films, including designs for antisubmarine netting, maps for aircraft bombing-raid practice, and mural restoration for Westminster Boys School. The modest handful of film credits she and others like her received—men as well as women—belie the extent of their involvement in British wartime film production. The Crown Film Unit was based at Pinewood Studios alongside the service film units, and Gick recalls undertaking design work at this time for both the army and the navy, whose representatives "used to come in and want bits and pieces done every now and then. . . . I did so many different sets for so many different people, all at the same time. . . . It was very hard work, Crown."[73] This adaptability stood her in good stead after 1944, when she was married with two small children, and she switched to working from home, producing illustrations for trade publications such as "The Builder" and hand-painting cels for film titles in her drawing room, although she described the latter as a "hideous job!"[74] She would later work on commercials and children's films, and returned to design for feature films and television in the 1960s.

Gick's employment pattern is mirrored by those of other women in Britain's art departments. Colleen Browning worked as a set dresser and scenic artist on half a dozen high-profile films in the late 1940s, as did matte artist Joan Suttie, whose credits included David Lean's *Oliver Twist*, which won an award at the Venice Film Festival for its art director, John Bryan. After a seemingly short but intense period of work, screen credits for

Browning and Suttie dry up and it is not known how their future careers unfolded. Perhaps, like the documentary directors, they retrained or took their skills and talents into other professions, including raising children. Certainly, good assistants were invaluable, probably too valuable to promote, as they could be relied upon to temporarily step in for art directors. With the exception of Carmen Dillon, and to an extent Olga Lehmann, no individual woman sustained a career as an art director in British film production, but collectively the more than one hundred women—including Peggy Gick, Colleen Browning, Iris Wills, Betty Pierce, Joan Suttie, Sheila Wilson, Isabel Alexander, and many others—who joined the union through art department roles were essential members of the teams whose professional skills shaped the visual quality of Britain's film culture in the 1940s. Their work was no less valuable than that of men in the art director role; it was just paid less as befitted its "assistant" status.

Conclusion

Opportunities expanded and retracted for women during the 1940s, especially in nontraditional positions such as camera, sound, and art direction. There were some important shifts during the war years, including better access to a wider range of jobs, quicker movement through the ranks, and a broader range of assignments on offer. These resulted in some women building a body of work as documentary directors, while others in art department roles were able to develop an impressive portfolio that worked to their advantage in their later careers. But despite these shifts, wartime opportunities did not lead to lasting structural change, and women were only ever accepted as second-choice technicians, their duty to ensure that, as the union put it, "the full rights of [male] employees have been preserved."[75] The system that supported male domination of remunerative employment opportunities and privileges remained intact, coupled as it was with prejudice concerning women's technical and managerial capabilities. In the light of these conditions, some women made pragmatic choices—Kay Mander shifted from directing back to continuity—while others left to have children, with some coming back into the film industry later (Peggy Gick) or moving into more "family-friendly" professions such as teaching. These women were not "lost" to the labor market—indeed the country was desperate for female labor in the postwar years—but they shifted into more conventional feminine roles. In this respect, the business of making films was no different from other industries, which, as established social histories of the period have shown, were steeped in the structural inequalities of gender.

4

The 1950s

Rebuilding Britain

The decade of the 1950s saw the feature film industry in a state of flux. The country's biggest film company, Rank, a vertically integrated corporation, was in considerable financial difficulty and survived only by scaling back its operations. It closed its Gainsborough and Two Cities studios in 1949, concentrating its production base at Pinewood, where it also dismissed staff in its bid to rationalize production and balance the books.[1] The film industry was at various points in the decade both supported and hamstrung by government intervention. A 1947 tax on Hollywood imports had led to severe reprisals by the American film industry, which boycotted the British market, drastically reducing the supply of Hollywood films into the country. This precarious arrangement was overturned in 1948 by the Anglo-American Film Agreement, which supported production activities by the Hollywood majors in Britain. The postwar Labour government also intervened in film affairs through the creation of the National Film Finance Corporation (1949) and the Eady Levy (1950). These interventions, which underwrote bank loans and created an entertainment tax, respectively, were intended to help British producers raise funds for film production.[2] All three measures had varying degrees of success, but as the film union itself recognized, "the indigenous base of British feature production" was shrinking, with implications for its workforce.[3] This chapter focuses first on production context and women's union representation as shop stewards—within the broader social context of debates about women and work—before providing an overview of women in the film industry through union membership application data. I then move on to four complementary case studies that characterize women's work in film production during the 1950s: the production secretary, publicity assistant, paint and trace artist, and editors in the documentary sector.

The Film Industry and the Value of Women's Labor

The precarious nature of the production base in Britain had some profound consequences for film technicians, with one estimate suggesting that 25 percent were unemployed in 1949–50.[4] But this negative assessment has to be balanced with the fact that other sectors of the industry were more buoyant. The tradition of a double-bill/two-feature program in cinemas created the demand for a steady supply of low-budget supporting features, all of which provided much-needed work for technicians, often under the radar of the union's agreed minimum rates and crewing levels.[5] Nonfiction production continued to flourish in this decade, with the market for documentary and instructional shorts stimulated by growth in the British economy. Documentary was no longer the patriotic and pedagogic voice of the nation, but corporations such as ICI and Unilever, alongside the newly created National Health Service and the National Coal Board, commissioned films to communicate new ideas, products, and services to domestic and global markets. The increasing availability of television and the launch of commercial television in 1955 presented both challenges and opportunities for the film industry. It hastened the decline of the cinemagoing audience—with annual admissions falling from 1.6 billion individual visits in 1946 to 515 million by the end of the 1950s—but it also created work for film technicians.[6] Commercial television needed a steady supply of advertisements, and companies such as Halas and Batchelor—Britain's leading animation studio—readily obliged. The studio expanded rapidly in the 1950s to meet demand and played a central role in training staff to work in the growing commercials sector and children's television.

Faced with these circumstances, the main objective of the film union during this decade was to ensure job security for its members, something it sought to achieve through agreeing on minimum crew levels with film producers and maintaining a closed shop to control the supply of labor.[7] It also handled the launch of commercial television in 1955 by bringing its technicians into the ACT, relaunching as the Association of Cinematograph, Television and Allied Technicians (ACTT) in 1956. Concerns about women were not at the forefront of the union's agenda during this decade. The debates about the "woman technician" that had preoccupied it during the war ceased to be a pressing concern, and the "For Women Technicians" column that Kay Mander had first edited in the union's journal in 1940 was long since defunct.

But women continued to have a voice in the union through their role as shop stewards: production secretary Teresa Bolland was chair of the continuity, assistant continuity, and production secretary section; Edna Kanter, steward for the publicity department; Rosalie "Wally" Crook for the cartoon sector; and Bessie Bond for the laboratories, one of the union's largest sections. Given that the sections they represented were well staffed with women, the issues they raised by their very nature had a gendered dimension. Teresa Bolland, for example, used the pages of the union's journal to argue for pay parity for women in continuity and production secretary roles, drawing comparisons between work done by men and women: "The pay of Continuity girls should be higher—the work is just as responsible as a 1st Assistant's [director], and should be on a level with his; a Production Secretary's wages are not bad, except when you consider she works alongside the Production Manager, and often has to deputise for him."[8] Bolland's argument is an early example of calls for role equivalence and the value of women's skills to be recognized by the union and appropriately remunerated by employers. Membership forms bring the issue of waged labor and value into sharp relief: the wages for women in continuity were approximately two-thirds of those earned by men in the first assistant director role. There is no evidence that Bolland's argument led to change; indeed, the only response in the pages of the journal was a lighthearted sketch of the role ("The Strange Life of a Production Secretary") that appeared in print four months after Bolland raised the issue of pay.[9] Its inclusion smacks of tokenism and a union ostensibly recognizing women's contribution to the film economy but in ways that did not disrupt the gendered status quo. It would be several years before job equivalence arguments would gain any traction in the UK.

Women who served as shop stewards regularly attended the Women's Trades Union Congress Annual Conference and published reports on these events in *The Cine-Technician*. The TUC conferences engaged with the debates of the day, including equal pay in the civil service and abolition of the last vestiges of the marriage bar, and reports penned by the ACTT's women shop stewards brought these wider social concerns into the film industry's orbit through the pages of the union's journal. But the pieces inevitably concluded with a self-congratulatory notice about the ACTT's established commitment to equal pay, an assertion that conveniently sidestepped the types of issues Bolland was raising about role parity and the economic value assigned to women in the workforce through the union's job-level system.[10]

Indeed, the wider debates taking place in British society about the national economy and the increasing numbers of older and married women in the workforce found no place in the union's journal. As social historians have demonstrated, attitudes about women working were in a state of flux in the 1950s. On the one hand, domesticity and motherhood was privileged in public discourse, most notably through publications like John Bowlby's *Child Care and the Growth of Love* (1953). On the other hand, it was widely acknowledged that women's labor was essential for postwar reconstruction.[11] A number of government recruitment campaigns targeted women (especially those over the age of thirty-five) at this time, seeking to encourage them into the workforce, in teaching, auxiliary nursing, and other roles in the new welfare state.[12] Studies like Alva Myrdal and Viola Klein's *Women's Two Roles: Home and Work* (1956) were part of a wider debate taking place in the 1950s about women's participation in the labor market. Increasing numbers of women were economically active at different stages of the life course, with the majority of married women found in either factory or white-collar occupations such as secretary.[13] While the film industry remained dependent on women's labor to sustain production during this decade, the union did not offer any official or coordinated response to the topical issue of women and work.

Women and Union Records: An Overview

Records from the union's database show how women's labor continued to support the film industry, although it did so in a narrowing range of roles. Just under two thousand technicians applied for union membership in the 1950s, of which just under five hundred were women (see appendix C). In the face of declining feature film production and the union's closed-shop grip on labor supply, these figures show that women continued to represent a significant proportion of the workforce. Britain's animation studios recruited large numbers of women, most through the traditionally femininized positions of paint and trace artist and colorist, while production secretary remained a common job for women. These roles, well stocked with female recruits, form two of the central case studies for this chapter. I explore how the production secretary married problem solving and emotional labor into a form of creative practice, while women in paint and trace reveled in the creative and artistic aspects of their work.

Women continued to join the art department as costume designers and draftswomen, and as continuity girls on the studio floor, albeit in much smaller numbers than in the previous decade due to the shrinkage in feature film production. Others joined the industry as librarians, working in the film libraries of companies specializing in nonfiction film (British Transport Films, Rayant Pictures), and a handful joined as scriptwriters and script secretaries. There was a sharp downturn in the numbers of women joining the union through camera department roles, with only a handful joining the industry this decade, most of whom were employed to retouch film stills. One positive development in the 1950s was the increased number of women joining the union through publicity and casting roles, a trend that first emerged in the mid-to-late 1940s. Several of the casting directors worked for the industry's leading studios, including Peggy Smith at Twentieth Century Fox, Thelma Graves at Ealing, and Jenia Reissar at Romulus. The increase in recruitment through publicity jobs, at senior and assistant levels, was strengthened by a 1952 union resolution that publicity for all first or leading feature productions must be handled by an ACT publicist.[14] The presumed suitability of women for this occupation, due to the feminized characteristics of the role, form the third case study of this chapter. Finally, women continued to be recruited in substantial numbers to editing positions, both by the larger film studios such as Ealing, Rank, and MGM, and to the many companies specializing in nonfiction filmmaking. Women working in editing is the chapter's fourth case study, which examines freelance editors in the nonfiction sector and how they combined work with domestic responsibilities in a sector that they found had enhanced scope for professional autonomy.

The Production Secretary

Many of the women who joined the union through jobs in the Floor category were employed in secretarial roles, either as production secretaries or secretaries in a production department. Some worked for established companies such as Realist, Butcher's, and Associated British Picture Corporation, while others joined through the smaller production companies that proliferated at the time. The role of production secretary had a higher status than generic secretary, and this was reflected in salary: production secretaries were paid between ten and twelve pounds per week, while secretaries in production earned around eight pounds per week in the mid-1950s, although there was variation depending on employer and levels of experience. A trainee starting work at a small production company might earn as little as six pounds while an experienced secretary to a director could earn fifteen pounds per week. The majority of women were in their twenties (often twenty-five or over) and single; because the average age at marriage for British women in the 1950s was twenty-three, the demographic profile of these production secretaries suggests that many were opting (either through choice or necessity) for a career over a domestic role.[15] Their pay was above average by the standards of the day, where an average weekly wage was six pounds in 1950 and eleven pounds in 1960, and certainly higher than wages for women in manufacturing roles.[16] But the comments on pay by Teresa Bolland cited earlier illustrate the many occupational tensions concerning wages, and, as I will demonstrate, pay relative to responsibility was a recurring theme in women's accounts of their work.

Contemporary accounts of the production secretary role are limited, and there were few descriptions published in the British film trade press during the decade. This is in sharp contrast to the many accounts of the continuity girls' workday that appeared in print in the 1930s when the union and the film industry were modernizing the sector after the introduction of sound. While the production secretary may have been largely absent from film press, secretarial training was in fact booming in the 1950s, and young women were being actively encouraged to acquire skills in shorthand and typing. By the time Viola Klein was researching her famous sociological studies of British women's employment, office work was the main occupational destiny for women. Secretaries appeared regularly in the popular press—with features on the "Fastest Typist Competition" and the "Secretaries Conference at PERA [Production Engineering Research Association]" being broadcast on British independent television—while Helen Gurley Brown's best seller *Sex and the Single Girl* (1963) popularized the secretary as a figure of autonomous and capable womanhood.[17] Male-generated descriptions of the role emphasized how the performance of administrative duties deemed minor (typing, shorthand, answering the telephone) contributed to greater office efficiency, as secretaries took responsibility for "time-consuming minutiae," leaving the male manager to direct his energies to higher tasks.[18] In the context of the film industry, these "higher tasks" were associated with (male) creativity, which was sharply and hierarchically contrasted with the noncreative work of the (female) secretary. However, as always, these official, male-authored accounts leave out as much as they reveal, and another, more complex picture emerges when women describe their work. Oral histories provide much-needed insight into the role of the production secretary, and this case study draws on interviews with three women: Pamela Mann-Francis, Ann Skinner, and Sheila Collins. All three worked as production secretaries on British feature films in the 1950s and 1960s: Mann-Francis worked with director David Lean; Skinner on mid-budget British films that received critical acclaim; and Collins on the glossy, international coproductions that proliferated during the decade. What draws their experiences together are the common threads of organizing, problem solving and prevention, and emotional labor; in this respect their work has much in common with the continuity role: tasks may differ, but the underpinning skills of detail work and interpersonal communication remain the same. This is another role where understanding the workflow process helps us rethink the distinctions between jobs designated "creative" and "noncreative." While these three women were some of the most highly achieving in the profession—with Skinner later progressing to the role of producer—the services they performed are typical and thus illuminate a workplace culture that was duplicated across British feature production more broadly.

If the continuity girl's role was on set, sitting at the director's right hand and prompting him through her encyclopedic knowledge of the script, the production secretary, by contrast, was an office-based role that, though it rarely strayed onto the studio floor, was nevertheless intimately connected to the mechanics of film production. The role is best understood through a description of the production manager's job, for whom the secretary often substituted. In production manager David Cousland's words: "The production manager organises the film's production office . . . and helps gather together the film's production unit. He co-ordinates the work of the various studio departments . . . and acts as a liaison officer . . . fit[ing] together the complicated jig-saw puzzle of his firm's production plans."[19] This involved ensuring that props, costumes, and sets were in place before shooting commenced; keeping an eye on costs and making all necessary preparations for location shoots, including not only hotels and meals but also locals for crowd scenes along with permissions and permits where required. Working closely with producers and director's assistants, the role, in Cousland's estimation, gave one "an all-round, thorough knowledge of film-production," which required initiative, efficiency, and "an elasticity of thought and of action," as well as being able to "get the best out of people."[20]

The production secretary was to facilitate the organization and orchestration of these back-room functions, and while some of this involved mundane aspects such as typing up call sheets and preparing progress reports for financiers, Ann Skinner's claim that "you did a bit of whatever was needed" captures the inherent variety of the role, certainly as it was experienced by many women in the 1950s and 1960s.[21] Skinner started in the film industry as a publicist's secretary in the Rank Organisation and from there moved into the role of production secretary. In her experience, the specific demands of the job depended on whom you worked with, and she claimed to have learned much from working with what she described as an "incompetent" production manager, whose inadequacies enabled her to take a larger role. This involved checking multiple locations and creating a shooting schedule that broke the script down into sets, actors, and locations in the most cost-effective and efficient manner. By the time she had drawn up the schedule, she claimed that "you know your script pretty well," and she had learned how to problem-solve the organization of film production, essentially fitting together all the elements of what Cousland termed the "complicated jig-saw puzzle." She found that people increasingly came to her office and talked to her as though she were the production manager and described it as "a wonderful experience . . . [and] a very satisfying job."[22]

Sheila Collins was similarly creative in her role. Like Skinner and Pamela Mann-Francis, she started as a secretary in the publicity department at Rank before moving into a production secretary role in the mid-1950s. She carved out a career specializing in running the London production end of big, international coproductions. Working on films such as *The Vikings* (1958), *Tarzan's Greatest Adventure* (1959), and *The Longest Day* (1962), she was responsible for a diverse number of tasks, including arranging the overseas shipping of equipment, which ranged from cameras to firearms; engaging artists; and arranging special permits. As she says, she became "quite an expert on shipping," working with the newly emerging companies in Britain that specialized in shipping for the film industry, where you had to "move in a hurry," and skilled at getting special permits to go into other countries, which she described as "quite an art."[23] Working across multiple international sites was challenging, and she recalled a "horrific shipping" incident in which she managed to lose a Churchill tank for ten days during the shooting of *The Longest Day*, when it was shunted into a railway siding en route between Germany and France due to strikes at the French railways. But being the key contact person in London gave her significant scope to get involved in every department of film production because "anything they wanted they'd have to come through me, because they were all miles away." Much of Collins's work involved the accurate identification of equipment or processes, and she delighted in the research aspect of the role. This ranged from sourcing the correct "military equipment," digging out original designs for grapnels (small, fluted anchors), and "trotting off to the Admiralty" to talk to people involved in the D-day landings.[24] The research side of the job was also commented on by other production secretaries, including Teresa Bolland, who remarked that she especially enjoyed the challenge of tracking down items such as a 1945 Spitfire because it was "almost like C.I.D. [Criminal Investigation Department] work."[25] All women described the importance of being able to "think on your feet," demonstrating that "elasticity of thought and action" was not the sole preserve of the production manager. Women in the production secretary role used their initiative to come up with creative solutions to the many problems that film production presented.

The job also required significant emotional labor and the performance of what Erin Hill describes in her assessment of studio secretaries as "tact, discretion, and a gingerly managing style."[26] Nowhere was this more evident than in Pamela Mann-Francis's professional dealings with the famously temperamental director David Lean. Mann-Francis worked with Lean on a number of films, including *Summertime* (1955) and *The Bridge on the River Kwai* (1957), where she was faced with relaying messages from producer Sam Spiegel to Lean over the casting of Alec Guinness in the lead role, knowing that Lean found the decision contentious: "I remember getting a taxi out . . . to tell David this and he wasn't very happy."[27] Lean's moods were notoriously difficult to handle, and those with the most responsibility, like Mann-Francis, had to judge which information to disclose, and when, and deal with any emotional fallout. That she worked with Lean on several films indicates how skilled and trusted she was professionally. She arranged for special shampoo to be flown in for Lean's wife when she visited him on location (a decision Mann-Francis described as "absolutely ridiculous") and drew up a list of the best Parisian nightclubs for Lean's son when he honeymooned in the capital.[28] These small but important tasks that bridged the public/private divide were an essential part of the oil that greased the wheels of film production.

Being sensitive to social norms, including the workings of racism, was equally crucial, as Ann Skinner discovered when she arranged accommodation for Black actor Brock Peters in the early 1960s, a time when British landlords still practiced overt racial discrimination.[29] Many secretaries performed the type of behind-the-scenes invisible labor that facilitated the professional lives of others. Personal secretaries Pam Rippingale and Mary Harvey were remembered for holding a discreet "open house" at the offices of directors Roy Boulting and Frank Launder, where established film technicians—typically freelancing in the 1950s and between jobs— could pop in for tea at a time engineered by the secretary to coincide with the director's availability. Features editor Teddy Darvas recalls, "Pam didn't say 'There may be a film for you' but she made absolutely sure you were there when she knew you were wanted. . . . It was a terribly nice thing . . . [a]nd they were frightfully discreet."[30] Not only were the secretaries discreet, but they also acted as gatekeepers, permitting or denying access to employment and presumably other opportunities and absorbing both the positive and negative emotions that inevitably accompanied those decisions.

Despite performing such a complex role, where their resourcefulness and creative problem-solving skills were in high demand, many women found the pay disappointing, not least because the job required long hours with no paid overtime. Mann-Francis vividly recalled being paid only nine pounds per week in 1956 for her work on the big-budget *Bridge on the River Kwai*, describing it as a "ridiculous" sum because Lean was "very demanding" and she had to spend a year in Ceylon for the shoot. Being on location meant there was little opportunity for her to detach from work at the end of a day's shooting, and she was called upon to assist with script revisions and other tasks in the evening. She had been left further out of pocket on *Summertime*, as "David didn't have a car. . . . I used to drive him everywhere . . . [and] he never paid for the petrol or anything."[31] Nevertheless, compensation came in the form of perks—such as occasional first-class travel—and the status that production secretaries accrued when attached to big-name directors. For Mann-Francis, "Working with David was great and you did feel you were at the top of the [film] industry, even if you were only a secretary." Professional standing was matched by familial approval, her father being "absolutely thrilled when I worked for David . . . because this was . . . the top."[32] Being close to the center of power, when women could rarely wield it themselves, was very appealing, as Mann-Francis was aware, although the danger she observed was that secretaries became "so devoted to the director or producer . . . that they give up their whole lives to it."[33]

In the face of limited career progression, this was hardly surprising. Despite having what David Cousland described as an "all-round, thorough knowledge of film-production," few women made the transition to production manager, let alone producer, with the secretary role an end in its own right rather than an apprenticeship. Ann Skinner was alone in progressing to producer, although it took her seventeen years to make the transition in the face of considerable skepticism from the male elite. That Richard "Dickie" Attenborough openly doubted her capability to handle what he described as the "tough" producer role illustrates his lack of real understanding about what her role entailed and how her labor enabled his.[34] David Cousland may have described production manager as a "progressive job" that led naturally into more senior producing roles, but women had a rather different occupational ladder. Their progression might come from moving into continuity—as both Mann-Francis and Skinner did—or from working for a more prestigious director, but here they remained in a supporting role, providing service to those in more senior creative positions. In many respects, they were too valuable to promote, like their continuity girl counterparts or editors such as Thelma

Myers, whose ambitions to direct in the 1950s were thwarted by the male directors with whom she worked (see chapter 2). Erin Hill makes the point that it was precisely the "lack of avenues to more satisfying work" that led many women in support roles to put their considerable creative energies into what was available to them, doing far in excess of the job description and expecting little by way of recognition in return.[35] This is not to imply that women meekly accepted their lot; Mann-Francis's complaints about her salary, for example, reveal that she was only too aware (at least later) that she had been exploited.[36] And clearly not every production secretary enjoyed the power Sheila Collins wielded. Nor were the opportunities Ann Skinner grasped, in the face of an incompetent production manager, always available. But their accounts make us reassess the creative/noncreative divide and reveal the multiple ways that the production secretary contributed in very significant and concrete ways to film production. Along with Skinner and her peers were the many other women who joined the union as production secretaries in the 1950s. That so many of them were single suggests that at a time when women's domestic role was privileged in popular discourse, some opted instead to carve out the best available professional role for themselves in what was a deeply gendered and patriarchal working context. In the next section, I continue the thread of ancillary or support work, examining the role of women in the studios' publicity departments.

Working in Publicity

Publicity was another area where women found opportunities for employment in what were commonly thought of as nontechnical roles. Women had been involved in film publicity since the early days of cinema, where the popular opinion was that they were well placed to address female cinemagoers due to an assumed shared interest in the feminine pursuits of fashion, star biographies, lifestyle, and gossip. During the Second World War and the recruitment of men into the armed forces, women increasingly held senior positions in British studios, including Margaret Marshall, publicity director at Two Cities; Betty Callaghan at Gainsborough; and Enid Jones at London Films. One estimate suggests that by 1949 there were at least twenty-five women publicists in executive roles at British studios, and applications to the union support this assessment, showing dozens of women joining as publicity directors and assistants.[37] By the late 1940s to early 1950s, women were an established presence in the profession—with some winning industry awards, such as Jean Osborne's award for her promotional work on *The Sound Barrier* (1952)—but this needs to be understood in the broader context of an increase in the workforce overall: vertically integrated giants like Rank expanded and needed publicity departments and their personnel to play their part in realizing the organization's national and international ambitions. By 1946 the workforce was sufficiently large to attract the interest of the union, which established its publicity section, ensuring those in the trade were brought under its closed-shop agreements.

Despite the visible presence of women in publicity roles, this is not to claim that publicity was a female-dominated or feminized profession like continuity. In fact, many of the biggest names and most famous campaigns of the decade were led by men. Theo Cowan, Rank's controller of publicity, was responsible for the campaign that launched *Doctor at Sea* at the Venice Film Festival in 1955, where the sight of the bikini-clad British star Diana Dors gliding down the Grand Canal in a gondola was the toast of the festival. Rather, publicity needs to be understood as a place where there was a greater tolerance of women in senior roles. This was not the result of some newfound egalitarianism but, rather, conventionally gendered institutional thinking. Witness John Myers, one of British cinema's leading publicists, proclaiming in 1947 that women had "a greater facility than their male colleagues . . . [for] the specialised spheres . . . [of] fashion publicity, biographical and profile writing, and research work," helping himself to the well-worn assumptions about "natural" feminine competencies that proliferated at the time.[38] Under these conditions, women's options were limited, but many did turn these gendered assumptions to their advantage, using them as leverage into what was one of the few well-paid and interesting jobs available to them at the time. Applications to the union show women holding positions as head of biographical, feature writer, and fashion writer at the Rank Organisation in the late 1940s, all of which were industry-designated specialized spheres that did not attract male applicants.

Where women did dominate was at the lower levels, and here women were brought into junior positions to perform highly feminized tasks. Ann Skinner, who joined the publicity department of Pinewood Studios in 1955, remembers answering the phone and typing up the publicity press kits but also relaying messages and information between the publicity department and stars on the studio floor. Communicating with stars was one of the most important parts of the job, and Skinner and other women like her were the public face of the office, tasked with greeting stars, making tea, and caretaking between appointments, at all times striking a balance between being cordial but not overfamiliar in what was a hierarchical and gendered workplace. Not only were good people skills and considerate manners an unwritten part of the job description—all of which had a class dimension, of course—but young women were also expected to be pleasant to look at and dress and behave in ways that were highly feminized. According to Skinner, the expected convention was to "dress properly in nice shoes and stockings" and be willing to masquerade as a "fan" in the staged shots the publicity department organized around star autograph signings.[39] So women's entry into and success in publicity departments, at both junior and senior levels, was conditional on their performing a version of femininity that was highly coded by a set of gendered norms.

Indeed their very success in the role worked against their promotion, something that was recognized at the time by publicist John Myers. Not only were women recruited into what he termed "blind alley jobs," but the industry's expansionist pressures were such that "there is no time to train, and anyone who can do a good job cannot be spared to be taken off it."[40] So women were both the recipients and cause of their own occupational discrimination; it was always this way. Under these conditions, junior women like Ann Skinner, Pamela Mann-Francis, and others like them were unlikely to progress to publicity director roles and therefore took the occupational ladder sideways, moving into production secretary and continuity work. Women in senior roles, such as Jean Osborne, worked steadily through the 1950s, but their careers stalled in the next decade, possibly because middle-age women were seen as anathema to the overtly masculinist and youthful discourses that were shaping British cinema culture in the 1960s. We have seen how women supported the film industry through secretarial and publicity roles, which demanded emotional and other forms of feminized labor, but how did they fare in jobs that were deemed more technical, especially away from the particular demands of the feature film sector, with its big budgets and stars? In the next section, I examine women's work in shorts and documentaries, first in Britain's burgeoning animation or cartoon industry, and then in live-action, nonfiction shorts and the work of freelance editors. What was the nature of women's work in these sectors, and to what extent did the structure of these industries facilitate greater creative involvement by women?

Working in "the Haggery": The Paint and Trace Girls of Animation

The British animation industry had grown rapidly during the Second World War, when instructional and training films were in high demand. Skilled technicians were highly sought after, and with a shortage of male personnel, women had been pulled into the animation workforce.

Animation was one of the key recruiting sectors during the Second World War and notable for the number of women in senior creative roles, including Joy Batchelor, who cofounded the Halas and Batchelor studios in 1940, and animators Kathleen "Spud" Houston, Rosalie Crook, Christine Jollow, Vera Linnecar, and Elizabeth Williams, all of whom worked at the Halas and Batchelor studios in the 1940s.[41] Collectively these women made significant creative contributions to the studio's output, including the well-respected *Charley* series (1946–47) and the *Abu* series (1943), among others, and formed the core of the studio's animation team.[42] Their careers continued into the 1950s, but opportunities narrowed as more men moved into the company.

While the animator Joy Batchelor has been the subject of revisionist scholarship, this case study focuses on the less senior position of paint and trace, as it was in this job where most women in the animation industry worked.[43] In the 1950s just over two hundred people joined the union through animation positions, of which 44 percent were women, mostly working in paint and trace roles or as colorists and paint mixers. By comparison, men were recruited across a broader range of roles, including the more senior positions. Britain's animation studios were among the biggest recruiters of women's labor in this decade, and by 1957 members of the trade press were referring to paint and trace as "an entirely feminine process," although it was there that their interest in the profession stopped.[44] This case study explores how paint and trace has been marginalized in critical discourse and then goes on to examine it as a craft skill in its own right, one that problematizes the distinction between creative and noncreative labor. It also considers career progression within animation studios and how access to higher-level jobs was regulated in ways that disadvantaged women. I draw on oral histories with British women in paint and trace roles (Jill Clark, Gaumont-British Animation; Pamela Masters, Pearl and Dean), as well as published memoirs and reminisces of leading figures such as Joy Batchelor and Vera Linnecar. I connect these with stories of women working in Hollywood's animation studios, as there are many similarities in how workflow was organized. By drawing together these voices, a more nuanced and detailed picture emerges of women's craft skills in animation.

Painting and tracing are junior positions in the production hierarchy. Tracers were responsible for copying the pencil drawings generated by animators onto celluloid frames using ink, which would then be passed to painters to color in the traced outlines (see "Paint and Trace" in glossary). These roles were associated with the finishing, rather than creating, stage in the animation process and were paid accordingly, with tracers in

Britain's animation studios earning roughly half the wage of an animator. The wages reflect the value the industry accorded the work, and because paint and trace roles were held by women, the economics of the profession were sharply gendered: men dominated the remunerative employment opportunities in this sector as they did in all others in film production.

The association in Britain of paint and trace with women's work is replicated in other national cinemas. Kirsten Thompson's research on classical-era Hollywood has shown how women were "almost entirely restricted to the Inking and Paint department" at studios such as Disney, Warner Bros., and MGM and indeed were regularly rejected as applicants to other, more senior roles in animation production ("inking" is the American equivalent of the British term "tracing").[45] Scholars have found similar employment patterns and gender discrimination in other national cinemas, with notable animation industries including Japan and China.[46] The high proportion of women in these roles and the feminization of the labor sector has worked against serious critical engagement with their work processes and a lack of understanding of what the work entails. Frequent descriptions of inking and painting as "tedious and detailed work . . . best suited for women" have obscured a full understanding of the role.[47] This has been exacerbated by the industry's own vocabulary, which saw workspaces colloquially designated male or female, with Disney's ink and paint department known as "the Nunnery," and its female workers "stinkers and fainters," descriptions echoed in other Hollywood studios where the ink and paint department was referred to as a "hen house."[48] As Mindy Johnson explains, male animators looked on the ink and paint department "as a pool of potential dates [rather] than as a workplace of comparable artists," while the clever nicknames "cloaked the artistry" that took place there.[49] Designating workspaces via gendered attributes ("tedious," "detail work") has elided their place in critical debate.

Echoes are found in the British animation industry. At Gaumont-British Animation, one of the country's leading studios between 1944 and 1950, the paint and trace department was nicknamed "the Haggery" and its female workforce colloquially referred to as "the cattle corps," terms allegedly imported by American animator David Hand, who helped set up the studio.[50] Terms such as "hens," "hags," and "nuns" point to how women's labor was routinely understood in ways that naturalized it, constructing it as an extension of women's (hetero)sexual and reproductive functions rather than a craft skill in its own right. This was despite animation more broadly being the subject of serious critical interest in Britain in the 1950s. After the success of Britain's first animated entertainment feature, *Animal Farm* (1954), publications like Roger Manvell's *The Animated Film* (1954) began to appear in print along with journal articles and commentary, many of them written by Joy Batchelor's husband, John Halas. Despite the growing critical interest in animation in the country, this did not extend to what were deemed the lowly functions of paint and trace. There are no descriptions of the role comparable to those penned by continuity girls in the 1930s for the fan and trade press of that decade (see chapter 2). Nor is there any evidence of a trade voice advocating for change through leading figures in the union as Teresa Bolland attempted to do through the pages of *The Cine-Technician* when she called for the wages of production secretaries to be raised. So the invisibility of paint and trace is shaped by ideologies of gender that obscured women's work in animation while taking that of their male coworkers more seriously.

Women who worked in paint and trace describe how employers placed a premium on speed and accuracy while, for the women, the creative and artistic aspects of the role were most important. Jill Clark, who worked as a painter for Gaumont-British Animation (GBA) in the late 1940s, remembers "turning them [cels] out extremely quickly" while being "absolutely accurate" and making sure she "didn't go over the edges at all"; it was, she recalls, "quite complicated really." To achieve both quick and accurate results required total concentration on what was "quite exacting work," and to ensure that "everything moved like clockwork," it was "head down ... [without] much chance to chat or anything" (see fig. 7).[51] It was, she concludes, not a nine-to-five job. Clark's experience finds echoes in the Hollywood studios where women were expected to produce "8–10 cels an hour" while supervisors urged them to work faster with phrases like "Come on now, quick—like a bunny!"[52]

Despite the relentless pressure of the production process, Clark nevertheless described the working environment at GBA as "restful," and with a radio playing in the background, she "thoroughly enjoyed" her job. At first glance her description might sound odd, but it is repeated in other women's accounts of paint and trace. Auril Thompson, who worked at Disney in the 1940s, acknowledged that although the repetitive nature of the work was demanding, "once I got into it, to be able to ink and just swing into a lot of cels, there's something almost euphoric about it."[53] Women's descriptions communicate the satisfaction that comes from mastering the work process and the rhythmical harmonies that come from hand, eye, and technology working in perfect coordination. This is skill-as-art and, in fact, there are strong parallels with the negative cutter Queenie Turner (discussed in chapter 2), who described in intimate detail the creative rhythms she found in hand joining, another female-dominated role that has been widely maligned as repetitive and low-skill work.

Figure 7. Paint and trace at the Halas and Batchelor studios, circa 1940s.
Source: British Film Institute.

The scope to control color and tone was another of the attractions mentioned by women. For Jill Clark, the challenge in paint mixing was getting "the colour exactly right. . . . That was quite a job," and she preferred painting to tracing because "it was more varied, . . . [and] you were using the colour, which was nice," and perhaps all the more welcome after the austerity years of the war.[54] Pamela Masters, who worked at Pearl and Dean in the mid-1950s, recalled that one of the central challenges of the role was understanding tonal values and how to layer color between cels to give the impression of consistency. For example, if a character's body stayed still but their arm moved, "you had to change the colour of the paint just a little bit to match the colour of the body . . . very hard to do."[55] Women at Disney were similarly enthusiastic about the creative potential of color, with Sylvia Roemer, supervisor of the color department in the 1950s, recalling, "You had quite a bit of leeway in what you could do as far as designing the colors. . . . We made so many more new colors that the paint can never had."[56]

Finally, women repeatedly emphasized their skills in brushwork. If the application of paint was too light, the effect would be streaky; too heavy, and the brushstroke would show.[57] There was a skill in producing consistent work across multiple cels to create the impression that, in Jill Clark's words, "each drawing flowed into the next." Similarly exacting were the standards set for line drawing (tracing or inking). One Disney employee recalled how "Walt demanded shaded lines in his inking which made it even harder to do."[58] Part of the success Pamela Masters enjoyed at Pearl and Dean came from her training at art school, where she had excelled at anatomical drawing. Her ability to produce accurate, detailed drawings for the company should be understood not as the result of her gender and a "natural" facility for detail work, but of her rigorous art training at Hornsey College, London.[59] As Clare Kitson has shown, women at Halas and Batchelor were "especially proud of their brush-tracing technique—which . . . was acknowledged to be hard to master—and felt the whole art of the film was in those immobile cells, not in the movement they generated."[60] Certainly there seems to have been some recognition of this technique as a form of skill-as-art in the industry at the time. Promotional materials produced by the Halas and Batchelor company in the early 1960s name its tracers—all female—in the staff listings alongside the company's camera operators, designers, and animators (all men). For the record, the tracers were Josie Roxburgh, Mary Izzard, Mary Lasbury, Jeannine Hirst, Joyce Smith, Patricia Shiers, and Susan Bailey. That the women were listed as prominently as the men suggests that the role attracted a degree of respect and recognition within the industry, with companies happy to trade on the craft skills of a section of their workforce, even though they paid the women low wages compared to their male coworkers. In sum, women like Masters, Clark, and the hundreds of others like them had a strong sense of how their craft was underpinned by both technical skills and aesthetic sensibilities.

Given the high standard of women's skills, what opportunities existed for career progression, or was paint and trace another "blind alley job" like publicity assistant? The occupational pathways for some women appear to have gone upward rather than sideways. Pamela Masters started her career at Pearl and Dean in the paint and trace section and was then promoted to paint mixing before moving up to the drawing side as an assistant animator, responsible for in-between drawings (see "In-Betweener" in glossary). She recalls there being both men and women animators at the studio, and in her estimation there was "every opportunity to become a designer if you wanted to stay there long enough and get up the ladder"; you just needed to "integrate yourself into the department."[61] Another woman who moved up the ladder was Alison de Vere (fig. 8), who started at Halas and Batchelor in the mid-1950s as a color paint mixer and progressed from there to artist and designer for the studio, working on *World*

Figure 8. Alison de Vere (seated, left) at Halas and Batchelor studios, 1950s. Source: British Film Institute.

of Little Ig (1958), after which she left the company to become head of the animation unit at Guild Television Services. She would later win awards for her animation in the 1980s. So there seems to have been some scope for women to progress, perhaps more than their counterparts at Disney.

It does not do to overstate the case or present animation or certain studios as a protofeminist idyll. Women were more likely than their male counterparts to start at entry-level positions and take longer to progress, despite being more highly trained than men.[62] Masters's art school training was matched by that of her female coworkers at Pearl and Dean; two had been to Ruskin College Oxford and the rest had been through art college. Alison de Vere studied at the Royal Academy (London) and Joy Batchelor at Watford School of Art before turning down a place at the prestigious Slade School of Art to go into commercial art. Pamela Masters may have enjoyed a degree of progression at Pearl and Dean, but one wonders why the company failed to take her on at a higher level in the first place. As Kitson acerbically observes, it was easier for "an enthusiastic young man to bypass that step and talk himself into a job in-betweening."[63] Moreover, it seems that opportunities narrowed for women animators already working in the industry as the 1950s progressed. Jez Stewart has shown how an influx of men from GBA into Halas and Batchelor changed the gender dynamics of the studio, with most of the male animators being moved into a separate unit under the leadership of Allan Crick and tasked with producing the company's most prestigious sponsored films.[64] And Joy Batchelor herself was a less visible presence in the company during the mid-1950s, turning her creative energies to producing and scriptwriting while she cared for her and her husband's two children. Under these conditions, women could either stay but work on less high-profile commissions, or they could leave, and by the early 1950s both Vera Linnecar and Rosalie Crook had joined a rival company, Larkins, and Kathleen Houston had moved to New Zealand, where she worked with her husband, also an animator.

Not only did women with career ambitions have to surmount gendered hurdles, but there were also risks associated with moving into more senior creative roles. Stella Harvey, who worked for Halas and Batchelor as an in-betweener during the war, remembers one of the company's camera operators being "a bit of a groper and we all dodged going into the dark room with him," something that her male peers in the role presumably did not have to deal with.[65] Women also reported high levels of camaraderie in the paint and trace department, and, given the relatively pleasant working environment—background music, one's own workspace—it is no wonder that many were reluctant to leave a female-dominated environment to face an uncertain future and possible sexual harassment. Moreover, there was little need in the role for the "soft" skills of tact and discretion that characterized the work of continuity girls and production secretaries. Paint and trace might have been poorly paid and of low status, but women could work next to their female friends, and, like many other support roles, it offered an outlet for their creative energies, one they turned into a highly skilled craft. This creative potential is duplicated in other facets of work in the shorts and documentary sector, and in this final section I return to the figure of the editor.

Mining a Seam: The Editors of Nonfiction Film

Chapter 2 discussed the role of the editor and how women's employment in this field narrowed in the 1930s after the introduction of sound and the creation of new, hierarchical job levels that pushed women toward junior/assistant roles. Women now faced prejudice in British cutting rooms, but the Second World War had given them greater employment opportunities as scores of women were drafted in as assistants, while those already working in the industry (Thelma Myers, Vera Campbell) moved up through the ranks. By the end of the war, there was a widespread impression that "cutting room crews . . . generally . . . were 100% female," and women editors were certainly a visible presence in both the specialist and lay press.[66] One of Britain's leading magazines for a middle-class female readership, *Good Housekeeping*, included a special feature on editing for feature films in its June 1947 edition, while the union's journal, *The Cine-Technician*, carried advertisements by freelance editors such as Margaret Cardin, suggesting her business was successful enough to justify the advertising fees (fig. 9).

Some of the women who entered the industry during the war would go on to forge successful careers. Noreen Ackland, for example, started as an assistant to the well-respected editor Reginald Mills in the cutting rooms of the Army Kinematographic Service in 1942. After the war she moved with Mills to edit for the prestigious Archers production company and also worked during the 1950s for director Muriel Box, who had a policy of employing women in her production team where possible.[67] Anne V. Coates (niece of movie mogul J. Arthur Rank) started her career in the late 1940s as a cutting room assistant, first for Religious Films at Elstree and then at Pinewood Studios, where she progressed to full editor, establishing

Figure 9. Advertisement for Margaret Cardin's editing services. Source: *The Cine-Technician* (Jan.–Feb. 1948): 16.

a reputation for her work on *Lawrence of Arabia*, which won her an Oscar. Their achievements, however, always took place in the face of opposition, with Ackland and others recalling male directors who would simply not employ women in the cutting room and male editors who refused flat-out to hire women assistants, prejudices that denied women access to both employment and training opportunities.[68] Those, like Coates, who did succeed, felt that their ability to "disagree in a certain way"—that is, nonconfrontationally—was a skill that women of her generation brought to the director-editor relationship, an observation that points to both the emotional labor that editors performed and the expectations under which women labored.[69]

Although women enjoyed some success as editors of feature films in the 1950s and have been the subject of some revisionist scholarship, my discussion here concentrates on those who worked in the shorts and documentary sector, as their contribution to film production is less well-known.[70] This case study focuses on the work of three women editors whose long careers in the British film industry stretched from the Second World War to the 1980s: Kitty Marshall, Kitty Wood, and Monica Mead. Collectively their editorial work contributed to the production of several hundred shorts, children's films, and second or minor feature films, although the exact number is impossible to quantify. The women came from broadly similar middle-class and educational backgrounds and spent much of their professional lives as freelancers, providing contract editing services in the 1950s and 1960s for companies such as the National Coal Board, World Wide Pictures, British Transport Films, Basic, the BBC, and others. After the war nonfiction film production was flourishing in Britain, and the sector created many work opportunities for film technicians. Some saw nonfiction shorts as a training ground and stepping-stone into features, while for many others it was an end in its own right, one that offered plenty of opportunities for regular, well-paid, and interesting work, albeit under freelancing conditions. That is how the three women in this case study saw their work. This analysis addresses three topics: pathways into editing and training, how the women understood their creative practice as editors, and their reflections on being women in the industry. Together these topics illuminate career profiles that were typical for women in this sector of the film industry and help us to understand both the constraints women encountered and the opportunities they found for creative expression and professional autonomy.

For all three women, their pathways into editing came after a spell working as a general assistant to a director. As Kitty Marshall described it, this "jack of all trades" role introduced her to different aspects of filmmaking, including location scouting, organizing crew, and continuity work, all tasks typically deemed appropriate for women.[71] The early years of their careers were characterized by variety: Marshall did animation drawing during the war; Mead worked as a production assistant in the early 1950s, where she did everything from picking up lunch for the crew to editing sound; and Wood took continuity work when editing was in short supply. All three freelanced extensively. Kitty Wood recalled, "There were a lot of little jobs you could get then in . . . children's films or second features."[72] Mead similarly moved from job to job, initially knocking on doors "on spec" and then surviving on short-term contracts "bit by bit."[73] Kitty Marshall had a long-standing association with the National Coal Board but nevertheless described herself as a "temporary worker for thirty years" who sustained her career through a series of short-term contracts. None of the women served formal apprenticeships as editors; rather they learned on the job by working as a general assistant. While on-the-job training was a characteristic of the film industry more broadly, this type of training presented particular challenges for women, who found themselves excluded or taken less seriously as trainees because of their gender. In the face of such difficulties, women with any kind of ambition had to create their own opportunities. The award-winning editor Lusia Krakowska started at the British-based production company the Polish Film Unit during the war, and when not cataloging films in the company's library, "spent a great deal of time . . . upstairs [in] the cutting room [with] the negative cutters," where she "watched with great fascination" and "everybody taught me a little bit" (another example of the pedagogic labor of the negative cutter's role, discussed in chapter 2).[74] These experiences illustrate the typical work pathways available to women in the mid-twentieth-century film economy.[75] Kitty Wood felt that working in what she characterized as "the very bottom rung of the feature world" gave her a type of training that worked to her advantage when she later moved into documentaries and commercials. In her estimation, directors of second features were used to working very quickly and were therefore well trained and very efficient. She felt that working alongside them had "sharpened me up," leaving her in a good place to take advantage of work in the new commercials sector in the mid-1950s, which needed editors who could turn things around quickly.[76] Marshall and Mead likewise recalled that working quickly was a highly regarded occupational skill and that those who could work accurately at speed were in great demand.

Enterprising and skilled women like Wood, Marshall, and others found that the short film sector offered scope for creative input into filmmaking, especially because it was customary to edit after shooting had finished rather than during, as was the tradition on feature films. In this respect, Kitty Marshall's reflections on her experience at the National Coal Board are particularly illuminating. The NCB produced *Mining Review*, its premier in-house cine-magazine that was shown in miners' welfare halls and pit canteens as well as commercial cinemas. It was a highly regarded cine-magazine with good production values and had a reputation for turning out some "crisply fluent little movies" that were popular with audiences.[77] Marshall recalled one occasion as NCB editor when she was given "something like 30,000 [feet] of 35 mm material on the sinking of shafts for a certain pit, highly technical . . . shot higgledy-piggledy . . . and trying to work out what the exact process was . . . in what order it would come."[78] With no more than a one-page outline of the film's general story to guide her, Marshall's first challenge was to undertake research to decipher the technical processes behind mine-shaft sinking before deciding how to edit the filmed footage. A chance encounter with a coal board engineer on the London Underground confirmed that her technical assessments were correct, and she went ahead and edited the footage accordingly. The finished film, likely to have been *Bevercotes New Mine Part 2 Sinking the Shaft* (1958), would have been widely distributed, both domestically and overseas. Marshall embraced what she saw as the creative potential of editing, saying, "Your most exciting times as an editor are when you get this material [that] hasn't been connected . . . and putting it together yourself, it's great fun."[79]

Marshall's experience is echoed by Monica Mead, who reflected that the creative input she had working on documentaries was "enormous" because "they'd go off to a factory or a location somewhere and they'd shoot everything in sight and then come back . . . and say 'Make something out of it.'"[80] The opportunity to "make something" out of raw footage in nonfiction production provided women like Marshall, Mead, and others with scope for considerable creative license, something they actively embraced. Kitty Marshall's thoughts on the editor's role are insightful, likening it to "a glassblower"—in other words, someone who responds to another's design brief but who "would have quite a bit of effect on the design, and he [*sic*] was an artist craftsman."[81] Equally valued was professional autonomy and control over one's work. Good editors were in high demand and could expect a more equal working relationship with a director. Kitty Wood recalled that when the well-known documentary director Mary Field was late for a prebooked editing session, Wood "put her work away and got out somebody else's work," much to the consternation of Field, who lost her place in Wood's schedule.[82] This brief anecdote is revealing, giving insight into how freelancers like Wood regarded both their own time and their position in the creative hierarchy.

The scope to manage one's own time was especially important for women with children. By the early 1960s, Monica Mead had three children and, with a cameraman husband away on location, sole responsibility for their care. She managed this over the years through a combination of working from home, doing part-time work, and employing live-in help. When the children were small, she worked from home "doing tiny little jobs in the spare bedroom" for small companies, which "didn't require elaborate equipment."[83] As the children got older, she worked on *Mining Review* as a contract editor for the NCB, hired out cutting rooms on an ad hoc basis, and found that by working quickly she could finish "two weeks' work . . . in about three or four days if we were clever." She found contract working on "short-time jobs" fit with her family life and would "work for four or five weeks, and have a few weeks off." Mead's preference for what she characterized as "episodic work" is echoed by feature film editor Anne V. Coates, who chose editing because it afforded a degree of flexibility: "If one of the children was ill and I went in a couple of hours later, it didn't really matter."[84] Other women, however, struggled to combine work with child care, and for some it was the end of their careers in the film industry. For Lusia Krakowska, "I tried when the children were very small, but I was always away when they were at home on holidays, it's an impossible situation," something made all the more poignant for her, as "I used to miss the smell of the cutting room terribly. . . . I had withdrawal symptoms."[85] Such was the pull that editing exerted over Krakowska that she was tempted out of "retirement" in 1953 to work unpaid on two documentary shorts for director Anthony Simmons, *Sunday by the Sea* (1953) and *Bow Bells* (1954). These were poetic documentaries with loose, impressionist scripts and camera work by Walter Lassally, a cinematographer famed for his photographic sensibility. Lassally and his team shot the footage for *Sunday*, and Krakowska edited it into what is a lyrical portrayal of working-class families enjoying a day at the seaside. Later described as a "virtuoso display of precise frame cutting," Krakowska's editing helped *Sunday* win the Grand Prix in its category at the Venice Film Festival in 1954.[86] Editing's loss was education's gain, and after Krakowska left the film industry, she retrained as a teacher in order to accommodate paid work and family commitments. She would go on to specialize in the care of children with autism, becoming principal of one of the National Autistic Society's flagship schools in Ealing, London.[87] These anecdotes illuminate the lived experience of middle-class women in the 1950s and how they navigated what Alva Myrdal and Viola Klein characterized as the "Two Roles" of home and work.

While editing was more open to women than other technical jobs, it was not immune to gender discrimination. Women reported being refused work or feeling that they had to work harder than men to prove themselves. Kitty Wood recalled how her gender-ambiguous name (Kitty/Kit) would get her an interview only to then be turned down for work when the male employer discovered she was female. She experienced a generational divide in the 1960s with some older men from a features and shorts background "very much against . . . employ[ing[women as editors," while "the commercial people" had no such reservations, suggesting how emerging production sectors could create new professional openings for women.[88] Conversely, Wood found that some male directors preferred women editors, if only because it was assumed they must be very good to have survived in what she described as a professional "atmosphere of not liking women." Monica Mead similarly struggled to get a toehold with some companies who were more suspicious of women in the role and less inclined to offer work. She described the head of editing at Movietone News as "a bit horrified at the idea of a woman" on the team, because they were "an alien species to him," and was persuaded to give her a chance only because a male colleague vouched forcefully on her behalf.[89] Once she was in the role, Mead still had to battle discrimination. She was not allocated an assistant or given access to specialist equipment (professional privileges her male coworkers automatically enjoyed), which left her in the unenviable position of having to devise work-around solutions in order to succeed in the job. It was for this reason that Mead believed "women had to be that much better . . . [whereas] men could busk it a lot more."[90] And in addition to overt discrimination were the informal work networks that especially disadvantaged women with children. As Krakowska found, it was "very difficult to freelance because unless you are around with the boys and have a drink, you don't get the work."[91] Pub culture has always been one of the key routes through which workplace intelligence was disseminated and one that worked against those with care/domestic responsibilities.

As these oral testimonies illustrate, women may have been a visible presence in the editing workforce, but they still operated in difficult professional circumstances. In some contexts, cutting crews might be female-dominated; in others, such as Movietone News, women were in a minority. To succeed in an "atmosphere of not liking women" they needed to be tenacious, highly skilled, and extremely professional; there was no "busking" for women in the industry. Despite these challenges, editing in the shorts and documentary sector seems to have afforded these women a high degree of creative agency. Women took the opportunity to exercise professional autonomy and, by "mak[ing] something of it," took the creative lead in a way that challenges the privileged position afforded the director in much film scholarship. Editing work also enabled women, where necessary, to combine paid work with family responsibilities. Topics such as mine-shaft sinking may have been less obviously glamorous than feature filmmaking, but the sector had its compensations. This may explain why women's recollections of the mining industry were so enthusiastic: Marshall described it as "marvellous . . . I adored it"; for Wood, it was "extraordinarily interesting"; and for Mead, "Why did I keep going? . . . Because I enjoyed it." Editors like Wood, Marshall, Mead, and the forty or so others granted ACT union membership in the 1950s as full editors would not have the high-profile career of the Oscar-winning Anne V. Coates but, like their contemporaries in paint and trace or the production secretaries in features, did succeed in carving out a space in the film industry to do professionally satisfying work.[92]

Conclusion

The defining characteristic of the 1950s shows women taking what opportunities they could to do interesting and meaningful work that they made creatively rewarding. This was often in roles that men did not want (production secretary, paint and trace) or sectors like nonfiction film, which had lower status relative to features. Some women called for the union to regrade jobs held by women, arguing that this was skilled labor on par with male-dominated roles and should be compensated for accordingly. Wider recognition and acknowledgment of women's skill sets in these roles would have helped them earn promotions—from production secretary to production manager or publicity assistant to publicist—but these calls fell on deaf ears. The union patriarchy saw no reason to reassess its remunerative structures or revise its prejudicial assessment of women's technical and managerial capacities. This clash between expectations and experience, opportunities for women and union authority, would reach a head in the next decade, when a small number of "pioneer" women began to elbow their way into male-dominated positions.

5

The 1960s

The New Pioneers

The 1960s are commonly perceived as a decade of change in British society. For social historian Arthur Marwick, the decade ushered in a "cultural revolution," and, while other historians have been more circumspect, there were many new developments that impacted people's personal and public lives in these ten years. The country enjoyed full employment and high wages, and there was an increase in disposable income being spent on new consumer goods. Contraception became more widely available, enabling couples to control family size and untie sex from marriage, while greater numbers of women entered the workplace than in previous decades. The expansion of education for girls led to a corresponding rise in expectations that interesting work would follow, with many anticipating that they would enjoy greater life opportunities than their mothers. Many women had been through the new art schools that proliferated in Britain in the 1960s, and, equipped with training in commercial art, graduates of the system looked to the new creative industries of film, television, popular music, and advertising for employment.[1] As this chapter shows, it was this new generation of art school–trained women who began to test the film industry's traditional working practices in fundamental ways. Changes to censorship rules meant that new themes could be explored more fully in film, television, and other media forms, including a corresponding increase in the sexualized imagery of women's bodies, especially in advertising. The film industry and the trade union were slow to respond to the ambitions of a new generation of women, although they were quick to publish sexualized imagery in their journal, now published as *Film and Television Technician*, where a raft of "pinup girls" appeared in print in the mid-1960s. Of course, much remained the same—the 1960s did not necessarily "swing" in small towns and rural areas—and a more realistic approach to the decade is to see it as one of "transformation and tradition," where new ideas and ways of thinking butted up against established habits.[2] Taking this idea as a touchstone, this chapter examines key developments in the film industry before describing some of the film-related jobs in which women worked. Four case studies follow in areas that characterize women's work during this decade: costume, makeup, special effects, and women's experiences of working in the commercials sector, one of the decade's growth markets.

The "New" Film Industry

The film industry was experiencing its own transformation. The trend of declining cinema audiences, which had started in the 1950s, accelerated in the 1960s, and by the end of the decade, annual cinema admissions were down to around 500 million individual visits in the UK, from a postwar peak of 1.6 billion.[3] Under these precarious conditions, producers had to look beyond domestic audiences for sales, with export and television being the most obvious markets.[4] Many film companies increasingly created products for television (short films, serials, and children's entertainment), while the export market for features was supported by the influx of American capital that poured into the film industry in Britain. As Margaret Dickinson and Sarah Street have shown, a favorable exchange rate provided affordable labor costs and studio facilities and made Britain an attractive investment opportunity, and by the late 1960s between 80 and 90 percent of films made in Britain had American backing.[5] American investment reached a peak in 1968 with companies such as MGM, Disney, United Artists, Twentieth Century Fox, and others pumping over 31 million pounds into their British subsidiaries. The industry enjoyed some high-profile successes, including the James Bond films and big-budget productions like *Lawrence of Arabia*. In addition, the decade saw an emerging independent sector with small companies such as Woodfall and Vic Films producing innovative "New Wave" fare, feature films such as *A Taste of Honey* (1961) that brought the stories of young working-class people to the screen for the first time. But under these market conditions, the film industry became increasingly volatile, and established production companies such as Rank and the Associated British Picture Corporation struggled to survive, with stalwarts including Ealing Studios and British Lion closing in 1959. These were replaced by numerous one-picture companies that rented studio space and hired crew on short-term contracts. Over the course of the decade, American financing dropped sharply—down to just under 3 million pounds by 1974—and production levels noticeably dwindled.[6]

Against this backdrop of boom and then slump during the 1960s, film technicians had to adapt to survive. On the one hand, there was work: British crews were needed to produce the feature films financed by American capital, and studios like Pinewood kept their construction and camera staff on contracts, providing a labor force that outside production companies using the studio's own stages were then obliged to employ.[7] But on the other hand, the conditions of employment changed, with increasing numbers now working freelance on a film-by-film basis. Looking beyond the feature film sector, production of short films continued to flourish, albeit under increasingly difficult distribution arrangements, and the commercials sector offered film technicians opportunities for work, especially in camera and editing roles. Applications for union membership reflect this drift to freelance status, showing greater numbers of technicians now describing themselves as "freelance" or "self-employed" on their membership forms relative to previous decades. While total applications (combined figures for men and women) remained high—over two and a half thousand were processed between 1960 and 1969—as the decade progressed, the union became increasingly concerned about the levels of unemployment and eventually put an embargo on new entrants to the film production branch in 1969.[8] This shook the confidence of the workforce and, as we will see, left men even more determined to protect jobs in the industry from outsiders, especially women.

Women and Union Records: An Overview

What did these developments in the film production landscape mean for women in the film industry? Just under five hundred women applied for membership in the 1960s, a figure that represents around 18 percent of all applications. This is the lowest percentage since the 1930s and can be explained by the expansion in the workforce that was taking place in jobs traditionally occupied by men (see appendix C). Women's applications continued to follow the usual pattern, with the majority joining through traditional feminine roles, such as production secretary, assistant editor, and in paint and trace, although with the exception of production secretary, these were no longer in the large numbers that had characterized previous decades. Women continued to have a presence in the art department as draftswomen, in publicity as assistants, and in film libraries as assistants and librarians. Small numbers joined as scriptwriters, casting directors, and set dressers, with a handful gaining their union ticket as assistant directors, all for small companies specializing in nonfiction shorts. These women were paid on average between fourteen and sixteen pounds per week, comparable to a production secretary role and reflecting the junior/supportive function of the grade. And despite the gradual shaking loose of the old studio system, with its hierarchical job levels and tightly structured ways of working, this had no impact on the long-established male dominance of the camera department, which remained resolutely closed to women, perhaps unsurprisingly given the mounting concerns about unemployment.

At first glance, the profile of women's employment in the film industry suggests, at best, stasis and, at worst, regression, certainly when set in the wider context of the departure of established women film technicians, who, as Sue Harper writes, "left the film industry in droves."[9] This was especially true of directors and screenwriters, who, finding themselves out of step with a volatile industry, either retired or opted for television or children's filmmaking. The careers of established directors such as Muriel Box and Wendy Toye, producer Betty Box, and screenwriter Anne Burnaby all faltered during the 1960s.

But a more detailed examination brings a different picture into view, one that suggests women's employment was more robust and diverse than has been widely recognized. Alongside the production managers and assistant directors were a handful of women joining the union as directors, notably Mai Zetterling, Estelle Richmond, and Midge Mackenzie. These women brought with them several years' experience gained either abroad or in acting. The numbers of women costume designers in art departments went up this decade: nineteen in total (as well as three men), notably greater numbers compared to the handful who joined the union in the 1950s. Many of the costume designers in the 1960s were freelancers, gaining their union ticket through small, independent production companies such as Romulus, Grand Films, Apjac Productions, and Woodfall. So the burgeoning independent sector provided women with employment in traditional femininized roles. Costume and wardrobe form the first of this chapter's case studies, with particular emphasis on the creativity of the wardrobe department.

Trade union records also show that new areas of employment were opening up for women in the 1960s. In the Art and Effects category were approximately two dozen women who joined the film union as either puppeteers or matte artists and model makers. Most puppeteers worked at either Grosvenor or AP Films (later Century 21), companies that specialized in producing serials like *Thunderbirds* for children, which were broadcast through independent television companies. Matte artists and model makers were recruited into departments of special effects through companies such as AP Films, MGM, and others. Such jobs had previously been closed to women, but as demand for skilled workers grew during the decade, some companies were willing to employ them, a decision that was not without its critics. The matte artist in special effects forms another of this chapter's case studies.

Departments of special effects were not the only new employers of women in the 1960s. As the film industry navigated a volatile landscape, makeup departments—long-established bastions of male power—began to open their doors to women, albeit slowly and reluctantly. Oral testimony shows how a small number of women began to get a toehold in makeup departments in the 1960s, crossing into the film industry after training in television. As the case study here shows, they were usually greeted with displays of overt discrimination and prejudice from the majority-male workforce. And while much of the film industry was leaden-footed in the face of women's increasing aspirations, the burgeoning commercials sector was more welcoming. Oral histories shed light on women's experiences of working on commercials—as editors, continuity girls, and art directors—a sector one woman described as "brilliant" and "exciting," and this forms the final case study of the chapter.[10]

Taking the narrative of tradition and transformation as a touchstone, this chapter examines both customary areas of employment for women (costume and wardrobe) and newer opportunities in makeup, special effects, and commercials. Case studies of wardrobe and commercials are important to reclaiming women's work in areas commonly thought of as noncreative. Conversely, makeup and special effects as male-dominated departments have not suffered the same level of critical marginalization. Here my interest is in recounting women's experiences on the studio floor, a history told primarily through men's opposition to women. Because these positions were associated with masculinity, with men's identity as workers heavily invested in them, men had much to lose by women's incursions, especially as the job pool was beginning to shrink. As the case studies show, the union as a regulator of labor did much to limit women's progression in these fields.

Costume Design and Wardrobe

In chapter 2 I explored how in the 1930s British studios paid greater attention to costume design as part of a wider move to increase the quality of British films. The case study of costume designer Gordon Conway and her call for "better dressed pictures" opened up some of the work-flow processes around costume and its mix of costume hire, adaptation, and original design, alongside the challenges designers faced in terms of resources and status. It also highlighted how roles within costume teams were often gendered, with construction and maintenance functions (cutting, sewing, repairing, ironing) falling disproportionately to women while design and supervision roles were more readily available to men. These distinctions were often aligned with creative/noncreative values that, as we have seen throughout this study, were less rigid than has commonly been understood.

This case study builds on that analysis and has two main goals: (1) to outline some of the core elements of the costume designer's role as described by women in the 1960s, focusing on their emotional and physical labor, and (2) to examine the costume department from the perspective of the wardrobe mistress, attending to questions of creativity. The 1960s present a new development in the history of women's work in costume as an upturn in the number of women designers coincided with an international appetite for British culture, especially popular music, films, and fashion. In this decade British films were the subject of widespread popular debate, and because they often showcased fashion, costume was a central part of that discussion, which, as we will see, placed women's work center stage.

The nineteen costume designers who joined the union in the 1960s were working in a professional context that was very different from that of their 1930s peers. By now, costume was well established in British studios, its status having been boosted during the Second World War, when costume dramas enjoyed immense popularity, especially those produced by Gains-borough Pictures and its leading designer, Elizabeth Haffenden. Costume designers had been formally recognized as members of the art department, with membership of the ACT granted in 1947, and facilities at studios had been built up and developed over the years since Conway's tenure. By 1956 the wardrobe department of MGM British Studios at Elstree was suffi-ciently noteworthy to be profiled in the cine-magazine *Film Fanfare*. This boasted of the department's resources, including its costume holdings and staff (both designers and wardrobe supervisors), and showcased the work of wardrobe mistresses as they fitted actors—and even chimpanzees, with costumes for the studio's current *Tarzan* film, *Tarzan and the Lost Safari*.[11] The wardrobe department at Rank's Pinewood Studios was seemingly as impressive. An article published in a leading fan magazine, *Films and Filming*, trumpeted the studio's "vast selection of off-the-peg uniforms, with accessories to match," while its ladies department used "lace by the mile" to produce glamorous gowns for the studio's female stars, all under the creative supervision of its leading designer, Julie Harris.[12] As chapter 2 illustrated, similar profiles in the fan magazines of the 1930s had turned to Hollywood studios and their designers to showcase advances in costume departments. By the mid-1950s, studios like Pinewood were showcasing their own facilities.

It was into this professional context that costume designers entered in the 1960s. The union records show three distinct groups of women being accepted for membership in this decade. The first group were in their mid-twenties and at relatively junior levels, with between nine months' and two to three years' experience under their belts, a status reflected in their salaries, which were between twenty and thirty pounds per week. This included Yvonne Blake, whose career as a costume assistant started in 1961 on the low-budget horror film *The Terror of the Tongs* (1961). Over the next decade she would graduate to *Nicholas and Alexander* (1971), for which she won an Oscar. The second group of women were at the other end of the pay and experience scales and included older women between the ages of forty-five and sixty who had expertise gained outside film, notably stage designer Jocelyn Herbert and renowned costume historian Doris Langley Moore, who in 1963 established the Museum of Costume (since 2007 known as the Fashion Museum) at Bath.[13] With their expertise they could command high salaries for film work, between £100 and £150 per week, although costume design for film was only a small part of their professional portfolio. The third group were in their thirties and, with experience across theater, film, and television, commanded salaries of between £50 and £75 per week, a respectable wage and similar to that earned by men as lighting camera operators or producers. This group included women such as Jocelyn Rickards and Emma Porteous, who would go on to establish long and fruitful careers as costume designers, specifically working in the feature film industry. Rickards designed for some of the most eye-catching films of the decade, including *From Russia with Love* (1963), *Blow Up* (1996), and *Morgan: A Suitable Case for Treatment* (1966), for which she was Oscar nominated.

Rickards and her contemporaries Shirley Russell, Julie Harris, and Phyllis Dalton enjoyed high-profile careers in the 1960s. Dalton's and Harris's careers were well established by this point, and they won Oscars this decade for, respectively, *Doctor Zhivago* (1965) and *Darling* (1965). Russell had started her career working as an assistant to Doris Langley Moore and joined the film industry in the early 1960s, earning a BAFTA nomination for *Women in Love* (1969). She ran her own costume company, The Last Picture Frock, which she later sold to the costume house Angels, and was such a widely acknowledged expert on period costuming that art dealers called on her to help date paintings.[14] Married to a more famous husband, director Ken Russell, she was positioned in the popular press as "Mrs. Ken Russell" and "Ken's wife," and described herself at work as costume designer, "continuity girl, sandwich-maker, the lot" in her early collaborations with Russell.[15] Notwithstanding this adjunct status, women's opinions were frequently sought in the popular press of the day as the latest British films interested their readership. Statements about design principles were a common feature of their remarks, with Jocelyn Rickards describing costume as "a means of conveying by a visual signpost the background of each character," while Russell cautioned against designs that left the audience "more aware of the costume than of the actor."[16] What is also laid bare in their accounts of their work is the emotional and physical labor the costume designer's role involved, especially when working with actors. Jocelyn Rickards described her job as that of the actor's "whipping boy," responsible for "coax[ing] nervous performers into skin-tight leather trousers, dusting their privates with talcum powder to ease the fitting, without speaking a cross word."[17] The consequences of doing so had been made apparent to her early in her career when she lost her temper with a performer about to go on stage, who then gave "an awful performance— I felt dreadful, personally responsible."[18] In order to succeed in her job, Rickards had to learn the lesson that one of the functions of the costume designer's role was, to quote Arlie Hoschchild, "produce the proper state of mind in others"—in other words, undertake the type of emotional labor that is one of the defining characteristics of much of women's professional work.[19] Rickards's experiences were echoed by Shirley Russell, who had to persuade the infamously short-tempered actor Oliver Reed into collar studs for the period film *Women in Love*, leading to what she later described as "some very nasty sessions with him first thing in the morning."[20] Far from being just amusing anecdotes, Russell's comments remind us that, BAFTA nomination or not, her work came at a price, where skills of tact and diplomacy had to be married with a capacity to absorb emotional blows if, like Rickards, she was to perform successfully in her role.

A costume designer's work also involved significant physical labor, something that is rarely acknowledged in accounts of women's work in filmmaking. Rickards recalled a particularly long day that ended with her "kneeling on a dusty floor hammering away on Coca-Cola bottle tops" to create military medals for a modestly budgeted production.[21] Of her work on *Doctor Zhivago*, a period drama with a large cast and heavy costume demands, Phyllis Dalton recalled how she and her team had to "walk and hump clothes" around on a location shoot when the wardrobe bus had been "left too far away" to transport them.[22] Shirley Russell summarized her work on the 1920s-set musical *The Boy Friend* (1971) as "physically hard. It wore me out."[23] Comments like these by leading designers touch on the emotional and practical aspects of design, often sidelined in film studies that are more concerned with questions of artistry and aesthetics.

But what of the much larger workforce who worked under designers like Rickards, Russell, and others who were themselves only the most visible face of the costume department? While recent research has opened up costume design and the core elements of the designer's role, much less is known about the labor of wardrobe staff and their collective contributions to film production. It is difficult to be certain of total numbers, as wardrobe staff in British studios were members of the union NATKE, and no union records survive of their membership.[24] But there are clues about the size of the workforce and its perceived value to be gleaned from ACT documentation. When the ACT accepted costume into its ranks in 1947, it took only three jobs—supervising dress designer, dress designer, and assistant—while categorizing ten jobs for membership of NATKE: wardrobe supervisor, wardrobe master/mistress, and their staff members, as well as costumers, dressers, dressmakers, cutters, needlewomen, and assistants.[25] The distinctions being drawn between these positions seems to mirror the design-versus-construction/maintenance functions introduced at the beginning of this case study, and implicit in the ACT's decision are certain assumptions and hierarchies about what types of work have value in the production economy.

These assumptions seem to have been reflected in the popular press, where, despite costume designers being highly visible in the 1960s, there was no equivalent correspondence detailing the work of, for example, a dressmaker or needlewoman. We have to go back to 1950 to find a brief profile of a wardrobe mistress, Vi (Violet) Murray, published in the pages of *Picturegoer*. Emphasizing Murray's skills in sewing, dressmaking, ironing, and improvisation, the article's author, John Farleigh, praises the wardrobe mistress as "the housewife of the studios," effectively suggesting that her professional skills are little more than an extension of women's presumed natural talent for domesticity.[26] Later descriptions would be equally vague, with a 1981 delegation of British costume designers describing wardrobe staff as "responsible for the servicing, upkeep and continuity of the clothes, once the film is under way," although they were less forthcoming about what this involved in practice.[27] What were the challenges of servicing clothes when faced with, for example, location work, multiple takes, or a cast of extras to dress? How did the wardrobe department ensure continuity when costumes went missing or were misplaced? To begin to address these questions, I have drawn on interviews with costume designers and wardrobe mistresses to piece together a picture of women's work in this underreported area of production. I focus on the careers of two women: Betty Adamson (career span 1949–87) and Rosemary Burrows (career span 1958–2005). Both had extensive careers in the wardrobe departments of Britain's film studios, but I want to focus on Adamson's work on large-scale international coproductions and Burrows's work for the smaller-scale Hammer Film Productions, as these open up how wardrobe departments functioned on productions of varying size and budget.[28]

In accounts of work given by the costume designers Julie Harris, Phyllis Dalton, and Jane Hamilton, wardrobe supervisor Betty Adamson emerges as a key figure, remembered with enthusiasm and praised for her organizational skills and problem-solving abilities. In 1969 Julie Harris was working as costume designer on *Goodbye Mr. Chips* (1969), a musical drama set in a boy's boarding school. With several hundred schoolboys to dress, Harris ordered identical stock costumes for the opening scenes but was horrified to discover that "when the clothes were unpacked none of the ties and hatbands had any stripes on them."[29] She credits Adamson with getting the production out of a tight spot: "We had a wonderful wardrobe supervisor called Betty Adamson, who found art students in Sherbourne and lots of pots of white paint and brushes. And they all sat down and painted the stripes . . . on all the ties and boaters. It went on almost all night."[30] Adamson's skills appear to have been the stuff of industry legend.

Some years later, costume assistant Jane Hamilton was taken on as a junior to Julie Harris, who was designing for *The Great Muppet Caper* (1981). Shot in Pinewood Studios, the film presented a number of wardrobe challenges, as it mixed together humans and puppets in a live-action musical setting. In Jane Hamilton's account, one of Adamson's many talents was her ability to successfully coordinate the wardrobe needs of large casts on big productions. Shooting on the Muppet film involved an ambitious underwater musical number where Miss Piggy was accompanied by two dozen professional swimmers dressed in silk capes, bathing suits, and flowered bathing caps to perform a synchronized routine that moved from poolside to underwater. Multiple takes were made possible by Adamson rigging up huge heaters on the set to dry off the outfits and coordinating a team of dressers to get the swimmers quickly out of the costumes and back into them again ready for shooting. Hamilton recalls that the director "kept taking takes," leaving the wardrobe department to get the swimmers "in and out and in and out. . . . It was unbelievable. I couldn't have supervised that in a million years."[31] For Hamilton, Adamson was "a brilliant supervisor . . . really efficient . . . really practical and knowing,"

Figure 10. Wardrobe supervisor Betty Adamson's work on *The Great Muppet Caper* (1981).

whose professional skills were clearly invaluable. Her labor enabled the director's "vision" and saved the production shoot considerable money by keeping cameras rolling (see fig. 10).

Nowhere was this more than evident than during location shooting, where the "servicing, upkeep and continuity of the clothes, once the film is under way," brought particular challenges. Adamson is remembered by Jane Hamilton as a frequent coworker of costume designer Phyllis Dalton, who designed for large-scale international coproductions, including *Lawrence of Arabia* and *Doctor Zhivago*, although, as was often the case for wardrobe staff, Adamson was not granted a screen credit for these films. On these types of productions, specialist facilities had to be carefully preplanned and, unlike cameras, lighting, and other technical equipment, were rarely at the forefront of the director's mind. Getting up to five hundred extras into period dress for a day's shooting on *Doctor Zhivago* meant a significant amount of forward planning by the costume team, from setting up wardrobe tents where extras could be dressed to laying out uniforms in the sun to break them down and give them the appearance of age. Costume was, as we have seen, hard work, with Dalton recalling heavy clothes to "walk and hump" around the shoot, often with little more than an "old hanging rail" to assist you.[32] Dalton found that practical problems soon arose when "you've got a crowd of extras in period costume . . . lying about on the grass . . . [because] no-one has thought of even a bench to sit on."[33] It was for reasons such as this that Dalton rated "a good wardrobe supervisor" as someone who would always ask "what's happening to the crowd," ensuring appropriate wardrobe facilities were part of the planning conversation from the outset. Here we see how wardrobe, as one part of the "complicated jig-saw puzzle" of film production, links to the work of the production secretary, discussed in chapter 4. In Dalton's assessment, Betty Adamson was not merely good but "a wonderful . . . wardrobe supervisor" who could manage, during location work, to rig up "a washing machine and everything going in the middle of the desert. How she managed it, I still don't know."[34] So wardrobe supervisors like Adamson had to work accurately at speed, have physical strength, good people skills, and excel at organization and logistics.

Adamson's ability to make the seemingly impossible possible comes through clearly in the recollections of those who worked with her. Indeed, her occupational talents resonate strongly with those described by Elizabeth Nielson in her assessment of costumers in the Hollywood studio system. For Nielson, what costumers often referred to as "creativity" was "synonymous with resourcefulness . . . [a] *spontaneous* productive sense of creativity . . . [that could] find cheap and fast solutions to production problems."[35] Although this type of imaginative, nimble thinking was rarely acknowledged by either award ceremonies or in an individual's paycheck, it nevertheless played a central role in achieving the finished look of a film. But Adamson herself was ably supported by a team of unhistoricized dressers, needlewomen, and many others, of whom little is known. Dalton recalls that "as many as fifteen or twenty" worked on costumes for *Doctor Zhivago*, which, as a prestigious production for MGM British, represented the high end of the market, but even this account excludes the Spanish costumers who embroidered the ball gown for the film's star Geraldine Chaplin, sent out from London to Madrid, where, Dalton recalls, it was "so much cheaper to have it embroidered."[36] Spanish labor may have been cheap, but the skills were second to none, as Dalton discovered when the dress went missing in transit between the two cities. It was the Spanish costumers who stepped into the breach: "They just did me another one, very, very quickly . . . an all-night job."[37] This meant creating a new ball gown from scratch—cutting, sewing, embroidering, and finishing entirely by hand—a feat that could be achieved only by highly skilled, experienced dressmakers (fig. 11).

Figure 11. Geraldine Chaplin in *Doctor Zhivago* (1965) wearing costumes designed, made, and maintained by Phyllis Dalton, Betty Adamson, and other unknown wardrobe staff.

While Dalton presents the anecdote as "one of the worst things that's ever happened" to her professionally, it also reveals the significant amount of outsourced labor that props up film production generally and costume specifically. We have no way of knowing how much the Spanish costumers were paid or the working conditions in which they labored. Nielson's research on the Hollywood studio system has shown how many of the "exquisite hand embroideries and decorations" that characterized MGM's productions were produced by "fine seamstresses from Mexico and Japan and Puerto Rico," often immigrant laborers who worked long hours in cramped conditions for very modest wages.[38] British studios may not have operated on the same scale as Hollywood, yet Dalton's story reveals how similar working practices were in play. Her designs for *Doctor Zhivago* won her an Oscar for Best Costume Design, but, like most industry awards, they fail to acknowledge the below-the-line labor—from Adamson's logistical skills to the unnamed dressmakers and embroiders—who made the glamorous production possible.

While Betty Adamson represents the experience of one type of wardrobe supervisor—working as part of large team handling crowd scenes and extras alongside principal players—Rosemary Burrows's experience in the 1960s was at the other end of the spectrum. Interviewed in 2010 for BBC Radio 4's *The Film Programme*, Burrows gives a fascinating insight into the production culture of a small studio producing films with modest budgets.[39] Burrows was a student at the Berkshire College of Art in 1958 when she was asked to help costume crowd extras on a film being shot at Hammer's Bray Studios, for which she was paid £11 per week ("I thought I'd died and gone to heaven"). Hammer specialized in horror films made in the studio rather than on location, budgets were modest (Burrows recalls £230,000 being relatively generous for the studio), and with a six-week shooting schedule, she had to work quickly and efficiently.[40] Hammer's productions used a small roster of actors, notably Christopher Lee and Peter Cushing in lead roles, and the crew members were salaried, earning modest pay in exchange for regular employment. The wardrobe team was small, headed by the experienced Molly Arbuthnot (who had worked in the film industry since the 1940s), and the cast members were dressed in outfits from the studio's wardrobe stores, which Burrows would adapt and embellish according to the demands of the script. The only original design work Burrows recalls was for bespoke nightgowns for female stars, designed to reveal or obscure cleavage, buttocks, and legs according to the demands of the different national markets across which the films were distributed.

With no prior experience in costume (Burrows had been studying pottery before she joined Hammer), she had to learn quickly and described her apprenticeship as "a pretty incredible initiation."[41] Instrumental to her learning was the actor Peter Cushing, whom Burrows described as "quite fanatical about period. . . . He taught me a lot." Cushing's most iconic roles for Hammer were Baron Frankenstein and Doctor Van Helsing in the studio's iterations of *Frankenstein* and *Dracula*, respectively. This meant the character had to appear in the debonair style of a nineteenth-century gentleman, but satisfying Cushing's period demands was challenging not least because, as Burrows recalls, "there was no budget" for wardrobe. Unfazed, Burrows, under Cushing's tuition, used a series of eye-catching frock coats, polka-dot cravats, velvet jackets, and satin-trimmed waistcoats, complete with tiepins, cufflinks, and other accessories to visually signpost the character's professional background and social standing. Burrows's recollections suggest how the costume "look" of Hammer's films—renowned for their visual style—was a combination of the actor's input with the wardrobe team's creativity—that is, resourcefulness (see fig. 12). Her account gives a brief glimpse into how a wardrobe department functioned on small-scale productions where small teams with minimal resources built up close working relationships with actors. Burrows's experience is far removed from the large-scale washing, drying, and dressing facilities that Adamson orchestrated on location, but the

Figure 12. Rosemary Burrows with Peter Cushing on the set of *Arabian Adventure* (1979).

underlying skills are the same: resourcefulness and great skills in inter-personal communication.[42]

Burrows passed her "initiation" at Hammer, if her subsequent career is any indication. By 1967 she was acting as "Mother Confessor" (her description) to Marlon Brando during the making of *A Countess from Hong Kong* (1967)—presumably performing the same kind of emotional labor as Shirley Russell and Jocelyn Rickards—and would later advise Christopher Columbus on special effects when he was directing *Harry Potter and the Philosopher's Stone* (2001). But despite the wealth of experience and knowledge Burrows and many others held, costume and wardrobe continued to suffer from a lack of proper recognition in the industry. Costume assistant Jane Hamilton, who started in films in the 1970s, found that "the male sex . . . [were] always a bit patronising, about women doing 'frocks,'" an attitude that dogged her career in the 1980s. And Shirley Russell, who costumed amazing fantasy sequences in *Lisztomania* (1975) and *Tommy* (1975), still struggled to convince her director husband, Ken Russell, quite "how much work is involved" in delivering her designs.[43] This was more than merely status; it had real material consequences for women who continued to be underpaid relative to the value they added to the production team. The "housewife of the studios" still had an uphill struggle for equal wages.

Makeup

If costuming represents one strand of women's work in an area with an established tradition of employing women, how did they fare in areas of feature filmmaking such as makeup that had long functioned as bastions of male power? There was little tradition of women working in this area, which had been dominated by men for decades, possibly because of a tradition stemming from early cinema of male barbers doing studio hair and makeup for film. In Hollywood the Westmore brothers (Perc, Ern, Monte, Wally, Bud, and Frank) ruled the studio system, along with Cecil Holland and Jack Dawn at MGM's studios, a state of affairs that reflected the masculinization of the wider beauty industry. Women's labor, where it was permitted, was confined to supportive tasks such as body-painting extras rather than chief makeup artist or heads of department.[44] Conversely, women's hairdressing—categorized as a subdivision of the makeup department—was staffed by women, with the department functioning as a social space in the studio, where actresses congregated and gossip was shared.[45] Britain followed a similar pattern; hairdressing was staffed by women while men held senior makeup positions, headed departments, and took the lead in defining the craft. Harry Davo, chief makeup artist at British International Pictures, wrote "The Art of Makeup," published in *The Cine-Technician* in 1935, while fan magazines regularly profiled men in their pages: "Gerald Fairbank, the make-up expert at Beaconsfield Studios," in *Picturegoer* (1936), and Billy Partleton, the "master of make-up," in *Films and Filming* (1957), among others.[46] Other leading figures included Robert (Bob) Clark, chief makeup artist at Elstree Studios (from the 1930s to the 1970s) and Walter Schneiderman, whose career started in the 1940s and who worked at many of Britain's leading film studios.[47]

Men did not have it entirely their own way, however, and this case study has two aims: to sketch a brief history of women's makeup work in British films before turning to the work of Linda de Vetta, whose career illustrates how a small group of women broke through into feature film makeup in the 1960s. There are no ACTT records to support this case study, as makeup artists and wardrobe staff were members of NATKE, meaning crucial evidence about wages and workforce demographics is missing. Oral histories, however, provide a valuable insight into this under-researched area, revealing how makeup represented a new area of work opportunity for women in the 1960s, albeit one fraught, once again, with male prejudice and discrimination. I examine women's entry into the profession; their workday, skills, and expertise; and how they were treated by their male peers and the unions. Makeup is now one of the most popular jobs for women in film, with recent statistics showing that 85 percent of makeup artists working in Britain are female. What this case history reveals is how women like Linda de Vetta had to surmount considerable male prejudice to build successful careers in the British film industry, paving the way for subsequent generations of women.[48]

The size of the makeup workforce in Britain was relatively small compared to camera departments or editing. In the estimation of Walter Schneiderman, there were between fifty and sixty makeup artists working in the British film industry as a whole during his career, with no more than six to ten of them being women, mainly at the larger studios of Shepperton and Pinewood.[49] In such a small-scale and niche profession, it was particularly difficult for women to make any inroads once men had established their dominance. Women's function in British makeup departments rarely extended beyond support roles, with the wives of makeup artists drafted in to do body makeup on actresses on some of the bigger productions.[50] Only occasionally were they tolerated as assistants. Peggy Rignold was taken on as an assistant to Elstree's makeup chief, Harry Davo, in the mid-1930s and became sufficiently competent in the role to be "hired out" as an assistant to other men.[51] But any ambitions she may have had for career progression were interrupted by the outbreak of the Second World War, and by 1942 she had joined the Film Production Group of the Army Kinematographic Service as an assistant editor. Jill Carpenter enjoyed a long career as a makeup artist in the 1950s, '60s and '70s, although her screen credits show she was predominantly working on second features, a profile suggesting that for a woman to progress beyond assistant was a more realistic option in low-budget filmmaking.

One of the few women to work on prestige productions for any length of time was Connie Reeve (figs. 13 and 14). Born in 1924, she had attended art school and worked as a commercial artist before World War II. Family connections helped Reeve gain entry into the film industry, as her sister was married to Harold Fletcher, head of makeup at Shepperton Studios, who invited her to train as a makeup artist after the war.[52] Earning a wage of around six pounds per week in the late 1940s (comparable to an editor or senior secretary), Reeve worked on some of the most iconic British films of the postwar period, including several Michael Powell and Emeric Pressburger films—among them *The Red Shoes* (1948), *Gone to Earth* (1950), and *The Tales of Hoffmann* (1951)—as well as *Moulin Rouge*

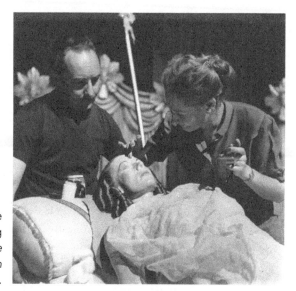

Figure 13. Connie Reeve applying makeup for *The Tales of Hoffman* (1951).

Figure 14. Connie Reeve applying makeup to Barbara Bain on the set of *Space 1999* (1975–77).

(1952) and *The Prince and the Showgirl* (1957). The quality of her work was such that, by the early 1950s, she was entrusted with making up leading star Gina Lollobrigida in John Houston's *Beat the Devil* (1953), but despite (or because of) her talent, she struggled to progress to chief makeup artist and later claimed that women were neither "welcomed nor supported" in the industry.[53] Career progression became more difficult after her marriage in 1956 and the subsequent birth of two children, but she found a way around the child-care conundrum by having her infant daughter cast in the television series *Swallows and Amazon* (1963), allowing her to work on the production. Imaginative solutions to child care were one thing, but early mornings and long days were not conducive to family life, and she took a step back from her career when the children were small, although she would later return to work in television and occasionally features.

Although Reeve had family connections, even she experienced prejudice, which suggests how feature films were less than hospitable to women in anything other than assistant roles. Conversely, one of the peculiarities of the British system was that makeup in television was dominated by women, who benefited in the 1960s from selective and comprehensive training schemes run by the BBC and independent television companies such as ATV (Associated Television). One BBC employee claimed that television companies at this time had a policy of employing women only in their makeup departments precisely because "the film industry refused to employ women" in the role and "all the other areas of television were male-dominated."[54] While television might have served as a relative oasis for women with professional ambitions to work in makeup, any attempt by them to move across into films was met with a hostile reception. As one woman recalled, "We were considered very inferior" by the film industry, a classic example of women's skills being downgraded by men to exclude them from entry into a profession.[55] Despite this prejudice, it was the "television girls" who were to bring pressure to bear on the male dominance of the feature film industry.

As British cinema enjoyed a production boom in 1967, its film studios were scrambling around for additional freelance labor. The industry's small roster of makeup artists were fully engaged, and with another big film with a large cast about to go into production at Shepperton (on the period comedy *Great Catherine*, 1968), the studio was desperate for additional skilled workers. It was under these conditions that they turned to a small group of television-trained women who were freelancing at the time: Linda de Vetta, Ann Brodie, Heather Nurse, Jane Royle, and Sandra Sylvester. In this case study, de Vetta serves as an illustrative example, as she is one of the few women working in the field whose life story has been recorded, and it is through these recollections that we can map the labor practices of this unique moment in film history. De Vetta started her career in television, training at ATV Studios between 1962 and 1963, and subsequently worked on live television shows for the company before leaving in 1966 with the ambition to work freelance and learn more about prosthetics. She quickly found work as a makeup artist on commercials and fashion shoots but was approached in the spring of 1967 with an offer of freelance work on *Great Catherine*. Along with four other women (all of whom had trained in television) she was signed up for eight weeks' work on the film. The conditions of employment were strict: the women were to work only on "specials"—that is, actresses in supporting roles—and at a salary that was half of what the makeup men received, justified on the grounds that the women were merely "assistants." At the end of the shoot, they were to be granted membership of NATKE, although even then strict conditions would be placed on their employment. As de Vetta recalls, the women were not to be "allowed to chief a film, we weren't allowed to do commercials, because it meant we would be working on our own and unsupervised. . . . In essence . . . we could only be a makeup assistant under a union membered makeup artist."[56] This is despite the fact that the women had all completed formal training programs in television and had built up several years' experience by the time they signed the contracts. Once again, the industry handled the need for labor by creating junior positions, at lower wages, into which women could be recruited (see chapters 1 and 2 for further examples).

De Vetta quickly proved herself invaluable, however, and in the next few years she worked on a number of feature films, including *Charge of the Light Brigade* (1967), where she and her coworkers set up temporary tents on location in Turkey to process the hundreds of Cossacks and officers requiring makeup for battle scenes. She was sufficiently skilled to be appointed chief makeup artist on *Performance* (1970) by the film's director, Nicholas Roeg, but this contravened the conditions of her union ticket, and the makeup branch of NATKE responded by taking her to a union tribunal to revoke her membership. De Vetta eventually won the case—thanks to some nifty legal footwork by her father's lawyer—but at this point she found herself ostracized by some in the makeup community.

Over the next few years, she continued to find work, but it was difficult, and she was often forced to take productions that had been rejected by makeup artists who were more established in the business. She joined the makeup team on *Ryan's Daughter* (1970) because few other people wanted the job; she recalls, "They'd asked other makeup artists [but] they wouldn't go to Dingle in Ireland for six months!" She worked again with Nicholas Roeg on *Walkabout* (1971), this time uncredited and operating under the radar as "Linda Richmond" (her married name) on what was a shoestring-budget shoot where, in addition to doing makeup, she cooked meals for the second unit when the catering truck got stuck in a sand dune. And she often found herself tested by the male establishment, many of whom had a thinly veiled dislike of women, especially television-trained "girls." She recalled one incident where Charlie Parker, chief makeup artist on *Ryan's Daughter*, refused to speak to her until she had created three rubber prosthetic ears for John Mills's character in the film, a test to prove she was capable of the job; she passed it with flying colors. Parker would later apologize to her, but, as de Vetta recalled, such treatment "wasn't uncommon."[57] She later proved useful to Parker on the film when he fell out with leading actress Sarah Miles on the shoot and gratefully delegated her to de Vetta. Young pretenders like de Vetta clearly had their uses, absorbing the emotional fallout of on-set debacles and pacifying the crew with a home-cooked meal.

De Vetta was not alone in experiencing attempts by the union to block the careers of women. Christine Allsopp, daughter of makeup artist Connie Reeve, was similarly treated with hostility when she applied to be a trainee member of the makeup branch in 1977, forced to endure several meetings with "mostly men complaining about the 'television girls' and trying to defend their turf from these 'interlopers.'"[58] Makeup artist Mary Hillman had a comparable experience when she tried to work in films after serving an apprenticeship with the BBC and working extensively in television and the commercials sector in the 1960s. Director Alan Parker asked her to be makeup chief on *Bugsy Malone* (1976), but she found herself ostracized on set: "I was a member of the union [but] no-one in film would work with me because I was a television girl."[59] With the support of Parker and NATKE's president, she stayed on the film, but it was an uncomfortable experience, where "no-one . . . spoke to us because we were television."[60] While it is a function of unions to regulate the supply of labor, these examples suggest that the terms used to achieve that were highly feminized, indicating it was the sex of the applicants—as much as their labor—that represented a threat to the department.

Despite the many obstacles that the union placed in the way of women, de Vetta and others put up with male prejudice because they found working on feature films particularly engaging. For de Vetta, it satisfied her desire to learn new skills and experiment with techniques, opportunities that she felt were less readily available in television at the time. Not content with refashioning John Mills's prosthetic ears, she created the look of a badly decomposed cadaver on *Walkabout*, scarred actor James Fox's body for his drug-fueled character Chas in *Performance*, and, most famously, created a modified lens for David Bowie's iconic yellow cat's eyes on *The Man Who Fell To Earth* (1977).[61] Because she was employed freelance and frequently worked on location, it was up to her to supply her own equipment, and her pride and joy was a Max Factor box, brought from

America in 1967 by her then husband, which she stocked with makeup, brushes, specialist chemicals, and dental tools for modeling (see fig. 15).[62] Her workday was arduous, with long hours and heavy responsibilities. For de Vetta, this meant getting out of bed at 5:30 a.m. and doing her own makeup before driving herself across London to Shepperton Studios for a 7:00 a.m. start. This was no mean feat, as the trend for women in the 1960s was for full makeup with two sets of false eyelashes, and de Vetta drove at such speed that the crew nicknamed her "Leadfoot Linda" for her ability to get to the studio in under an hour.[63] The rewards were plentiful, however. The pay was good—forty-five pounds per week in 1967 ("a fortune"), one hundred pounds in 1970 ("more than my old male friends")—so, unlike the underpaid production secretaries discussed in chapter 4 doing more traditional forms of women's work, long hours in

Figure 15. Linda de Vetta on the steps of Pinewood Studios, circa 1969. Source: Photograph in author's possession.

a "man's job" were generously remunerated with a "breadwinner's" wage. And she relished the technical aspects of the job. This included not only working with prosthetics, latex, and other materials but also liaising with camera and lighting crew, checking, for example, that her makeup work harmonized with director Tony Richardson's choice of film stock to produce the required sepia tones on *Charge of the Light Brigade*.[64] Once she had children, she found the long hours and location work unsustainable and, like countless women before and after her, switched to working on commercials when the children were small, returning to features in the early 1980s with the support of live-in help. She enjoyed a long and successful career and later worked on high-profile films with leading directors including James Cameron, Roman Polanski, and David Lean, and as a personal makeup artist to A-list stars including Sigourney Weaver, Jeremy Irons, and Judi Dench.

What of the other "television girls" who were recruited alongside de Vetta in early 1967? Their profiles suggest mixed fortunes. Jane Royle, like de Vetta, enjoyed a high-profile career in features, winning a BAFTA for her work on *The Company of Wolves* (1985), and Ann Brodie continued in feature films through the 1970s before moving to Canada and the United States to develop her career. The career of Heather Nurse was more modest, with half a dozen screen credits to her name, including working with Bette Davis on *Madame Sin* (1972) before her credits petered out, a similar profile to that of Sandra Sylvester. But the 1960s represent a turning point when women finally began to get established in feature film makeup. A brief expansion in film production, coupled with the women's experience in television (which made them a ready-made and well-trained workforce), created the conditions of entry that, once under way, were difficult to reverse and would lead, over time, to women's current dominance of the field. In the 1960s, however, to be a makeup artist was to be a woman in a man's world, and that was no easy ride. To paraphrase editor Monica Mead (see chapter 4), you had to be better than most men and tenacious to survive as an "interloper," something that is mirrored in the experience of women in special effects, the next case study.

Special Effects

Trade union records show other new areas of employment opening up for women in the 1960s, with around two dozen joining the union in the roles of puppeteer, trainee matte artist, and model maker. Most of the women were employed by either Grosvenor Films or AP Films, the latter being best known for popular series such as *Supercar* (1962), *Fireball XL5* (1962–63),

Thunderbirds (1964–66), *Stingray* (1964–65), and *Captain Scarlet and the Mysterons* (1967–68) that screened on British and American television. Other employers included MGM, Hawk Films (Stanley Kubrick's British production company), and Bowie Films Limited, a British company specializing in special effects.[65] Special effects was a growth area in British film production in the 1960s. AP/Century expanded rapidly from 1962 onward, after the successful export of *Supercar* to the United States, while the production trend in Britain for horror and action films meant that special effects were in high demand. The filming of Stanley Kubrick's *2001: A Space Odyssey* (1968) at MGM British Studios and Shepperton Studios in 1967 created work for film technicians and served as a showcase for their craftsmanship. By the end of the decade, the profile of special effects was sufficiently high to warrant the formation of a specialist committee within the ACTT union to protect and promote the section's interests.[66]

Over eighty technicians joined the union through AP/Century during the 1960s, the majority of whom were men in the positions of special effects technicians, clapper loaders, and set artists. But women took the lead as puppeteers: fourteen women and seven men joined AP Films in the 1960s.[67] Salaries were around fifteen to seventeen pounds per week in the mid-to-late 1960s, comparable to an assistant director role but less than a special effects assistant in the company, who earned twenty to twenty-five pounds and was a job that was filled exclusively by men. Headed by Gerry and Sylvia Anderson, AP/Century has been the subject of revisionist history, and while much of that history has focused on the Andersons, more recent interviews with production personnel, including Mary Turner, have provided an invaluable insight into this area of media production and the role of women in the workforce. Turner was a leading figure in the studio, often credited with "puppetry supervision" on a number of the company's series. She trained in sculpture at art school in the 1950s before joining AP in 1960, and her role in the company was varied. She sculpted figures for *Thunderbirds*, *Captain Scarlet*, and others; supervised puppetry operation during filming; and was responsible for the general care and maintenance of the puppets—no mean feat when the special effects team kept blowing them up. In addition to these operational duties, she was instrumental in developing both the design and mechanics of the puppets. Sylvia Anderson would give Turner a general description for new characters, but the interpretation of that was often Turner's own; she recalled, "I was modelling the puppets . . . the way I thought they should be."[68] This description of working partnerships echoes that found in the art department (discussed in chapter 3), where the technical skills and aesthetic sensibilities of assistants played a key role in the creative process. Turner also took the lead in developing controls for the puppets on the *Thunderbirds* series. The challenge was to develop a mechanism that could turn and tilt the puppet heads using a control underneath the torso, and Turner "spent time working that out in my own time and managed to get it to work."[69] Turner was one of a number of women at the company, alongside Christine Glanville, Judith Shutt, Yvonne Hunter, Heather Granger, Joan Garrick, and Turner's sister Carolyn. Many of these women were in their twenties or thirties when they joined the union, suggesting a more mature and probably highly educated workforce. Turner's account suggests how the role of puppeteer provided women with interesting and relatively well-paid creative work in an environment that seems to have been less hostile to their presence, certainly compared to the dynamics of the makeup department discussed earlier.

If puppetry provided some women with a supportive working environment, how did others—specifically matte artists—fare in special effects, a sphere dominated by men because of its links with technology? There is little by way of archival evidence, not least because so few women worked in the role. The union processed only six applications by women in the 1960s: Elizabeth Hague, Anne Sanderson, and Gillian Culham at MGM; Joy Seddon (later Cuff) at AP Films; Lynnette Scott at Bowie Films; and Hilary Randall at Hawk Films. By comparison, almost fifty men were recruited to special effects departments, principally as matte artists, technicians, and camera operators. Although no archival material has yet come to light on five of the women, Joy Cuff has recorded a number of oral accounts of her professional life as a matte artist/model maker, and these, in addition to her film credits, allow us to piece together a picture of women's contribution to this very male-dominated sphere of production. Cuff provides a case study through which to trace one woman's movement through British film culture in the mid-to-late 1960s. She started her career at AP Films before moving on to Hammer horror films, Stanley Kubrick's *2001, A Space Odyssey*, and television commercials, thus working across popular, domestic, and international productions in a way that is characteristic of the decade. The following discussion focuses on what Cuff's work entailed and her experience of the studio floor, with its risks and challenges for a woman in a male work environment.

Cuff entered the film industry in 1964 after studying at Kingston School of Art, London, where she specialized in painting and pottery. Her first commercial role was as a sculptor for AP Films, where she worked in the puppet workshop modeling puppet heads for *Thunderbirds*. The workshop was in charge of set design, special effects, and puppet/model making for the company, and the team was predominantly male; thus, Cuff, as a woman, was in a minority in the puppet workshop. It is likely that she was taken on because she was exceptionally talented, and her father, a commercial artist, had connections in the film industry. Certainly, her reflections in interview communicate her significant achievements as a painter during childhood, adolescence, and young adulthood.[70] Her work for AP Films at this time was varied and included puppet making, input into costume and hair design for the puppets, and occasionally standing in for live-action shots (fig. 16). Perhaps the real value of the role for an ambitious young recruit is that it gave Cuff a union ticket, which was her passport to future employment and introduced her to people in special effects. Through her work on *Thunderbirds*, Cuff met Wally Veevers, a leading figure in British special effects, and the matte artist Bob Cuff, for whom she would later work as an assistant. She married Bob Cuff's son Paul in 1969. These contacts provided her with a way into the male-dominated field of special effects and opened up offers of freelance commissions. These included modeling the medallion the actress Ursula Andress wore around her neck in the Hammer film *She* (1965), designing and building the iconic temple entrance for Hammer's sequel *The Vengeance of She* (1968), producing a series of illustrations for François Truffaut's *Fahrenheit 451* (1966), and matte painting and artwork for the western *Mackenna's Gold* (1969).

As a matte artist and model maker, Joy Cuff was not office-based but worked in the special effects workshop, where she reported to the

Figure 16. Matte artist Joy Cuff at work, late 1960s.

department head, who, in turn, reported to the director. The work was often dirty and messy, involving working with paints, plaster, plastics, acrylics, putty, and other materials, and the nature of the job meant she often spent long periods of time working on her own. Her job was craft-based and involved skills in painting on glass, the ability to render backgrounds in different styles (documentary, impressionistic, fantastical, etc.), fabricate scale models, and have a working knowledge of how filmmaking shaped perspective, depth of field, and color tone (see "matte artist" in glossary).[71] Unlike the production secretary, continuity girl, editor, and many other roles held by women, emotional labor and the underpinning skills of tact and diplomacy were not prerequisites for success in Cuff's role. Nor did she require the kind of skills in interpersonal communication that characterized women's labor in costume and wardrobe, where they worked in close proximity with actors. There was a degree of problem solving and creative resourcefulness, which Cuff relished—working out which material would give the best finish and adapting household/everyday materials for model making—but this relied on technical know-how and aesthetic sensibilities rather than the "softer" skills of persuasion and negotiation. In this respect, Cuff and the handful of other female matte artists posed a challenge to the norms of femininity that dominated the film industry, something I return to shortly.

Commissions helped her build up a portfolio of work that showcased her skills. But that in itself was not enough to build a career in a man's world; she needed connections. She credits the well-respected matte artist Bob Cuff as having a significant influence on her career. Not only did she, in her own words, "learn a lot from him, in doing matte work and model work and design," but his validation permitted her entry into the male world of special effects.[72] Joy Cuff faced gender prejudice from industry giants like Wally Veevers, who, she claimed, "didn't think women should be out there working" and had the power to block her career progression. But because Veevers held Bob Cuff in high regard, Joy found she was tolerated: "That's why I managed to stay, really, because I was working for Bob."[73]

Tolerance was one thing, acceptance something else, and when Cuff moved from AP Films to big studio work, the gender politics came as a shock. Between 1966 and 1967 she worked at MGM British on Stanley Kubrick's *2001, A Space Odyssey*, taken on as a special effects department assistant and working with Bob Cuff. The film was a significant coup for the British film industry, providing work for hundreds of technicians over a prolonged period of time. Shot at Shepperton Studios, it was famed for the cost and complexity of its production design, which included a

revolving drumlike set, the "stargate" sequence, and multiple settings ranging from the prehistoric to the futuristic. The film was a showcase for
British special effects, with a large team led by Wally Veevers and Douglas Trumbull and comprising over twenty-five crew members in roles as
varied as special effects technician, engineer, coordinator, and airbrush
artist.[74] With the exception of Joy Cuff and Hilary Ann Pickburn, all the
special effects crew were men; in fact, the whole shoot was overwhelmingly
male, from the rank-and-file jobs of plasterers, carpenters, electricians,
and stagehands to the more senior technical and creative roles. This was
the type of male homosocial world from which women were rigorously
excluded, and working on the production was, in Cuff's words, "an eye-
opener" in terms of sexual politics.[75]

She was involved in producing the film's moonscapes and painted matte
model shots, which put her at the heart of the production process; as such,
she quickly found herself an object of curiosity for male technicians, who
were used to seeing women only as secretaries, continuity girls, or in
designated female spheres such as wardrobe. First of all, Cuff had to deal
with what she described as "constant banter." This included being given
the nickname "Chelsea," a reference to her art school background and a
term that served as a popular euphemism in the 1960s for a number of
perceived countercultural attributes that ranged from taking drugs to
sexual permissiveness. Such was her novelty status that as word spread
that there was a woman working on the sets, men would take a detour to
walk through the stage, where, Cuff recalls, "they'd just stop and watch
me work." This objectification was further intensified when "the chippies [carpenters] built a little fence in front of me, so that people could
come along and lean on it and watch me working [. . . the] stage hands,
electricians, the grips, the plasterers. . . . It was kind of patronising in
a way."[76] Her experience recalls the scholarship on male homosociality
and its "exclusionary practices," discussed in chapter 1, where men use
banter and other tactics in an attempt to undermine women's confidence
and sense of competency when they are doing "men's work." Here sexual
objectification is used to "other" Cuff as a worker and to oppose her presence as a woman in a job heavily bound up in masculinity.

Cuff developed strategies to enable her to work against a backdrop of
"banter," including "put[ting] my blinkers on," but not all attention could
be readily ignored.[77] The assumption of sexual availability took a more
sinister turn when she was sexually assaulted by one of the male technicians. Working alone one afternoon to finish a set, she felt "this little
finger come up my bum. I turned around and I hit him right around the
face." This was followed by a "big uproar, everybody laughed. . . . And

then it went dead silence [*sic*], and the guy just stormed off the stage."[78] Cuff's completely justifiable reaction led to her assailant—a shop steward—inventing a trumped-up charge against her that claimed she had broken union regulations governing job demarcation by using plaster in her work. The situation escalated with Cuff's sets being "blacklisted"—that is, camera crews refusing to shoot them—and was resolved only when Kubrick agreed to hire a separate plasterer and laborer to work with Cuff, which appeased the union official, allowing him to back down while his authority went unchallenged.[79] She remained on the production for the rest of the shoot and later worked alongside plastics expert Roger Deakin, which made things "a bit easier because I had an ally then . . . another guy [and] I wasn't all by myself."[80]

Cuff's experience illustrates what was at stake for a woman who entered a male domain and how union regulations could be mobilized to serve the interests of men holding power. How representative was her experience? Certainly, there were few female peers on the studio floor in nontraditional roles. And those who did enter the fray could expect to deal with harassment or, like makeup artist Linda de Vetta, have to "double up" on tasks, cooking food for the crew in addition to her makeup duties. Those in senior creative positions were by no means exempt from gender-based bullying. Cuff recalls the male crew describing producer Aida Young as "a dragon" and being "warned off" from working with her on the Hammer film *The Vengeance of She*, which Young was producing.[81] Young herself had previously been publicly humiliated by male crews who mockingly mimicked her female voice when she worked as a features director in the 1940s, forcing her to turn to the somewhat more female-friendly role of producing.[82] And stars were not exempt from misogynistic backlash, as actress Geraldine Chaplin found when she entered the canteen at MGM British while shooting *Casino Royale* in 1967, the year that Cuff worked at the studio. In Cuff's account, the canteen was dominated by below-the-line technicians, nearly all men, with above-the-line labor using a separate restaurant. Cuff recollects that when Chaplin entered, accompanied by four other women, "the whole of the canteen, which was full, was in an uproar. They [men] were banging the tables, knives and forks," in an attempt to intimidate her.[83] Chaplin stood her ground, picked up her food, and sat down, and gradually the noise subsided, but Cuff's account brings into view precisely how women's labor was regulated and policed in spaces that were heavily tied to men's identity as workers. Cuff, a brilliant artist, was one of the few successful entrants who survived, because she had the protection of established men, practitioners like Bob Cuff and, later, Roger Deakin.

Commercials

This chapter, so far, has focused on the feature film industry of the 1960s, showing how costume and wardrobe offered women professional opportunities, albeit of low status compared to the majority-male job of camera work, and how women navigated gender discrimination in the male-dominated bastions of makeup and special effects. In this final case study, I examine the experience of women in the new industry of commercials and the extent to which this type of work proved to offer a more positive experience for women technicians. This ties up some important themes in the history of women and film and prepares the ground for the next chapter, on the 1970s and 1980s. Commercials have been relatively absent in the history of British film, not least because of industry and critical hierarchies that have positioned feature films as the main goal of creative ambition. Work in commercials, where it figures at all in film history, is presented as a training ground for directors—that is, a place to learn their craft before they move onto the real business of feature film production. Nowhere is this more evident than in auteur studies of male directors, where their commercials are scrutinized mainly for emerging signs of their authorial signatures.

Women have a rather different relationship with commercials as a place of work. Coming from a position on the margins of mainstream filmmaking, commercials offered women employment opportunities that were less readily available to them in features. Women looked to the commercials sector for a number of reasons: to earn money, to exercise their creative talents, and to balance work with domestic responsibilities. And the commercials sector itself found in women a plentiful supply of highly skilled professionals, many of whom had extensive experience in fields ranging from animation and features to shorts and documentaries. The sector grew rapidly after the introduction of commercial television in 1955, and by the 1960s the commercials industry was awash with money and creative ambition. Alison Payne has shown how new advertising companies were quickly established and, by being less hierarchical and conservative than traditional employers (the BBC, civil service), were open to recruiting personnel from more diverse social backgrounds.[84] But there was a prickly relationship between the film industry and commercial television over the making of commercials. As television executive James Garrett recalls, "We were pariahs to the feature film industry; they wouldn't lend us their equipment or rent out their studios to us. . . . The absence of facilities and services . . . was very difficult."[85] And those in more junior positions were likewise aware of the divide. Editor Pamela Power, who joined one of the new commercials companies in 1959, found that "people outside the advertising industry used to look down on people in the advertising industry."[86] The low status of commercials and the sector's appetite for skilled labor and specialist equipment seems to have worked in women's favor. Working for World Wide Pictures in the late 1950s, editor Kitty Wood recalled that the company's documentary unit "wouldn't employ women as editors . . . but the commercial people were allowed to."[87] This case study examines how the new sector of commercials benefited women in two key ways: (1) it gave work to established technicians who were no longer or only intermittently employed in features, and (2) it provided an invaluable training ground for new recruits who would otherwise struggle to get a footing in the mainstream industry.

For women like art director Peggy Gick and continuity secretary Pamela Mann-Francis, commercials offered a much-welcome boost to their careers. As I discussed in chapters 3 and 4, both women worked steadily through the 1940s and 1950s, but their careers took a backseat when they married and had children. Commercials offered Gick a way back into work when her children were older. By the mid-to-late 1950s, she found "masses of it [work]" and could pick and choose her commissions. Working on the Camay soap advertisements gave her the opportunity to stretch herself creatively, because the work demanded "very elaborate sets"—glamourous settings and locations—as the company sought to position the soap as a luxury brand in the marketplace. Camay ads were widely regarded in the industry as, in Gick's terms, "the Ben-Hur of commercials."[88] On smaller productions, Gick described herself as "the whole art department," which involved her supervising the building of a set from her own drawings, then painting and dressing the set to get ready for shooting. Being able to work quickly was an asset, as a set build might be allocated only one day in the schedule, and Gick recalled that working from 8 a.m. until 10 p.m. was not unusual, but the job was well paid and short-term contracts suited her.[89] Commercials were, she recalled, "an absolute joy because . . . they were two or three days' work, and usually in the West End, so I could combine that with looking after the children."[90]

Gick's sentiment was echoed by Pamela Mann-Francis, who, as chapter 4 illustrates, had spent much of the 1950s working as a production secretary for Britain's leading director, David Lean. She married cinematographer Freddie Francis in 1963 and switched to working on commercials as a continuity secretary for a number of years. Recalling this part of her career in an interview, her comments reveal not only her own opinions but also how commercials were perceived by other film technicians. Interviewer Alan Lawson, a former camera operator, is quick to describe work on commercials as "soul destroying," and Mann-Francis reported that her cinematographer husband "hates commercials."[91] Her experience, however, was more positive: "I never minded commercials," she recalled, because they gave her "a great career" that she could combine with being married. More specifically, she found, "You worked quite closely with the director, which was nice . . . [and] people were slightly more in awe of what I did, slightly more respectful . . . and therefore I quite liked that."[92] Far from being "soul-destroying," commercials offered women like Mann-Francis the type of close working relationships and professional recognition that were all too often missing for women in the feature film sector.

Other women of the same generation as Gick and Mann-Francis found in commercials opportunities that were more difficult to secure in more mainstream filmmaking. Women who had worked professionally in the 1940s and 1950s as animators (Vera Linnecar, Nancy Hanna, Beryl Stevens), directors (Wendy Toye, Margaret Thompson), and editors (Cynthia Whitby) picked up work directing television commercials in the late 1950s and early 1960s. Alison Payne has shown how listings in the trade publication *TV Mail* (1960) record these and other women producing commercials for some of London's most prestigious advertising production companies.[93] As Payne observes, "The development of a new area, of advertising film production, appears to have offered an opportunity for women in the production industry," certainly one that was less readily available to them in the feature film industry.[94] While many male directors and cinematographers also worked in the commercials industry—including Joseph Losey, Ken Loach, John Schlesinger, Richard Lester, and Jack Cardiff—it seems that the sector, if only through necessity, was less gender prejudiced than feature filmmaking. And, of course, women, unlike men, were granted fewer opportunities for work. For this generation of women, commercials need to be understood as an important aspect of an episodic career (discussed in the introduction), showing how they worked freelance across a variety of projects and media, often combining paid employment with heavy domestic responsibilities. But more than that, commercials for these women had value, occupying an important position in their accounts of their working lives.

Commercials played an equally significant role in the professional lives of the next generation of women. While women like Peggy Gick and Pamela Mann-Francis were experienced technicians, working in commercials as middle-age women with many years of professional experience in hand, the industry also offered plentiful opportunities for younger women, such as Pamela Power, who started working in the sector in 1959 at just seventeen. Interviewed in 2014, Power's account offers a complementary picture, opening up a window onto what it was like as a young single woman to work in the new industry. She started work as a Girl Friday at Keith Ewart's studios on London's King's Road in 1959. Ewart, a well-respected photographer, established one of the first companies in Britain to specialize in commercials for television. Power recalls the studio being exceptionally well equipped with several cameras, including a rostrum, a 35 mm sound machine, a flatbed Steenbeck editing machine—which was not widely introduced to feature film editing until the late 1960s—and a Sellotape (CIR) film tape joiner, which came to the market only in 1964.[95] Ewart continued to innovate, hiring an opticals specialist to do dissolves and titles, and his cutting-edge technology put him ahead of the game, placing him at the vanguard of the commercials industry in the 1960s. Ewart would also regularly hire out his studio space to leading photographers of the day, including Norman Parkinson and Irving Penn, which made him exceptionally well connected with the mix of bohemians and old and new money that characterized British (i.e., London) society in the 1960s.

That aside, the facilities provided Power with an excellent training ground. She quickly moved into editing and learned her craft from the company's established editor Marianne Temple, who she described as "incredibly generous" with her time, adding, "She taught me a lot."[96] The company was small but perfectly formed, and the studio provided ample space for sets and props and a dressing room for the makeup artist, along with facilities for camera, editing, and lighting. As Power recalled: "Because it was such a tiny place, everybody knew everybody else, and . . . you could wander in and pass the time of day with them or watch them putting the make-up on . . . all that sort of stuff. . . . I saw so many different aspects of the film-making process. . . . It was such a brilliant environment."[97] And while camera and lighting remained male domains, Power was not totally alone as a woman in the company, recalling other women as editors, makeup artists, secretaries, and in senior roles from the advertising agencies.[98] By the time she left the company in the later 1960s, she was highly skilled as an editor and had absorbed a wide variety of filmmaking processes and technologies.

Her recollections of moving to Shepperton Studios in 1968 reveal much about gendered working cultures of filmmaking. Employed to work as an editing assistant to Tristan Cones on *Oliver!* (1968), not only did Power find the studios big and impersonal after a small company, but she was also the only woman on the editing team. This meant the gender dynamics of the work environment were different—"you don't have the same camaraderie with a lot of chaps as you do with . . . a mixture of men and women"—and she had to deal with "jokes from the guys about a particular dress I was wearing that day, or something like that."[99] Even though she was quick to describe these comments as "nonthreatening," she reflected that it did make her aware that at Shepperton—the heart of British filmmaking in the 1960s—she was a woman in a man's environment. Here it would be more difficult to forge the close working relationships she had enjoyed at Ewart's studios.

In sum, there is evidence to suggest that commercials offered women good opportunities for work, often of the type that was harder to come by in more mainstream filmmaking. It gave established technicians like Peggy Gick, Vera Linnecar, and others the chance to direct, to combine paid work with family commitments, or to take on interesting commissions on their own terms. Commercials also helped women move up the career ladder, providing them with opportunities that were difficult to attain through other means. A case in point is the career of Ann Skinner, who harbored ambitions to produce while working as a continuity girl. Not only did she have to face the skepticism of directors (see chapter 4), but she also had to work out how to raise funds at a time when both banks and male film executives refused to take women's business plans seriously. Women had fewer employment rights than men in the 1960s, and banks and other lenders saw them as risky propositions, usually asking for male guarantors (fathers, husbands) when women took out loans, even when they financially outperformed their male relatives. Requirements like these forced women into a position of dependency on men, and women's work needs to be understood in this context.[100] In the face of these obstacles, Skinner turned to working on commercials to raise the funds to bankroll her professional ambitions, which finally came to fruition in the 1980s when she produced her first feature, *The Return of the Soldier* (1982). And for the next generation of women like Pamela Power, commercials provided a type of apprenticeship that was difficult for young women to obtain in features. Power was able to capitalize on her training, later working on commercials and features with director Ridley Scott, including campaigns that produced iconic commercials for Benson and Hedges cigarettes and Hovis bread, and films such as *The Duellists* (1977), before setting up her own successful company, The Film Editors, in 1976. While not every woman's career was as high-profile as Power's, commercials nevertheless provided women with a valuable platform for employment and are crucial to understanding the history of women's filmmaking in Britain.

Conclusion

Women experienced mixed fortunes in the 1960s film industry. As Sue Harper argues, established technicians left the industry "in droves," some retiring while others found their way to television, children's films, and, as I have shown, commercials, which was not quite the step backward that Harper's assessment implies. Some built their careers in feminine spheres like wardrobe/costume, and others elbowed their way into the male domains of special effects and makeup. For others, the commercials sector was a more welcoming space than features, enabling them to build a body of experience that was to stand them in good stead in subsequent decades. Most of these women had to put up with some form of sexual harassment by men, which was especially pronounced in areas where men perceived their identity as workers to be under threat. Comments about physical appearance, inappropriate touching, and catcalling were common, and such micro-aggressions created a workplace that was never a comfortable fit for many women. All of this took place against a backdrop of widespread sexualized imagery in the popular media. It was from this context that the women's liberation movement emerged, which had a profound impact on gender relations over the next two decades, in the workplace and in society more widely, and it is to this subject that the next chapter turns.

6

The 1970s and 1980s

Working with Feminism

In the 1970s production levels dropped in the British film industry, and employment opportunities were sporadic for the workforce. This change in fortunes was caused by a dramatic reduction in the American finance that had underpinned British film production, which was down to just under 3 million pounds in 1974 from a high of 31 million pounds in 1968.[1] Without finance, film producers struggled to survive, and film output fell by almost two-thirds, from ninety-eight in 1971 to thirty-six by 1981.[2] In the early 1970s, studio space at Pinewood and Shepperton lay idle for months on end, and many film technicians faced periods of unemployment. Some notable pockets of activity still remained in the film sector, with Britain's market in low-budget sex comedies and horror keeping busy, alongside the occasional blockbuster (*Superman*, 1978) and the James Bond franchise providing employment for Britain's special effects artists. And for technicians who were so inclined, the expanding commercials sector continued to supply avenues for employment.

But against this seemingly inauspicious background was wider social change that had a positive impact on women's employment in film production. There was a heightened awareness of equal opportunities in society, with several pieces of landmark legislation coming into force—notably, the Equal Pay Act (1970) and the Sex Discrimination Act (1975). And women were more vocal this decade, demanding not only equal pay but equal access to jobs and training as well. Women in media production were particularly outspoken in this regard. By the early 1970s, feminist campaign groups such as Women in Media (WiM) and the London Women's Film

Group (LWFG) were putting pressure on the ACTT union for change, reopening the wartime debate about "the woman technician" with renewed energy. In 1972 the front cover of the union's journal featured a woman juggling a camera and a small child under the caption "Would you work with a female camera operator?" The article by the WiM group posed a number of challenging questions to the journal's readership, includ- ing "WHY have you never worked with a woman camera operator? . . . WHY doesn't ACTT insist that these grades be opened to women . . . [and] WHY is your reaction to this article unsympathetic?"[3] It called for recruitment quotas, a comprehensive review of the media industries, and a radical overhaul of employment practices and working culture. This kickstarted a debate in the union about gender equality, and at its 1973 annual conference, union women openly challenged the tired rheto- ric of equal pay: "There's nothing so wonderful about a policy that says women senior engineers will receive exactly the same money as men on the same grade if there aren't any women senior engineers in the first place. . . . The policy of equal pay had proven to be an empty one."[4] These and other activities led to the ACTT forming a Committee on Equality that pushed through a 1975 report titled the *Patterns of Discrimination against Women in the Film and Television Industries*, a landmark study that delivered the comprehensive review many women had been calling for, providing detailed evidence of discrimination in action in Britain's film and television industries. Although a combination of inertia and dis- sipated energies ultimately stymied attempts to successfully implement the report's recommendations in full, a major result from these activities was enhanced training activities for women in the 1973–75 period.

In 1974 the first "Women's Introductory Technical Workshop" was held at the newly formed National Film School (NFS) with the task of providing women from different areas in the film industry the chance to learn about professional camera and sound equipment.[5] Organized and delivered by women from the union, the BBC, and recent NFS graduates, this and similar training initiatives proved to be invaluable, providing women with credible alternatives to the tradition of "on-the-job" training, which had historically excluded them.[6] Moreover, such training provided women with the opportunity to learn about the history of women *as* filmmakers. Director/writer Conny Templeman remembers a series of workshops run by the then pioneering director of the Edinburgh Film Festival, Lynda Myles: "Lynda brought films that were either about women or made by women. . . . We analysed the films and talked about them. . . . That had a lasting effect on me." Myles herself remembers the workshops as being imbued with a "sense of solidarity and optimism" as women came together to learn about the history of film from a feminine and feminist perspective.[7] Women who attended day schools and workshops would bring their training and increased self-awareness into the workplace, and by the time the 1980s unfolded, two new important developments provided them with the opportunity to do so.

The first was the emergence of new independent companies in the mid-1980s. Companies such as Goldcrest and Handmade Films became important players in the business of filmmaking and invested heavily in film production during the 1980s, while the creation of Channel Four Television Corporation in 1982 was another significant boost to the sector, as the company established a separate film arm, Film Four International.[8] It earned a reputation for producing socially diverse content and an openness that extended to the technicians employed on its projects, and here women benefited. Sound recordist Moya Burns recalled, "Independent filmmakers . . . didn't have the old, traditional attitudes towards women and were very flexible," a feeling shared by director Melanie Chait, who found the independent sector to "have some tenuous understanding of women's issues."[9] With smaller budgets and a commitment to producing films reflecting social diversity, this production sector was more likely than mainstream features to understand how the context of production shaped screen content and therefore to be more open to recruiting women.

The other significant development of the 1980s was the workshop movement, which produced, distributed, and exhibited their films and supported collective and cross-grade working. They were able to access Channel Four funding for their projects, and it was through the workshops that many women and technicians from ethnic minority backgrounds secured work in media production. It was a combination of activism and training in the 1970s, coupled with new developments in the film production landscape in the 1980s, that shaped women's employment fortunes in positive ways.[10]

Women and Union Records: An Overview

Records from the ACTT union database show the routes through which women gained union membership in the 1970s and 1980s. The total number of applications from women did increase, from 18 percent in the 1960s to 25 percent in the 1970s, and reached 38 percent in the 1980s, the highest proportion of women joining the film workforce since records began in the 1930s (see appendix C). The majority joined the union through traditional roles such as production secretary/assistant, paint and tracer, assistant editor, casting director, costume designer, researcher, reader, and librarian. But there was a notable upturn across the two decades of women in more senior creative roles, especially in producing, directing, animation, and art direction. New pathways also began to open up for women. Jobs in sound had been notoriously closed to them since the introduction of the new technology to British film studios in the late 1920s. In the 1980s thirty women joined in sound jobs, as sound recordists, assistants, and boom operators, working in either the workshop sector or for commercial companies specializing in shorts and documentaries. From the late 1970s onward, women also begin to appear in the union records as clapper loaders, camera assistants, and rostrum camera operators. While the vast majority of applications to sound and camera continued to come from men, the records show women making small inroads and gaining traction in these positions, a process that began in the 1970s and gathered pace in the 1980s, all the more significant given their historically chronic underrepresentation in these areas.

In the light of such changes, this chapter puts these developments center stage, with case studies of women in camera jobs and the workshop sector. First, I look at the careers of several women, including Diane Tammes (cinematographer), Sue Gibson (clapper loader, cinematographer), and others, to explore how women navigated these male-dominated environments and their homosocial cultures. I then move on to analyze women's experiences in the workshop movement as the other major development in film culture of the period. Drawing on oral histories and contemporary press interviews, I investigate women's work in the Amber Film Collective, Leeds Animation Workshop, and the Black British collectives, including Sankofa and the Black Audio Film Collective. Five subthemes guide this analysis: cross-job working, child care, women-only spaces, Black women's filmmaking and pedagogy, working-class women, and cocreation. In a departure from earlier chapters, which focus on a single decade, here I combine the 1970s and 1980s, the rationale being that it took some time before the initiatives that had improved women's access to training bore fruit in the form of women's film careers taking off. In sum, the developments and opportunities of the 1970s had their widest impact on women's work in the 1980s.

Camera and Sound

My main focus in this case study is women in camera and sound jobs across mainstream and independent film. Women's entry into these male strongholds was sufficient to catch the attention of the specialist trade press of the day, which published several articles about women in these technical roles. Framing them as novelties, journals such as *Eyepiece* and *AIP* [American International Pictures] *& Co.* introduced their readership to Sue Gibson and Belinda Parsons (cinematographers), Harriet Cox (clapper loader, camera operator), Nuala Campbell (electrician, gaffer), Chyna Thomson (clapper loader, focus puller), and Moya Burns (sound recordist). With titles such as "Jobs for the Girls" and "Danger! Women at Work," these publications continued to rehearse the "exceptionalist" narrative that had framed women's work as directors in the 1920s, 1930s, and beyond.[11] A defining characteristic of the coverage was its emphasis on women's experience of working in a role typically occupied by men rather than any explanation of what the role of, for example, a cinematographer entailed. On one level this can be explained by the specialist nature of the press, as readers of *Eyepiece* (Guild of British Camera Technicians) would be familiar with the workings of the job. But on another level, the tone of the articles takes the significance of the role as a given; what needs to be proven is the figure of the woman in the role. Press commentary lumped the women together, but there were important differences in their career choices and pathways; Gibson and Thomson were closest to commercial filmmaking, while the others worked in the independent sector on film projects with much smaller budgets. What they did share in common, other than their gender, was the sexist treatment they received from many of their male peers. Indeed, the male culture of the camera department was notorious, leading the researcher of the *Patterns* report, Sarah Benton, to describe it as a "brotherhood" in order to reveal how its men closed ranks against women to protect their status.[12] In this case study, I examine women's access to and experience of training, getting jobs, and survival strategies as women in male-dominated environments, showing how they negotiated a myriad of "exclusionary practices" through which their entry to the sector was regulated (see discussion in chapter 1). This was the first generation of women whose careers unfolded in the light of second-wave feminism, and their experiences have a deep resonance with the recent and current conditions for women working in film industries today.

Getting Trained

For many women, their "novelty" status started at film school. Cinematographer Diane Tammes joined the camera course at the National Film School in 1971, making her one of the first women accepted for entry there. At this point Tammes was already in her late twenties and running a successful photography studio in Edinburgh but found herself being interviewed by a panel of seven men who had a "ha ha, what have we got here" attitude toward her.[13] Confronted with patronizing comments about "her snaps" (photography portfolio) and quizzed about "How much do you weigh?" she had the confidence to dismiss the questions as irrelevant. She was offered and accepted a place but found the male tutors singularly ill-equipped to work with women. In an interview Tammes recalled that the head of the school's camera department was "actually terrified of women picking up cameras. He just could not help himself. . . . He couldn't believe I wasn't going to drop it," concluding that she found his response "a bit daunting."[14] In an attempt to address women's perceived limitations, the school purchased a lightweight éclair ACL camera, known colloquially in the school as "the women's camera," but, as Tammes recalls "no woman wanted to use it, ever. We wanted to go on the Arriflex and use what everybody else was using." She survived this learning environment because as a photographer, "I knew about film stock, and cameras, lenses and so on. . . . I didn't need any tuition in that area." But her experience illustrates just how challenging it was for women to access training and equipment and to flourish in a context that had no confidence in their ability to succeed. It was for reasons such as these that the women-only training workshops, organized a few years later by the ACTT's Equality Committee, were such a success, with delegates enthusing how "being taught by women made an enormous difference—there was absolutely no putdown, no attitude of how stupid we were."[15] Tammes herself was a tutor for the first workshop and was keen to pass her technical skills on to other women. Upon graduation she worked in avant-garde cinema— including the feminist classic *Riddles of the Sphinx* (1977)—before carving out a successful career in documentaries for television.

Things had improved by the time Belinda Parsons entered the NFS camera course in 1977, at least in terms of total numbers of women. That was a peak year for women's entry, and Parsons recalled the school filling ten of the twenty-five new entrant places with women, a proportion that was "way higher than anything before" and that went some way to reducing their "novelty" status. In Parsons's account, "The mood, the climate, in '77 was really ripe for educational institutions to take a reasonable proportion of women."[16] The school's actions need to be placed in the wider context of developments such as the Sex Discrimination Act and the union's *Patterns of Discrimination Report* (both 1975), which threw a gendered spotlight on the recruitment practices of institutions like the NFS. Parsons found the training experience more supportive than Tammes, crediting the school with giving her "absolute confidence that I could light anything, handle any sort of location and studio work, and that . . . I could take any work that was offered to me."[17] For Parsons, at least, the value of training at film school was that "it gives women the chance to get in, which they couldn't very easily do under the apprenticeship system."[18]

The experiences of Chyna Thomson and Nuala Campbell offer a counterpoint to those of film school graduates, illuminating different training pathways and their conditions of entry for women. Thomson was one of the few women who did manage to progress under the apprenticeship system. Her entry into the film industry was supported by her father, Alex Thomson, the well-respected cinematographer, who, by all accounts, took her on as a camera trainee when she was sixteen because she "didn't know what to do with herself."[19] Starting out on Ridley Scott's fantasy feature *Legend* (1985), she worked her way up through the ranks of the camera department, from trainee to clapper loader and then focus puller by the early 1990s, earning numerous screen credits on many big-budget features, including *Raw Deal* (1986), *Alien 3* (1992), *Cliffhanger* (1993), and *Bridget Jones's Diary* (2001) among others (see glossary for role definitions). Thomson is a good example of an ordinary, professional woman carving out a career that is not spectacular but no less interesting because of it. She frequently worked on a camera team headed by her father, who, without any trace of irony, reputedly claimed that "no one took exception to his daughter joining his team."[20] In a manner similar to that of model maker Joy Cuff (discussed in chapter 5), Chyna Thomson was permitted entry into a homosocial world where she could access the requisite training because she was aligned with a senior male figure who held power. And, as with Cuff, powerful allies did not completely insulate her from discrimination. Learning on the job took place in the wider context of a male-defined filmmaking culture steeped in what she termed a "Oh yeah, she's just a girl" attitude and meant fending off inquiries about her sexuality ("You must be a dyke").[21] Thomson's comments suggest how women's novelty status in this particular work environment was expressed through explicit suggestions that her femininity was "deviant."

Lighting electrician Nuala Campbell offers a third example of routes into traditionally male areas of filmmaking. Campbell trained as an electrician through a government-sponsored scheme and learned her craft working as an installation and maintenance electrician on building sites in the 1970s before moving into freelance work in the television and film industries in the 1980s. Her credits include *Looking for Langston* (1989) and *Young Soul Rebels* (1991), both of which were modestly budgeted productions directed by Isaac Julien and key films in the representation of Black gay men on British screens. Campbell's entry into filmmaking was job-specific; training gained *outside* the film industry was more readily tolerated for jobs such as electrician, because it was generally regarded as a skill that was not unique to the film industry and therefore less jealously guarded than camera work. That said, the job of electrician was still seen as "man's work" because the role involved handling the heavy lighting equipment used to illuminate a studio/location set, attaching it to rigs suspended high above the film set, and working long hours. It was for this reason that Campbell described the working environment as more "macho" than a building site.[22] In her case, the combination of external training initiatives and what was deemed a non–film specific skill set facilitated her entry into the film profession.

Getting Jobs

If newly created film schools and external training courses were the principal means through which women were given, in Parsons's words, "the chance to get in" to nontraditional areas of filmmaking, this was only the start. The next challenge was getting a job. Often women were flatly refused work. Diane Tammes recalls that it was accepted practice in the early 1970s for any applications made by women to the ACTT union for membership as a camera technician to be formally rejected with a letter stating, "We do not accept women in these jobs."[23] Tammes's experience was corroborated by other women who reported being turned down for trainee camera operator jobs on the grounds of physical strength and that "the boys in the camera room would not like to have a woman around."[24] Such practices were formally outlawed when the Sex Discrimination Act became legislation in 1975, but there is some evidence to suggest that they continued well into the following decade; for example, a female location manager was turned down for union membership in 1989 on the grounds that "this was not a job for a woman."[25] Legislation did not lead to a rapid dismantling of the barriers women faced, which, as we have seen throughout this study, were multifaceted and expressed through languages, practices, and behaviors. Concerns about women's physical strength were frequently evoked by men to exclude women. Clapper loader Nienke Hendriks turned to the role because her attempts to work in lighting led to her constantly being dismissed with "Do you know how big film lights are?" while Chyna Thomson reported working out with weights to "keep herself fit and strong."[26] Public statements such as these are a type of preemptive strike, designed to acknowledge and head off common criticisms, but, as Thomson herself experienced, they ran the risk of her being demonized as "a dyke." As one of Thomson's American contemporaries, Catherine Coulson, observed, carrying a camera "doesn't require any more strength than carrying a child around," an activity designated as women's work, but the repeated reference to physicality in women's interviews highlights one of the ways they had to constantly prove their ability to work successfully with cameras and similar technical equipment.[27] So the response to the union's question—Would you work with a female camera operator?—was a resounding no from many quarters of the film industry.

In the face of gender prejudice, where women repeatedly found cameramen "very suspicious about using women technicians," they had to start at the bottom rung of the camera department and took a long time to progress.[28] Sue Gibson, for example, excelled at the National Film School, where she graduated from its camera course in 1981 with a clear ambition to work in cinematography. But Gibson found an absence of female role models: "There simply weren't any women cinematographers when I graduated so I became a clapper loader . . . much to the chagrin of the Director of the Film School who thought I was completely wasting my time."[29] This junior-level position is the bottom rung of the camera department, from which technicians move up through the ranks to focus pulling, camera operator, and, finally, cinematographer. Susan Jacobson (currently working as a clapper loader in British television drama) describes the job as fundamentally about taking care of "the little details"—more specifically, "making my focus puller's life as easy as possible . . . [by] taking away . . . the other things he would have to think about, like equipment, stock, stores or production office worries" (see glossary for role descriptions).[30] The role's supportive function—largely unchanged over decades—requires the clapper loader to be, in Jacobson's words, "diligent and efficient," a description that goes some way to explaining why it was one of the few jobs in the camera department that was more open to women in the 1970s and 1980s. It shares many similarities with the production secretary role in anticipating and meeting the needs of a senior creative figure (see the discussion in chapter 4).

While men in the clapper loader role would likewise need to prove their efficiency to succeed, women also had to deal with gendered "banter" and took longer to progress through the ranks. Gibson said, "I used to get all the quips and bullying you'd expect from a male crew with a woman in a menial role to order about," while one of her contemporaries, Genevieve Davies, noted that cameramen came to like women assistants, if only because "they find they make a nice pot of tea, and they don't put the boxes in puddles!"[31] Here the role is being reframed to align with women's presumed domestic knowledge about caring for objects and the workplace environment. And women's competence in the role (and willingness to make tea) could be double-edged, making them too valuable to promote. Gibson spent many years lighting commercials before she got her break into features. On one of the rare occasions where she openly criticized the film industry, she reflected, "I used to get frustrated seeing contemporaries coming along and getting movies; why not me? Perhaps it *was* the female hurdle."[32] Electrician Nuala Campbell reported similar experiences, observing "a tendency to assume all women are novices . . . [who've] only just got into the business," a common "exclusionary" tactic to downplay the skills and experience of outsiders whose presence threatens men's homosocial world.[33] Such misconceptions had very material consequences for women's careers. Not only did it take women longer to get promoted, but their gender also made them seem a riskier proposition to financial backers, who, as Sue Gibson found, "wanted someone with a track record."[34] As we have seen throughout this history, women often *did* have a track record, but men failed to see it, because its patterns and contours differed from their own. Such forms of gender blindness are insidious and continue to shape women's experiences of film industries, where, to this day, they are still seen as "riskier hires than men."[35]

The features industry seemed to have presented the greatest challenges to women working in camera and sound and was the sector most resistant to change. In 1983 the ACTT's Equality Committee requested that the union produce an equality handbook to address discrimination at the interview stage. The most vocal critics of the request came from the sound section and the film production branch, where union officials— all male—retaliated with calls for a men's conference and dismissed the Equality Committee as a "self-perpetuating matriarchy."[36] The request was adopted by twenty-six votes to nineteen (with six abstentions), but the narrow success gives a flavor of the hostility directed toward women in at least some quarters of the film industry.[37] In Nuala Campbell's experience, men's resistance to women as lighting electricians was far greater in the film industry than anything she had "ever encountered on building sites or in a factory . . . something to do with the fact that, in the film industry, electricians and grips are the macho element."[38] She concluded that "somehow the idea of a woman doing that job disturbs them quite a lot," an assessment echoed by sound recordist Moya Burns, who described features as a "hostile" area that was slow to change.[39] These comments show how women's presence was perceived as a threat by men in jobs that were heavily bound up in normative masculinity and hint at the strategies used to oppose women's entry. It was for this reason that Burns favored independent production, which relied on smaller budgets, often from bodies like Channel Four, which Burns credited as having "a different emphasis on the type of film they want to make, and this filters down to the type of crew they want to employ."[40] Burns went on to work with director Terence Davies on the feature films *Distant Voices, Still Lives* (1988) and *The Long*

Day Closes (1992), both of which benefited from Channel Four funding to tell the stories of marginalized or oppressed individuals.

Women in camera and sound were not the only ones to become exasperated with the macho culture that shaped the "brotherhood" of feature filmmaking. Script supervisor Penny Eyles, a contemporary of Moya Burns and Nuala Campbell, had worked on some of the decade's biggest features, including *Time Bandits* (1981) and *Brazil* (1985), but increasingly steered away from them in favor of what she described as "the little ones . . . the Sally Potters and the Stephen Frears," finding in them "a more democratic system . . . [where] we're all, you know, standing in puddles together."[41] So from different financial and production conditions, a different, more inclusive work ethos could emerge that benefited women. Such a change in philosophy was needed, as Britain's film studios clearly had a problem with women. American producer Gale Ann Hurd experienced this discriminatory attitude in 1986 when she was producing *Aliens* at Shepperton Studios. Some male crew members were "very upfront [about] their discomfort with women." They assumed Hurd was the director's wife and stated, "I won't take orders from a woman," a response that "happened quite a few times."[42] Hurd had sufficient power to back up her response of "Well, you won't be working on this film," but women in more junior positions had far less agency.

Survival Strategies

In the light of such hostilities, women frequently opted for a strategy of what one commentator called "fitting-in rather than fighting" as a means to progress in commercial filmmaking.[43] This was most evident in the career of Sue Gibson, who rose up through the ranks of the camera profession to become the first female member of the British Society of Cinematographers (BSC), in 1992. By 2004 she had been elected to the society's board of governors and served as its president between 2008 and 2010; the first and only woman to do so. Gibson worked in both feature films and television as a cinematographer; her screen credits include mid-budget productions *Hear My Song* (1991) and *Mrs. Dalloway* (1997) as well as the television series *The Forsythe Saga* and *Spooks* (both 2002). Cinematography has been defined as the "ability to convey a certain mood or atmosphere in the photography," which requires "the combination of sound technical knowledge of the properties of stocks, lenses and lighting equipment with an aesthetic understanding of composition, light and shade, texture and colour."[44] It also requires leadership, as the cinematographer instructs the crew of camera operators and lighting electricians and decides which camera, lens, and lighting to use for each shot. Gibson excelled in her profession, winning awards for her technical and artistic achievement on the first feature films she worked on as a cinematographer, perhaps not surprising given how long she had been waiting in the wings. By the time she tackled *Mrs. Dalloway*, she grasped the opportunity that the story's flashback structure offered for experimentation, switching between Kodak and Fuji film stock to create different looks and textures for the 1890s and 1920s. That she achieved this under difficult circumstances—the funding ran out halfway through the shoot, and camera crew members were replaced—is testament to her professionalism.[45]

Gibson's "exceptional" status meant she was frequently singled out for interviews by the trade press, in pieces that foregrounded her gender. Articles titled "Rising to the Challenge" and "A Woman's Place . . ." provide a taste of the discourses that framed Gibson's career. They also bear witness to how Gibson rehearsed a narrative of fitting in to the existing work culture as a means to explain her professional success. In interviews Gibson stressed how her sex "doesn't come into it" and that she had rarely been the victim of sex discrimination.[46] Notwithstanding comments about "quips and bullying" by men, Gibson categorized these as "part of being in the industry" and said the best strategy was "not rising to the bait . . . [and] being able to cope, to fit in."[47] For Gibson, this meant not "forcing yourself on someone who's suspicious or unhappy about it; it makes your job twice as hard," a tactic that, as we have seen, may have been anathema to producer Gale Ann Hurd but demonstrates the constraints within which Gibson was operating.[48]

Gibson gave questions about her gender short shrift in interviews—"I always end up being 'the only one,' or 'the first one' . . . give me a break"— and was reluctant to be drawn out on women's underrepresentation in the cinematography profession.[49] Interviewers invariably conclude that she "is an example of how to succeed by refusing to be treated differently to anyone else, and ignoring any obstacles that might be put in her way."[50] Scholars have found similar narrative strategies adopted by the high-profile Hollywood director Kathryn Bigelow, who is repeatedly quoted as saying she "ignores" any resistance or obstacles to women making movies and distances herself from questions about gender. Categorizing her approach as a "refusal-to-be-bothered strategy," Martha M. Lauzen shows how ignoring is a "face-saving" device that allows high-profile women in male-dominated industries to "avoid being overly concerned or defeated by the inequities they face," effectively allowing them to function as "neither victims of an unfair system nor somehow inferior to men."[51] The career of Sue Gibson, like that of Bigelow and others, demonstrates the extent to which acceptance and success in a "boys club" was, and indeed still is, predicated on never criticizing it and fitting into its existing culture.[52]

Other women adopted different strategies that edged more toward the "fighting" end of the spectrum. Nuala Campbell, for example, wrote graffiti on the pinups and calendars of naked women she found in the lighting technicians' tea room and actively sought to encourage other women into the role by "tak[ing] them out on a shoot."[53] Such activities were relatively small-scale attempts to change the culture from within but should not be underestimated in the face of a macho working environment. However, as Campbell admitted, she had to "work up the energy" for them, suggesting some of the emotional costs that came from challenging norms. And others steered their careers toward features in the independent sector or educational shorts, a pathway taken by camera operators Harriet Cox and Belinda Parsons and sound recordist Moya Burns. Cox, like Burns, worked on Terence Davies's films and political/feminist shorts, including *The Battle for Orgreave* (1985) and Sally Potter's *The London Story* (1986), before moving into higher education in the early 2000s. But even in the independent sector, women had to deal with discrimination. Sound recordist Melanie Chait could put up with "hav[ing] to prove yourself in a way that men don't" but found location work abroad a real hassle because she was often the only woman in the crew. Invariably "there's going to be some bloke who propositions you in some way," which put her in the unenviable position of "try[ing] to get out of it in as delicate a way as you can, because you've got to live with these people for three weeks and you don't want the whole crew dynamics to go sour."[54] So women performed emotional labor for the crew—ensuring group cohesion, shoring up male sexual egos—illustrating how they undertook additional, gendered tasks when employed in a "man's job."

Rewards

In the face of these challenges and demands, what did women get out of working in camera and sound positions? For clapper loader and focus puller Chyna Thomson, it was the opportunity to travel extensively, develop specialist skills in long lens shooting—recognized in the profession as especially difficult—and work with some of the industry's leading directors. In her role of focus puller, Thomson was responsible for keeping the camera lens in focus during shooting, manually adjusting it as the subject, or action, moved about in the scene (see role descriptions in glossary). This was no mean feat, and she enjoyed the professional challenge of pulling focus on the difficult 65 mm shoot of *Hamlet* (1996) and running backward to film actor Sylvester Stallone crossing a rope bridge in the alpine adventure *Cliffhanger*, an action film famed for its spectacular camera work.[55] Sue Gibson's motivation was her love of photography, which she described as "the way light played on things and how it creates a mood," which she married with the autonomy she found working on features where "you're . . . answerable to nobody but yourself. It's purely your judgement and your vision that counts." Gibson concluded that the experience was "very good for the psyche," a comment that perhaps offers us another route into creativity beyond the director's vision.[56] Lighting camera operator Belinda Parsons found that "working in film brought all my potential talents together," allowing her to combine her photographic and creative abilities with a preference for team working, while cinematographer Diane Tammes relished the "tremendous responsibility" that having "the visual side of a film in your hands" afforded her.[57] And for the more than sixty women who attended the first women's introductory technical workshop at the NFS, in 1974, it might just have been finally getting to handle cameras and sound recording equipment, an opportunity they described as nothing short of "liberating."[58]

Gibson, Campbell, Thomson, and the other women discussed here are the ones who did make a mark on the British film industry, often in the face of ingrained sexism. Positive discrimination continued to favor men, who secured the plum jobs on the decade's biggest features: *Gandhi* (1982), which won Best Cinematography Academy Awards for Billie Williams and Ronnie Taylor, and *A Passage to India* (1984), for which Ernest Day was Academy-nominated for his work. Both were historical epics of the type that the Academy board favored and, with budgets in excess of $20 million, were too expensive to "risk" a female hire.[59] But women collectively began to make modest contributions to camera and sound in this period, most often in the independent sector, where smaller budgets and a commitment to social diversity made for a relatively more hospitable environment for women. Success, however, in either mainstream or independent filmmaking was possible only for women of a certain class and race, and preferably "unencumbered" with children. Gibson was white and middle-class, as was Chyna Thomson. Harriet Cox found a career in education easier to balance with child care, joining the London Film School in early 2000, while Chyna Thomson stepped away from feature filmmaking in 2004 when she had her first child. Nuala Campbell was able to continue working only because, as a single parent in the 1980s, she was eligible for a local authority grant that enabled her to send her daughter to boarding school, something for which she said, "I can't feel grateful enough."[60] And all lived in London. Women who did not comfortably fit this profile—black, working-class, gay, northern—could anticipate an even more difficult time, given the challenges of the mainstream industry and its working cultures. No wonder, then, that some opted for alternative forms of filmmaking, such as the workshop movement, to build their film careers, and this forms the topic of the next case study.

The Workshop Movement

Film workshops had the potential to offer new production opportunities for women to work across different jobs and in roles that were not as readily available to them in mainstream, commercial filmmaking. Film workshops had been a feature of British filmmaking since the 1970s, but they really came to the fore in the 1980s, aided by the ACTT Workshop Declaration (1984) whereby the union formally recognized workshop practices and in doing so provided a basis for funding, much of which came from Channel Four, the British Film Institute, and the Greater London Council. The workshops were underpinned by a broad commitment to cross-job working, working collectively, egalitarian working practices, and fostering ongoing relationships with audiences.[61] With a flat, nonhierarchical structure, small budgets, and left-of-center politics, they were closer to the artisan model of production that characterized documentary filmmaking of the 1930s, with a production culture that had the potential to benefit women. Their main outputs were documentaries, shorts, and occasionally feature-length productions, many intended primarily for campaigning or educational purposes, with some screened on British television or through festival circuits. While the workshop movement has been the subject of extensive critical commentary, much less attention has been paid specifically to women's experiences of the workshop movement as practitioners and technicians.[62] The women who worked in this sector, like their counterparts in the mainstream industry, had been informed by second-wave feminism and discussion about gender roles, debates that were still unfolding. As discussed, these ranged from improved access to training and job opportunities to calls for state-supported child care and a critique of derogatory media-generated stereotypes. How did the workshop's stated commitment to egalitarian working practices coalesce with those of the women's movement and its call for equal job opportunities? To what extent, and in what ways, did gender roles and expectations play a part in shaping women's experiences of work in this sector? This case study puts such questions at center stage, focusing on the themes of cross-job working; child care; female crews/spaces; and class, community, and cocreation.

I draw on interview material with Elaine Drainville and Sirkka-Liisa Konttinen (Amber Film Collective); Gillian Lacey and Terry Wragg (Leeds Animation Workshop); Maureen Blackwood, Martina Attille, and Nadine Marsh-Edwards (Sankofa); and Avril Johnson and Lina Gopaul (Black Audio Film Collective). These women all trained outside the mainstream film industry and did not come to filmmaking through the National Film School as the women discussed in the previous case study had done. Some had been introduced to filmmaking through art school or photography courses (Drainville, Konttinen), while the others had studied subjects such as literature, sociology, and mass communications, the latter an important new subject area in higher education at this time. All shared a common commitment to an assessment of media images and media forms as powerful tools for negative stereotyping and sought ways to bring alternative voices and stories to the screen. Gender was not the only concern of these women, whose experiences and politics were intersectional, shaped by discourses of race, class, sexuality, and region. As a Black woman, Lina Gopaul, for example "read everything I could get my hands on to do with race and women," while as a white, working-class gay woman, Elaine Drainville felt there was no place for her in a London-centric film industry and settled in the North of England.[63] Gender was nevertheless a central preoccupation for these women and shaped their careers as filmmakers.

The workshops in which they participated shared a commitment to political filmmaking, but there were differences in their internal organization, their preferred genres or modes (animation, live action, experimental), and the roles in which the women specialized: Drainville is principally a sound recordist; Blackwood is a director and writer.[64] My primary focus here is not to explore whether one organizational structure is better than another, or to situate the women's work in a history of sound or animation, but rather to explore what the women could and did do within the workshop framework, their achievements and constraints, and how they experienced this mode of production. As filmmaker Margaret Dickinson observed, workshops were intended to be different from conventional film companies, and therefore: "In devising their own constitutions and working methods, group members confronted, in a very practical way … how to organise social relations in a way which is satisfying for the individuals involved, efficient enough to achieve objectives, tenable within a given external environment and allows for continuity and growth."[65] If workshops offered the opportunity to do things differently, how did this play out in terms of gender?

Cross-Job Work

Cross-job working was especially important for women who had so often been excluded from the full range of roles in the mainstream industry. It was a workshop principle that members were free to undertake different functions within or across productions—that is, they could direct *and* edit, or produce *and* write—an approach that was anathema to the mainstream industry and to the union, which was predicated on clearly defined job boundaries. In terms of technical roles, there does seem to have been a degree of flexibility in some workshops. At Amber, workshop members held distinct, specialist roles in, for example, editing, directing, camera, and sound recording, but were not limited to them; for instance, Sirkka-Liisa Konttinen was principally a photographer but also directed. Cross-job working often took the form of pooling or sharing ideas, or having an input into technical or artistic decisions. Avril Johnson described the process at the Black Audio Film Collective, where "from the word go we . . . argue about how a film should be made and when we go into the cutting room we argue about the cuts."[66]

That said, administration of the workshops does seem to have fallen disproportionately on women. At BAFC, Johnson admitted that "me and Lina and David [Lawson] do the administration," which led the interviewer to remark that "it does sound like there's a rather conventional gender division between being creative and providing back-up."[67] Johnson countered this by drawing attention to the examples (above) of how she and the others contributed to the creative process, but it remains the case that she and Lina Gopaul took the lead in performing the roles of administrator and producer, which were backstage supportive roles that had historically devolved to women. Administration at Amber was similarly undertaken by a woman, Lorna Powell, with the workshop's cofounder and director, Murray Martin, admitting that Powell was "sometimes exasperated by our lack of understanding of what was involved in her area of work."[68] His observation echoes that of an earlier generation of production secretaries and continuity girls, who, as we have seen, were similarly frustrated with how their work was misunderstood by men.

Looking beyond administration, women in other workshops were more openly critical of gender discrimination in the sector, suggesting that gendered values and norms were difficult to dislodge, even where there was the will to do things differently.[69] One of the founding members of the Edinburgh Film Workshop Trust, Sarah Noble, made the point that there were "more men working in the grant-aided sector than women" and that while workshops had been "set up specifically to counteract discrimination," it still existed but was "a very subtle form of [sex] discrimination."[70] Although Noble does not elaborate in her interview on what forms discrimination took, she and a female coworker, Cassandra McGrogan, set up "The Women's Unit" within the Edinburgh workshop, perhaps as a strategy to counter male dominance and ensure their voices were heard. And although Noble acknowledged that the Workshop Declaration allowed for cross-job working, she herself specialized in sound recording and editing, suggesting that accessing camera jobs could be as difficult in the workshops as it was in the mainstream. So women achieved modest gains in the workshops under the principle of cross-job working, with perhaps the key difference being that they undertook traditionally female roles in a structure that did allow for collective, creative decision making.

Child Care

The workshop movement's commitment to egalitarian working practices also had to recognize that the needs of individual members could differ, a concept that was thrown into sharp relief by the issue of child care. One of the demands of the women's liberation movement was for nursery provision to support women, and Laura Mulvey's questioning of motherhood and how to live it—made forcefully in her film *Riddles of the Sphinx*—was a central concern at this time. A recurring theme in this book has been how having children often signaled the end of a woman's filmmaking career or her movement into a different pattern of working. Women in some workshops faced the same dilemma, where the internal dynamics and logic of the group's structure seem to have been difficult to reconcile with child care responsibilities. Amber's cofounder Murray Martin, for example, admitted that "children were not an easy option" to accommodate in the workshop, creating a dilemma with "somebody wanting to have children but not wanting to give up work."[71] When pressed in an interview by Margaret Dickinson—"What about part-time work?"—Martin commented that although the group had "created that possibility," it was difficult to reconcile with the group's dynamics, which relied on "day-to-day communication," concluding, "It's a design problem."[72]

This does raise the question of whether it was women who were the design problem or the group's methods of communication. An interview with one of the women in the Amber collective, photographer Sirkka-Liisa Konttinen, sheds light on how she managed paid work and motherhood at the same time. When her daughter was born in 1979, she initially stepped back from the group to spend time at home. During this period, she collated her research on the Byker estate, a working-class area in the former shipbuilding and manufacturing city of Newcastle, drawing together photographs and oral history interviews she had taken in the early 1970s and transcribing interviews with her baby on her lap, and eventually published her work in book form (*Byker*, 1983). As with many other women discussed in this book, her home became her film studio for a period of time, and she chose projects or tasks that could be picked up and put down around the demands of children. There is a continuum from Konttinen's experience to those of her antecedents—women such as Peggy Gick painting cels at home and Monica Mead setting up an editing suite in her spare bedroom (see chapter 4). So is it clear that flexible and more imaginative ways of working that supported parents/mothers in the Amber workshop came from individual women adapting their practice rather than the workshop changing its internal dynamics.

Things took a rather different turn at the Leeds Animation Workshop, whose workforce was of a similar size to that of Amber but consisted of more women. For its founding member Gillian Lacey, "Our way of working was the product of its time," and the group "believed passionately in the ideals—the opportunities for women, a flat rate wage, no individual credits on the films, a collective work process."[73] Under these conditions a different approach to child care emerged. When one of its members, Terry Wragg, had her first baby in 1979, she initially worked from home "painting cels and things" or took the baby into the office "in a baby sling."[74] When her child was slightly older, she put into action a form of collective child care that she and a group of like-minded friends had devised: "We were six parents and three babies. . . . [For] three days in the middle of the week . . . one parent would have three children for half a day, and then they would overlap with their co-parent for an hour at dinnertime, because dinnertime was busy. . . . It worked quite well, in lots of ways." Wragg's was a practical solution to child care at a time when there was little formal, state-subsidized child care in Britain, and the wages in the workshop sector were not sufficiently high to cover the types of in-house au pair help that earlier generations of women filmmakers had relied on. Moreover, for women like Wragg, work was tied up with feminist principles: "We thought that it was a woman's right/duty/responsibility to the future, to work. . . . In order for women to have equal rights and opportunities at work, we thought that somehow childcare had to be done in such a way that we'd be doing childcare right, but childcare wouldn't be interrupting your work."[75] The solution was not perfect—Wragg recalls that colleagues visiting her in the hospital's maternity wing brought a grant funding applicant form for her to look at—but it did allow for flexibility. When she had a second child, she did more part-time hours and worked from home "doing what I could and keeping my hand in."[76] So in the case of the Leeds Animation Workshop, work and child care could coexist within the social systems that the group put in place. In Wragg's words, "In those days . . . we were making the revolution to some extent, as we saw it," and child care was a necessary part of that revolution.

Women in the workshop sector still experienced discrimination as women—through access to roles and child-care support—even while the sector shared feminism's commitment to egalitarian working practices. It was for this reason that women either banded together into subgroups (as Sarah Noble in Edinburgh demonstrated) or created opportunities to network in female-only spaces. Indeed, while the dominant narratives of the workshop movement put cross-job working center stage, what emerges from interviews with women is the premium they placed on working with other women. Often these were on projects that challenged gender and racial stereotypes and focused on women's stories. This next section looks first at the importance of all-female crews/spaces and then explores some of the stories that women in the workshops brought to the screen.

Women-Only Spaces

The concept of female separatism was central to second-wave feminism and ranged from experiments in all-women communal living to consciousness-raising groups where women came together to share experiences and form collective responses to patriarchal oppression. This thinking impacted the film industry, one outcome of which was the women-only day schools of the 1970s, where women practitioners created separate training spaces where they could learn and work in an environment free from male patronization. An extension of these ideas was the all-female crew, where productions were made with women technicians in all of the film's crew positions, from director and editor to camera, lighting, and wardrobe. This was a form of positive discrimination intended to counter the male dominance of the production team. Although their primary purpose may have been to support women into work, such arrangements also took the opportunity to create new forms of production culture that put women's needs and preferences first.

The best-known example of the all-female production is *The Gold Diggers* (1983), directed by Sally Potter, which was one of the key events for many women film technicians in Britain in the early 1980s. Funded by the British Film Institute and Channel Four, the film is a feminist adventure story that critiques the gendered history of cinema, along with its genres and imagery. It does this through the figure of Ruby (played by Julie Christie), who, through her relationship with Celeste (Colette Laffont), learns to deconstruct her status as the object of the patriarchal gaze, revered for her white beauty and traded between men. The film was made with a small, all-female crew, with no more than two dozen women working on the film and with some, like Sally Potter and Rose English, working across writing, directing, editing, and art direction roles. The crew requirements may have been modest, but Potter still had difficulties assembling an all-female crew. She found costume and sound relatively easy roles to fill, while lighting technicians came from theater, and set builders "tended to be women who had trained as domestic carpenters," itself an indication of the gendered gaps in production roles at this time.[77]

Once production was under way, the shoot generated excitement not only among its cast and crew but also within a wider community of politically engaged women working in film. Sound recordist Elaine Drainville did not work on the film but recalls it as "much talked about" among her filmmaking peers, and indeed she was taken by a friend to visit the film set during production, so special and memorable was the sight of an all-female crew.[78] Similarly, members of the Leeds Animation Workshop spoke of "the energy" given to women's filmmaking generally in Britain when Potter's all-women crew was making *The Gold Diggers* in 1982–83.[79] This was clearly event-filmmaking, which cemented itself in the consciousness of many women working in the industry at the time.

The all-female crew enabled women to inculcate a studio-floor culture that differed radically from the working environment of the mainstream industry and the studios at Pinewood and Shepperton, where, as Joy Cuff's experience has shown (see chapter 5), women had to deal with sexual harassment and the ever present banter. Moreover, there was no need for women to constantly prove themselves in the face of what cinematographer Diane Tammes described as the "ha ha" (that is, mocking and skeptical) attitude of men when confronted with a woman film technician. The experience of *The Gold Diggers* proved to be a revelation for the film's leading actress, Julie Christie, who was used to working with male-dominated casts and crews. Christie herself had been outspoken on women's issues in the 1980s and had become an increasingly vocal critic of misogynistic media representations of women. Her attempts to challenge misogynist attitudes in the profession were fraught with difficulty: "I have often found working on regular films that there's virtually no-one who shares my point of view. When you start talking about women in what is a male-dominated profession and you literally get laughed down, that's a lonely situation."[80] Christie elaborated on how women experienced the typical working culture of a male-dominated film set: "It's a slightly lonely position, which you tackle by bantering and creating a sort of bonhomie. It's a very flirtatious situation."[81] Her comments echo those of sound recordist Melanie Chait (discussed earlier in this chapter), who had previously found that location shooting often came with unwanted sexual attention from men in the crew. Christie's description of working on *The Gold Diggers* as "an amazing experience, the most satisfying film I've ever worked on" was no doubt shared by the other women on the shoot, who could finally work in a nonsexualized environment, create a culture on set that worked for them, and get on with the job in hand.[82] As Christie described it, this culture ranged from "scratch[ing] your bum" on set, to "communicat[ing] in shorthand" because the crew had a common language through the shared political experience of feminism.[83]

The experience of making the film had an impact on its cast, crew, and further afield, setting a precedent for all-female crews that other women were keen to duplicate. The following year Elaine Drainville was part of a team recruited by Melanie Chait to work on *Veronica 4 Rose* (1983), a documentary film about the experiences of young lesbian women, which was shot in Newcastle, London, and Liverpool. Commissioned by, and screened on, Channel Four, the film was directed by Chait, who had worked as a sound recordist on *The Gold Diggers* and was keen to support young women technicians. Drainville was just starting her career as a filmmaker and was taken on as an assistant to established sound technician Di Rushton. For Drainville, the shoot provided a "very supportive atmosphere" where she could extend her skills under Rushton's supervision: "Di . . . was just incredibly generous with her knowledge. . . . [She] taught me where the boom comes in, keeping out of frame . . . problem solving. . . . It was wonderful to work on an all-women crew when you were young like that, and you are also learning your skill, your craft. . . . We were all in it together."[84] Describing it as "new" and "exciting," it was a formative experience for Drainville, who would go on to specialize in filmmaking with a number of marginalized groups, including Palestinian women and children living with trauma.[85]

Terry Wragg was equally enthusiastic about the all-women environment of the Leeds Animation Workshop when she joined the group in 1977.[86] Working on the film *Who Needs Nurseries? We Do!* she spent her days painting cels, in a role very similar to the countless women whose labor had supported Britain's animation industry in the 1940s and 1950s (see chapter 4). The difference now was that rather than working in silence while listening to music, the women combined painting with talking. As Wragg recalls:

> A lot of talking was going on all the time . . . a lot of sharing of stories. . . .
> We were in a working environment . . . but it wasn't a million miles from
> being like a consciousness-raising group in some ways. Somebody would

say, "What was your experience like?" . . ."What was yours?" And so you'd kind of go round the room. I remember the feeling of those conversations. . . . I thought it was a brilliant place to work. It was really lovely.[87]

Equally compelling were film festivals that highlighted women's output as filmmakers. Both Wragg and Drainville recalled their participation in the first International Feminist Film and Video Festival in Amsterdam, held at the Melkweg, the city's concert hall, in the early 1980s. These events included screenings of films from Chantel Ackerman and Maya Deren, work by experimental feminist filmmaker Barbara Hammer, and discussions of Judy Chicago's installation *The Dinner Party* (1979), widely regarded as an icon of 1970s feminist art. Wragg described the festival as an incredible event, attended by women from all over the world, including Egypt, Mexico, and African nations, and with screenings and discussion, describing it as "mind-blowing, really amazing."[88] Drainville's experience was similarly exhilarating; she recalled passionate debates that ranged across lesbian sexuality, female sexual pleasure, and the struggle to get more women into the film industry, a topic felt sharply by British women who found themselves behind other countries—notably, Germany—that were "making quite radical films."[89] Both women went home exhausted and, as Drainville recalls, "stimulated on every blooming level: intellectually, emotionally. I was challenged, I was elated. I mean, it was incredible."[90]

The event did raise their aspirations as filmmakers. For Wragg, it "shook up my rigid ideas about a separation between politics and art and my belief that everything had to be easily accessible all the time," encouraging her to be more experimental in her work.[91] Drainville found that it stimulated her to reflect on the type of films she wanted to make and what she wanted to say as a filmmaker. And for someone who had studied Dziga Vertov at art school, she was delighted to be introduced to Yelizaveta Svolova, his wife and an editor and director in her own right, and other Russian women, including Èsfir Shub. Learning about and connecting with a longer history of women's filmmaking was an important part of Drainville's development: "When you start finding these women you just think, oh yippee, fantastic."[92] So female-only spaces in the form of all-women crews and film festivals played a crucial role in connecting women from the workshops with other women filmmakers, both past and present. The significance of this, and the positive impact it had on all areas of their life, is movingly communicated by Elaine Drainville, whose description is worth quoting at length:

[There was] a camaraderie in the industry amongst women because we were a rare species and we knew instinctively where we'd come from, how we'd got there and what it meant to be there . . . the battles we had to fight . . . what would get in our way, who would put us down. When you came across a woman in the industry, and then women came together to form women-only film crews . . . it was kind of an elation. . . . [There was] a unity of experience, we're talking the same language. . . . We didn't have to prove ourselves in the way in which we did do in an all-male crew. . . . [And] all the stereotyping, the sexist jokes had gone. All of a sudden you were experiencing what it's like to be a sound recordist on a shoot, not a woman sound recordist. When you're in an all-woman crew you don't realise you're a woman, you're just being you in your job. . . . It must be what men have a lot of the time.[93]

Drainville is careful not to give a false impression of a utopia—there were divisions and hierarchies among women that she acknowledges came to a head in subsequent years—nevertheless, there is a palpable sense of excitement for a generation of young women filmmakers who found themselves and each other for the first time in the early 1980s.

I now build on the theme of female spaces and use this closing section to examine in a little more detail how women used the new opportunities available through the workshop sector to tell stories from a female perspective. They did this through prioritizing media education activities and building long-term relationships with women's groups. Here I explore first the educational activities of Maureen Blackwood and Martina Attille, members of the Sankofa workshop, a London-based collective of Black British filmmakers who prioritized issues of race, gender, and sexuality.[94] Active between 1983 and 1997, Sankofa had a majority membership of women, although its most prominent member is perhaps Isaac Julien, who wrote and directed *Young Soul Rebels* about Black gay culture in London. I also examine the career of Sirkka-Liisa Konttinen, who worked through the Amber collective, using the photography project *Step by Step* to explore her working practice and her technical, curatorial, and interpersonal skills. Located in North East England, the Amber workshop had a specific interest in the region's working-class communities in what was rapidly becoming a postindustrial area in the 1980s. Still active to this day, its output included features, shorts, and photography, created through an aesthetic style that drew art cinema and documentary together with a commitment to social realism. Although all three women were involved in the production of films through their workshops (earning solo or codirecting and writing credits), I place emphasis here on media education, photography, and exhibition. Educational activities were a condition of receiving workshop funding, but they were categorized by the union as "supplementary activities" to the main business of production.[95] They seem to have been activities often undertaken by women, and this, alongside their ancillary status vis-à-vis the filmed image, means they have received less recognition in film history.

Black Women and Pedagogy

Blackwood and Attille were leading figures in a loose grouping of Black British filmmakers, artists, and cultural theorists who emerged in the 1980s. Journalists and writers such as Jim Pines, Kobena Mercer, and Stuart Hall were at the vanguard of the many debates about identity and Englishness that took place during the decade, while figures such as Isaac Julien, John Akomfrah, Karen Alexander, and Maureen Blackwood critiqued how the mainstream media represented Black people and, through the workshop sector, sought to create alternative representations and aesthetic modes specific to Black Britons.[96] They were part of a wider network of film collectives including Sankofa, the Black Audio Film Collective, Ceddo, and Retake that sought to bring the experience and stories of Black British and British Asians to the screen. At this time the representation of ethnic minorities in Britain's film, television, and video industry workforce stood at around 2 percent, and the workshop sector afforded opportunities that were less than forthcoming in the mainstream.[97] While films such as *Handsworth Songs* (1986, Black Audio Film Collective), *Passion of Remembrance* (1986, Sankofa), and *Looking for Langston* (Sankofa) are the most prominent and well-known examples of their work, the groups were also active in media education. This often took the form of workshops and discussion groups, many of which were led by women.

Interrogating gender politics was integral to Sankofa's ethos. For Martina Attille, the group's "particular character in terms of race, gender and sexuality meant that the unfinished business of the 1960s/70s (black, gay and feminist movements) was something that we felt needed prioritising in the present, particularly in relation to those three areas of experience."[98] Blackwood was equally clear-sighted about how Black politics historically had sidelined "thoughts around sexuality, black women's position within the structure of black political organisations, and so on," and that "politics in the 80s is much more about trying to bring these other concerns forward, and to grapple with all of those issues at once."[99] Their politics were intersectional, and as Black women they sought audiences with other Black women. Both were members of the Black Women and Representation steering group, which held a number of media education workshops in London in 1984, focusing on screenings and discussions around issues of representation. Workshops were advertised through posters and publicity materials with the tagline "For Black Women By Black Women," which were placed in local women's centers, colleges, and Black women's organizations, with advertising appearing in the specialist feminist and Black press, as well as the London paper *Time Out* (see fig. 17).

Specifically targeting Black women, on the grounds that they have "the least opportunity to use video equipment and talk about our relationship to the media," the purpose of the workshops was, in Attille and Blackwood's words: "[to] establish an ongoing forum for discussion around the social and political implications of the fragmentation of black women in film/video/television as well as a forum to talk about the kinds of images we want to construct ourselves, in an attempt to offer a more complete picture of our lives/politics."[100] The program's activities ranged from deconstructing dominant imagery in the mainstream media—Blackwood led a workshop on the "Mammy" stereotype and its circulation through historic and contemporary texts—to the politics of looking, using ethnographic

Figure 17. Advertising for Black Women and Representation workshop. Source: Reproduced in Charlotte Brunsdon, ed., *Films for Women* (London: British Film Institute, 1986).

documentary as a case study. Media education was an ongoing component of Blackwood's and Attille's practices as filmmakers. Attille became an active public speaker, leading a peer-to-peer seminar titled "Power and Control" in London (1985), contributing to the touring exhibition "Young British and Black" (1988), and participating in the conference "High Culture/Popular Culture: Media Representations of the Other" held at the Rockefeller Foundation in Italy (1989). In conjunction with Blackwood and another Sankofa member, Nadine Marsh-Edwards, the women organized a film production workshop called "Black (feminine)—Exploring Images of Black Women," held in London in 1986.[101] As was true for the women who went to the feminist festivals in Amsterdam, and those who accessed the first women-only training workshops at the National Film School in the 1970s, separate spaces were an important conduit for Black women's consciousness-raising and to build and foster networks between them.

The media education workshops also fed directly into Blackwood's and Attille's practices as filmmakers, shaping the images and stories of Sankofa's output. The workshop's best-known film, *The Passion of Remembrance* (1986), is an imaginative and intelligent film combining visually arresting images (drawn from both real and mystical landscapes) with astute social commentary to explore the diversity and richness of the Black experience. It also puts women in the spotlight, with Attille stressing that "the lead characters had to be black women (and not your traditional 'tart') and we wanted them to have the edge" in the narrative.[102] They were also instrumental in creating fully-rounded female characters who, for example, wore lipstick and were politically conscious, on the grounds that "it's a myth that feminism and lipstick are incompatible. We wanted to make a statement about pleasure and about women's culture."[103] These themes continued to find expression in other solo-directed projects that Blackwood and Attille made under the Sankofa umbrella. Blackwood used her short film *Perfect Image* (1988) to explore how Black women see themselves, each other, and their relationships with their bodies and how these are filtered through what she described as "a whole set of historical values [that] come into play, imposed on us from the outside" (see fig. 18).[104] The film depicts this through a gallery space that chronicles portraits of Black women, including a sculpted African head, a pseudoscientific document of the Black woman as "specimen," and a studio portrait of actress/ singer Lena Horne.[105] The film then deconstructs the images before returning to the space of the gallery to show "alternative" self-authored portraits, closing with a still from Vietnamese filmmaker Trinh T. Minh-Ha's *ReAssemblage* (1982), a film renowned for its feminist critique of ethnographic

Figure 18. Maureen Blackwood's *Perfect Image* (1988).

representational traditions. Blackwood plays with and problematizes representational strategies, combining satire with poetry and jazz to simultaneously question and celebrate Black women lives. Martina Attille's short film *Dreaming Rivers* (1988) likewise puts women's concerns center stage, tackling the theme of how women's desires are sacrificed to the patriarchal demands of the heterosexual, nuclear family. As Black critic and curator Karen Alexander argues, "The director sees the film as a warning for women always to make space for their own desires."[106]

Women like Blackwood and Attille found the workshop sector a constructive space where they could not only bring stories and representations as Black women to the screen but also reach out to other Black women and their communities, engendering dialogue and helping to build the next generation of Black filmmakers and audiences. But they were only too aware of the constraints they faced outside the workshop sector. As Karen Alexander observed, "Traditionally film—even independent black film—has been the cultural form which has most resisted black women's participation."[107] Blackwood seems to have been acutely aware of this, if her response to the question of whether she would step up to feature filmmaking is anything to go by: "Making the jump to features is a possibility, but there are trade-offs. It's incredibly expensive, it uses up your energy for several years, and I'm not sure I want to do that."[108] Even if she did opt for that route, she was astute in identifying that her chances of success were slimmer than those of her male counterparts:

> There are only a handful of black filmmakers who are commanding big budgets in the US and most of them are young black men. . . . Market forces see a film like *Posse* [a revisionist western about a group of male African American soldiers] as infinitely more marketable than *Daughters of the Dust* [a drama about three generations of African American women], which I would disagree with. There is an audience for both . . . but, we are at the mercy of external forces telling us what we want to see. Normally the people telling us this are white.[109]

In the face of racism and sexism, filmmakers like Blackwood opted for workshop production spaces and activities like media education where they stood the best chance of having the most influence. Film education and research continued to play an important part in the women's careers; Blackwood has been a writing mentor for a number of arts organizations, supporting young playwrights and screenwriters, while Attille worked with visual arts students at universities in California. Media education was an important aspect of the workshop movement, and in the Sankofa collective women were at the vanguard of this activity. It may have led to shorter filmographies, but it made an immeasurable contribution to British film culture, and the significance of women's pedagogy needs to be more widely acknowledged in histories of film.

Working-Class Women and Cocreation

Making connections with other women was also central to the work of Sirkka-Liisa Konttinen in the early 1980s. Her formal training in photography had given her an excellent grounding in the technical and artistic aspects of the discipline, and as a member of the Amber Film Workshop, she had played a central role in producing a series of images of working-class communities in the North of England in the 1970s, working as a photographer with female communities and cocreating work that examined women's social roles and expectations in terms of gender. Konttinen became a mother in 1979, and that experience, in addition to feminism, significantly shaped her thinking. The workshop sector gave her a space to explore motherhood and other themes central to women's lives, which she did through collaborating with working-class women's communities. In the early 1980s, the Amber workshop was involved in a number of projects in the North Shields area of England, and Konttinen became interested in the women in the area—specifically, the female communities that were built up around the many dance schools in the locality. Dance played a central part in the lives of working-class girls and women, from childhood through adolescence and into young adulthood and beyond. The dance schools were dominated by women; not only were the majority of the pupils female, but the teachers and owners were also women, with mothers and grandmothers playing an active role in these wider dance communities. Dance schools drew together women of different generations into a space where men and boys were absent or played a minor role. This gave rise to what Konttinen described as a "pretty feisty female community . . . around the dancing school," and as a young mother, she was "struck by the very intimate and close relationships between the mothers and the daughters" that she saw at the schools.[110]

This resonated with her because she was at a point in her life when she was questioning both the mother role and the negative representations of young girls and femininity in the mainstream media. In an oral history interview, she reflected that the dance project, which would be titled *Step-by-Step*, came about "because I had a young daughter myself who was clearly being moulded by her peer group and the aspirations thrown at little girls when they grow up." She also found herself questioning her own role as a woman, asking of herself, "What is the shape of a mother's role for children?"[111] This self-examination was trigged by feminism, with Konttinen reflecting, "As a young mother myself in the early 1980s I discovered feminism . . . honestly, with a big walloping crash."[112] Although she hadn't anticipated the dance project being long-term, she did, by her own admission, get drawn into the life of the women's dance communities: "The more I got to know them the more interesting it became."[113] The project unfolded over seven years, leading to several outputs, including a documentary film called *Keeping Time* (1983), a number of exhibitions, and the publication of *Step by Step* (1989), which drew together photographs and extracts from interviews with different generations of women who had participated in the project. Konttinen's practice was to work closely with communities, taking time to establish relationships and foster trust, something she believed came from being embedded in a place. Participants were active subjects in the process, not passive objects of the filmmakers' gaze, with dialogue and feedback an integral part of the process. Konttinen would take "the material back and forth to the dancing school, changing it, scrapping it, reshooting it, whilst listening to the experiences and comments of the mothers and daughters."[114] This required patience and active listening skills, and although this approach was consistent with Amber's ethos of "community engagement," what distinguished Konttinen and the dance project was that it focused on women.

For Konttinen, her ambition was that the photographs and stories would "serve as a springboard for both critical and sympathetic examination of women's lives in our society, and offer insight into our own dreams as well as others."[115] She sought to validate the cultures and experiences of working-class women while being critical of some of the social forces shaping women's lives, especially media representations. Describing the dance school as "a kind of finishing school for working-class girls," rituals in clothing, hair, and makeup along with lessons in elocution, modeling, and social graces enculturated pupils in feminine norms.[116] Success was the passport to dance certificates and trophies but also job interviews and "better" life prospects, emphasizing not only how the aspirations of young girls were molded but also the gendered norms through which economic security might be achieved. As her relationship with the community deepened, Konttinen found that feminism "started seeping into this project on the dancing school."[117] Actively researching across different media and their representations of women, she made a series of collages drawing on advertising, school books, and official reports, and then worked with the women to explore the images. These included advertisements from a pharmaceutical company for tranquilizers that depicted a struggling mother in a high-rise apartment with the caption "We can't change her environment but we can change her mood," and statements from male politicians calling for the closure of women's shelters.[118] Describing these images as "the misogyny women encounter in their everyday lives," Konttinen then staged an exhibition that brought together her photography, media representations, and statements by the women about how they "felt themselves being affected by this."[119] Konttinen described the process as "a form of self-reflection," and it seemed to function as consciousness-raising for herself and the group, as many of the educational workshops did at this time.

Through building relationships with women over an extended period of time, Konttinen fostered trust and mutual respect; thus she was able to give voice to the lives of working-class women and show their resilience and ambition, qualities that were rarely reflected in mainstream media representations. Some were single mothers, others married with unemployed husbands, many holding the family together through low-wage jobs or fighting for a man's wage. Konttinen was drawn to the life story of Margaret Bould, a mother who had been through a difficult divorce and had three children to support. Bould was adamant in saying, "I wanted a man's job and a man's wage to bring up a family," so she applied for a school caretaker's job that demanded "nine hours in the boiler room in the muck and the heat and the clart [sticky mud or grease] and the shit and shift[ing] a ton and a half of coal."[120] After she was turned down for twenty jobs—"they'd never heard of a *woman* caretaker"—she had "sharp words" with the superintendent and was soon shortlisted. As Bould put it, "The Equality law was out, but there was no equality down North Shields love!" Moreover, in her view, she was fighting not only for herself but also for a wider community of women with shared experiences: "I've fought for women in the Labour Party and in my union right through my two marriages and divorces, three kids, some rotten jobs and asbestosis. I don't want to see other women getting a raw deal."[121] An active member of the dance school, Bould had taken lessons alongside her daughters and described herself as "Nelly the Elephant in a tutu" but had no problem reconciling the two identities of caretaker and ballerina in her own mind. And other women showed how, through dance, they claimed an identity for themselves beyond socially accepted norms of femininity: "When I go dancing, I'm Denise. I'm not Quinn's and Shelley's mother and I'm not Dave's wife; I'm there to do what *I* want to do."[122] The dance project brought alternative representations of women into view, ones that highlighted women's agency while simultaneously pointing out the social circumstances in which life choices were made. For Konttinen, who was at a stage in her own life when she was discovering feminism, the project gave her access to a community where she could draw on her technical, artistic, and communication skills to create a space where she and other women could collectively reflect on social norms and put on the record more complex and nuanced portraits of women including their experiences and identities. At a time when media representations peddled images of feminine self-sacrifice, especially in the roles of mother, daughter, and wife, this was no small achievement.

In sum, the workshop movement did create opportunities for women to do things differently. While more of the administrative burden still fell to them, the principle of cross-job working did broaden their horizons, with some modest gains achieved. Combining paid work with child care continued to be a thorny issue, although those who signed up to it as a principle of the women's liberation movement managed to find solutions. And through the workshops, women did succeed in bringing the stories and perspectives of themselves and other women into view. For many, their experience of this mode of production was positive, with any negatives offset by the rewards they reaped.

Conclusion

One of the notable features of the 1970s and 1980s is how women created spaces to engage in dialogue with one another. While this is a widely recognized feature of the better-known feminist avant-garde cinema, what has not been fully acknowledged are the diverse and imaginative ways through which women in Britain's film workshops actively sought out and created opportunities for connection. These ranged from media education and community engagement activities to female-only film crews, feminist festivals, and training days. What is apparent in women's accounts is how exhilarating they found these opportunities, whether it was swapping stories while painting film cels, making sense of their own maternal role, or finding a "hidden" history of women filmmakers that had previously been unknown to them. They drew strength from these activities and seem to have used them to simultaneously assess and situate themselves in a longer history of women's labor.

This sense of exhilaration contrasts sharply with the experience of women in the camera departments of the feature film industry, who faced great challenges in work settings that were openly resistant to change and lacked the support structures that having other women around could bring. Small numbers of women did manage to elbow their way into the mainstream industry, but they had to not only navigate the many exclusionary practices that regulated access but also adopt strategies of either "fitting-in or fighting" to survive. In the feature film sector, the rewards were different, with opportunities for travel, better pay, and, very occasionally, industry prestige serving as compensation. But discrimination continued to be rife. Women took longer on average to progress through the ranks than their male counterparts, had to work harder to prove themselves professionally, and took on the additional burden of managing other people's gendered expectations, which ranged from making tea to dealing with the presumption of sexual availability. Through their collective efforts, they supported the film industry's outputs in myriad ways, from the clapper loader attending to "the little details" of equipment, stock, and stores, to the focus puller prepared to sprint backward to get the perfect shot. Their individual contributions were perhaps modest in scale, but they were greater than the sum of their parts and all the more significant given the context in which they were achieved. Women working cameras in the mainstream still labored under the overly determined "woman" prefix, a dynamic that arguably still operates to this day. With that in mind, the final chapter turns to the question of history, specifically legacies, and examines how a history of women in the British film industry might shape current and future debates about women and the media industries.

Epilogue
Legacies and New Beginnings

Finding a way to conclude this book has not been easy. This has been a personal project that I have worked on for several years, and it has taken a significant investment of time to analyze so much material and produce meaningful, interesting, and easy-to-understand findings. Endings, of course, invite reflection, and this process took me back to my initial motivation for the project, which was triggered by three distinct yet interrelated events. First, I was frustrated by the then current state of British cinema history, which was dominated by an overreliance on auteurist studies, an explanatory model that privileged men and male-defined notions of a successful career. That model was a blunt instrument for understanding forms of cultural production, like filmmaking, that are highly collaborative; it impoverished critical debate in the field; and it excluded women because they were rarely directors. Second, the more exciting discoveries were happening in early cinema scholarship, which was transforming the field, rediscovering many women directors and producers who were at the heart of movie culture. But in that area there were different frustrations. Scholarship focused on senior creative roles, and there was a sense that women contributed little of real value to cinema in the period between the coming of sound and second-wave feminism, a gap of over four decades. While it was acknowledged that women did not disappear from the business of filmmaking, there was a feeling that by moving (and being moved) into auxiliary, below-the-line roles, they were inevitably less interesting than the women pioneers of early cinema. This raised my concerns about implicit value judgments regarding labor.

Third, I was alarmed by the terms being used by industry stakeholders to discuss women's participation in present-day media production. At this time (2014–15) a number of UK government-commissioned reports were highlighting how few women held senior roles in media production and how many were leaving the workforce in their mid-thirties. At a round-table event organized by the Royal Television Society and led by leading industry figures, I was concerned to hear that the solutions proposed to address women's exclusion were mentorships and confidence training. This put the problem firmly at the feet of the individual and failed to engage with the structural barriers that had built up over time.

I started to research the role of trade unions in regulating labor in the film industry and came upon the membership application records of the ACTT. I thought that these, alongside oral histories, had the potential to open up the sound period of film and bring a new dimension to the debate about women's historical work. But I was not interested in writing a parallel history, one that sat next to the auteurist studies that dominated scholarship. As a feminist, I wanted to change the terms of the debate and—to paraphrase Joan Wallach Scott—use history as a critical weapon. As Scott argues, "The production of knowledge about the past, while crucial, has not been an end in itself, but rather . . . has provided the substantive terms for a critical operation that uses the past to disrupt the certainties of the present and so opens the way to imagining a different future."[1] The critical operation I envisaged was a future where practitioners and scholars might think differently about forms of labor associated with women and attach different values to it.

It was for these reasons that creating an archive of union membership data and women's oral histories was an essential part of the research process. These records documenting women in the workforce have enabled me (and will enable others) to explore and lay down both a different history of British cinema and a different methodology for doing film history. The data made me rethink the distinction between above- and below-the-line labor, to engage critically with the hidden processes and multiple inputs from the diversity of workers who shape the completed film, and to think differently about concepts of creativity. The distinction between above- and below-the-line positions is too rigid when it is predicated on a division between "creative" and "craft/technical," the latter too often deemed noncreative in production discourse. As this book has shown, it is a distinction that suited the needs of employers and unions, who had strict disciplinary definitions of jobs, and has since been adopted by film studies/history, but the reality on the studio floor, on location, in offices, and in editing suites was rather different. As teams worked together to a collective end, they were participants in a process that had a number of interlocking, codependent elements. The director or producer may have a "vision" (and, hopefully, a script) but this is realized by a team, and in ways that blur and cross the lines between the creative and the technical as these are commonly understood. Because women's labor was more readily assigned a noncreative status than men's in both industry and scholarship, our lack of understanding about what and how women contribute to the process has been particularly acute and demands our critical attention.

This book has shown ways to address that gap in our understanding. Peggy Gick (chapter 3), as an assistant to the art director, could produce the drawings and supervise the construction of a full-size submarine interior from nothing more than a photograph that "looked like a plate of spaghetti" because she had not only the technical skills but also the aesthetic sensibility to deploy them and to make creative decisions in the service of a shared understanding of what the film was trying to achieve. Likewise, editor Kitty Marshall (chapter 4) could interpret an outline brief and make creative decisions about how best to edit the reams of "higgledy-piggledy" material she received into a finished short film on a highly technical subject. And wardrobe mistress Rosemary Burrows (chapter 5) could develop Peter Cushing's iconic look through costume because she understood Hammer studio's visual style and could work within its budgetary constraints. This "resourcefulness," consisting of a number of micro-decisions, technical operations, and the aesthetic sensibility to engage them in the service of the film's goals, is creativity. In the paint and trace departments of Britain's animation studios (chapter 4), the impression that, in Jill Clark's words, "each drawing flowed into the next" was created by the women's brushwork and their skills in perfectly coordinating hand, eye, and equipment to unite the different elements of the work processes in a seamless manner that we, as audiences, do not see. As a form of skill-as-art, this is creative work. The same is true for the women in roles deemed "secretarial," the continuity girls and production secretaries, whom I have described as the linchpins of film production. Historical accuracy in *The Longest Day*—a film about the D-day landings of 1944—was the vision of the director/producer, but reconstructing this history fell not only to the actors, camera crew, wardrobe, and others during shooting but also to the film's production secretary, Sheila Collins, who knew how to identify and source the correct military equipment and which permits were needed to ship that equipment abroad in a timely manner. As I have shown (chapter 4), being able to do this successfully needed superb research skills and an overview of the "complicated jig-saw puzzle" of film production. But these skills alone were not enough.

Different elements of the puzzle needed help to interlock, to smooth over ragged edges and areas of tension. Women, more than men, provided the balm to make this happen through their emotional labor. They absorbed the director's bad temper, made tactful suggestions to the chief editor, and helped the actor into the right frame of mind for the next scene. Working out what to say, how to say it, when, and even to whom requires some creative mental gymnastics, drawing on advanced skills in communication and diplomacy, which were assumed to be naturally occurring in women but were in fact socially sanctioned areas they were encouraged to develop. Emotional labor and caring skills were and still are an essential part of moviemaking, as anyone who has worked on a bad shoot will confirm. Thus, insofar as film history focuses on the completed film as being the result of an individual—usually male—vision, what this book reveals are the multiple inputs from a diversity of workers, all of whom are making creative decisions through technical operations that influence the look and finish of a film. Creativity is not the work of a singular mind. Here, in giving priority to women whose work is the most poorly understood and marginalized in existing film histories, a new method for pursuing film history is offered.

To paraphrase Marx, women make films but in circumstances they do not choose. Individual work histories have revealed the determination of many women to seize what opportunities were available within the personal and professional contexts in which they operated. This study has shown how some were quick to take advantage of opportunities in commercials, a sector that many of their male peers disdained, while others capitalized on working with a weak male manager, using the experience to temporarily step in and learn new skills. Women were consistently paid less money than men, not because they had lower skills but because they were clustered into junior-level jobs or specific areas of work that were awarded less value in a production hierarchy that privileged male labor. Sometimes it was because of direct discrimination, as animator Anne Jolliffe found in 1965 when she compared her weekly paycheck with that of a male coworker. Women, more than men, had to deal with harassment and hostility in the workplace, and this came in a variety of guises. Overt sexual harassment took place beside a running commentary about clothing and physical appearance, while workplace behavior was regulated in accordance with gender norms, which were themselves underpinned by male prejudice concerning women's technical and managerial capacities. From the male instructors at the National Film School who were terrified that if women picked up cameras, they would drop them, to the male crew on the studio floor who publicly humiliated women who tried to give direction, women faced a minefield of obstacles and exclusions in the workplace that men did not. And they were almost always constrained in terms of responsibility, held back in positions that the industry itself recognized as "blind alley jobs." This made it more difficult for them to develop more specialized skills and build a case for promotion. This picture has echoes of Virginia Woolf's analysis of the many commonly occurring ways women are discouraged from artistry through being repeatedly "snubbed, slapped, lectured and exhorted. Her mind must have been strained and her vitality lowered by the need of opposing this, of disproving that."[2] In such ways is the image of male superiority sustained.

But women also found, and made, spaces for professionally satisfying work, where varying degrees of occupational autonomy could be exercised. This was especially noticeable in the shorts and documentary sector, in commercials, and in the independent workshop movement of the 1980s. Experienced women editors working freelance for the National Coal Board in the 1950s and 1960s, for example, were largely left alone to handle the reams of raw footage shot by men. Not only did they revel in the creative freedom of their work (described by one as "great fun"), but they also made it work around family and domestic responsibilities, reminding us that, for most women, working two jobs was the norm. In the 1980s some women opted out of the mainstream in favor of independent workshops that supported cross-job working and prioritized marginalized voices and media education. This generated a space where some women flourished and was especially important for a generation of Black British filmmakers who had few other avenues for accessing technical equipment and training and were constantly confronted with racist stereotyping in the media. Women like Maureen Blackwood and Martina Attille built an educational legacy that continues to have an impact to this day, but the experiences of many women highlight how much time and energy was expended on survival activities in what was a male homosocial world. The lighting electrician deciding whether to ignore or "work up the energy" to challenge men's sexism and the model maker who had to "put my blinkers on" on the studio floor were already working harder than their male contemporaries. Documentary filmmaker Anne Balfour-Fraser's observation that "women can achieve everything but it's appallingly hard work and it shouldn't be as difficult as it is" reminds us how women's professional achievements too often took place in the teeth of male opposition, whether that stemmed from prejudice, fear, or simply ambivalence about women in the workplace.[3]

What are the implications of these findings for the contemporary situation? In 2017 I took part in a symposium attended by academics, activists, and practitioners from different media backgrounds, its goal to showcase women's achievements in media production and debate the current landscape for women in the film and television industries. There was much to discuss, with industry-commissioned reports showing how horizontal and vertical segregation by gender continues to be an issue in the UK. Camera roles remained dominated by men, and less than one-quarter of postproduction positions were held by women, a figure consistent with data for the 1950s and lower than women's participation rates in the Second World War. As more young women pour into our universities and film schools to study media production, the promise of equal opportunities seems more remote than ever.

In my role at the symposium, I shared women's oral histories as a way to open up debate about the current media landscape. This included stories from many of the women who have been featured in this study: model maker Joy Cuff's experience of dealing with constant banter; continuity girl Ann Skinner's distress at the lack of on-location toilet facilities; makeup artist Jean Steward's fight to be reevaluated, her labor recognized—with appropriate remuneration—as skilled. The debate that followed was both fascinating and alarming, especially among the young women in the audience. Most were in their early twenties and were just beginning to navigate the workplace and its many forms of gender discrimination. This generation, born in the mid-1990s, had grown up with expectations of gender equality that their experiences of work were beginning to challenge. One woman, a freelance writer/producer, saw many parallels between previous generations of women and her own. She told how women were still infantilized through language—referred to as "girl" by the "higher-ups"—or afforded less status on set by men who were quick to (mis)introduce them as "assistants." Others recounted tales of inadequate restroom facilities, while another recalled a recent job interview for a junior position where she was asked to describe how she would "manage others' egos," suggesting how emotional labor is still expected of women in the workplace. The strength of the connection between past and present was emphasized in women's responses to a questionnaire upon which they underlined key words—"I've experienced the <u>exact</u> scenario"—and used exclamation marks ("Yes!") to amplify their message. These and other anecdotes, highly personal and easy to discount as minor infringements on individuals, coalesced to reveal a shared, collective picture of sexist workplace cultures and how they are experienced by young women in the industry today.

But what are the implications of young women in 2017 experiencing the "<u>exact</u> scenario" as women in the 1960s? Why should an anecdote about a fight for professional recognition—some fifty years earlier—retain its potency? That the women needed validation for their own experiences is clear, a vital process for those who lack the power to speak out against workplace discrimination, with young women being especially vulnerable in this regard. But the following statements, written by two young women, suggest that something more than validation was happening:

> Often I am self-deprecating in my choices of words and hesitate to call myself a "writer" for fear of not having enough experience. Hearing about women fighting for titles of "technician" or "artist" or "designer" inspired me to use terms that clearly indicate I am a professional and I owe it to those women to own it.[4]

Women looked for, and found in the stories, role models that they used to generate a sense of connection, solidarity, and female community. They also drew power from historical accounts, using them to build their own sense of resilience:

> Something very positive I took from listening to the oral histories was the importance and power of women using their voices and the way this creates support for other women in the industry. . . . I feel very moved by the sense of female community within the creative industries after today.[5]

These comments work on a number of levels, suggesting deficits and desires in present-day working cultures (for "a sense of female community") and how women were using history to stake a claim in the media industries as a profession that belonged to them. This is an important point, and one of the recurring themes in this study has been women finding their histories. Witness sound technician Elaine Drainville's delight in the 1980s when she discovered that Yelizaveta Svolova, wife of director Dziga Vertov, was also a filmmaker (see chapter 6). But Drainville's comment—"When you start finding these women you just think, oh yippee, fantastic"—also highlights how women are repeatedly written out of history, each new generation having to discover their predecessors anew.

Why should this be so? Undervaluing work associated with women and their wider history is deeply ingrained in our collective consciousness. This point was brought home to me sharply by two events. The first was an academic conference when I was challenged by an audience member to explain why I was writing what they described as a "losers' cinema"—here defined as a history of people (i.e., women) who had failed to attain director status—held up as the pinnacle of creative achievement.[6] The failure to see women's work in film production as *real* work has ensured it was, and still is, undervalued. The second event was an attempt to support present-day industry stakeholders to draw on women's film history as evidence in their campaigns about equality and diversity initiatives. Despite responses being initially enthusiastic, the collaboration failed to take off because, as one stakeholder described it, "the research, as it is historical, is not of great interest to the industry at present." While this was explained as a consequence of shifting priorities for the sector in the light of the emerging #MeToo movement (which began in 2017), what was being expressed was a deeper conviction that history was irrelevant. But, as my symposium conversations had highlighted, history was very much of interest to young women in the industry who used it to claim a professional identity. In their actions we could see history being mobilized as a critical weapon, as ammunition to disrupt the present and imagine a different future.

The archive and our uses of it—as researchers, educators, practitioners, and policy makers—is crucial. What I have presented in this study does not exhaust the materials in the "Women's Work in British Film and Television" resource, and indeed it was never imagined that it would. Archiving the ACT/ACTT union records and women's oral histories was a feminist act, an intervention intended to create a lasting record of the many and diverse workers who made up the film (and television) production workforce. There are many other findings that can come out of searching the resource: case studies of individual studios and how they recruited unionized labor at key moments in their histories; studies of entire jobs—for example, camera and sound technicians—that will be able to go into far greater detail than has been possible in this book. Histories of entire industries—television, film laboratories—that were beyond my remit. Individuals whose records remind us that the "British" film industry always relied on international labor, from the United States, Australia, New Zealand, Germany, the former Czechoslovakia, and India, among others. Applicants were asked to record their nationality on their union forms, and the number of India-born technicians accepted for membership in the late 1940s is both a document of their presence in the workforce and a reminder of Britain's colonial activities. Rich contextual layers are present in the comments of union officials who endorse the applicant, describing her as a "diligent worker" and him as "a bright young man." And the oral histories are rich and multifaceted, hundreds of hours of recorded reflections on the experiences, processes, achievements, frustrations, and meanings of work, all from women's perspectives. It is possible to engage critically with what the work of making a film entails, apart from the adulation of a director's "vision." And that is to sweep aside the outmoded frameworks of film history and approach work with a different value system, one that is in tune with more inclusive measures of success and creativity. We have in our hands the building blocks and methods to do so.

Appendix A

Application Form for Membership in the Association of Cine-Technicians (circa 1930s)

THE ASSOCIATION OF CINE-TECHNICIANS
30, PICCADILLY MANSIONS, 17, SHAFTESBURY AVENUE, LONDON, W.1.
Registered Trade Union No. 1995.

Studio or other Committee ....

APPLICATION FOR MEMBERSHIP

All Questions must be answered.   All Information is treated as Strictly Confidential.
Please Print Name and Address in Block Letters.   Please Write in Ink.

1. SURNAME   COOPER   Christian Names   Brigid Winifred Therese

3. Married, Single, Widow or Widower   Single   4. Age last Birthday. 23   Years.
5. Nationality   British
6. Employer's Name   British International Pictures Ltd.
    Address   Elstree, Herts.
7. Position held   Continuity   8. Department   Production
9. Rate of pay   £2.10.0.   Per   week
10. If not working, state Name and Address of last Employer and Date of leaving

11. How long have you worked in the Industry?   one year
12. If you are a member or should be a member of another Trade Union, please state its name

I, the undersigned, apply to be elected a Member of the Association of Cine-Technicians, and hereby pledge myself to abide by its rules and decisions, and to do my utmost to promote its welfare.

Date   24th October 1936   Usual Signature   Brigid Cooper

This application is endorsed by the undersigned Members to whom the Applicant is known, and they vouch for the qualifications and fitness for Membership of the Applicant.

Sponsors   Committee   No.
Sponsors   Flora Newton   Committee   No.
Sponsors   E Catchpole   Committee   No.
Sponsors   A. C. Kee.   Committee   No.
Studio or other Committee Secretary's Signature   Book   Date 27-10-36

Membership commences week ending ....   Membership No. 1626

[P.T.O.

Appendix B
ACT Job Levels, 1947

The following grades are properly recruited into the A.C.T.

(I) FEATURE PRODUCTION

Floor, Production and Casting
Associate Producer
Film Director
Unit Production Manager
First Assistant Director
Second Assistant Director
Third Assistant Director
Continuity
Assistant Continuity
Production Secretary
Casting Director
Assistant Casting Director

Scenario Department
Scenario Editor
Screenwriter
Literary Editor
Assistant Literary Editor
Reader
Research

Cine-Camera Department (including Trick and Special effects)
Lighting Cameraman
Outside Cameraman (without lights)

Camera Operator
Follow-Focus Camera
Chief of Camera Room (non-mechanical)
Chief of Loading
Clappers and/or Loading
Chief Cine-Camera Maintenance Engineer
Cine-Camera Maintenance Engineer
Assistant Cine-Camera Maintenance Engineer

Process and Special Effects Department
Process and Special Effects Cameraman
First Assistant Process and Special Effects Cameraman
Second Assistant Process and Special Effects Cameraman
Matte Process Artist
Assistant Matte Process Artist
Miniature Special Effects
Assistant Miniature Special Effects

Stills Department
Unit and Portrait Still Cameraman
Unit Still Cameraman (only)
Press Still Cameraman (only)
Assistant Still Cameraman
Retoucher
Finisher and Second Retoucher
Printer
Second Printer
Spotters, Trimmers and Glazers
General Darkroom Assistant

Sound Recording Department
Supervisor
Sound Recordist (Mixer)
Sound Camera Operator
Boom Operator
Assistant Boom Operator
Laboratory Contact
Sound Loader
Sound Effects

Sound Maintenance Department
Chief Maintenance Engineer
Maintenance Engineer
Assistant Maintenance Engineer

Sound Research Department
(As in Sound Recording and Maintenance)

Film Editing and Film Dubbing Departments
    Supervising Editor
    Editor
    Dubbing Editor
    Assembler (First Assistant)
    Second Assistant Cutter
    Laboratory Contact

Film Library
    Supervising Librarian
    Librarian
    Assistant Librarian

Foreign Versions Synchronisation
    Synchronisation Director
    Synchronisation Editor
    Synchronisation Dialogue Writer
    First Assistant Synchronous Editor
    Second Assistant Synchronous Editor
    Title Spotter

Negative Cutting Department
    Chief Studio Negative Cutter
    Studio Negative Cutter

Art Department
    Supervising Art Director
    Art Director
    Assistant Art Director (Design)
    Assistant Art Director (Set)
    Chief Draughtsman
    Chief Draughtsman
    Draughtsman
    Assists to the above grades
    Supervising Dress Designer ⎫
    Dress Designer   ⎬ not Wardrobe Mistress
    Assistant Dress Designer ⎭
    Scenic Artist
    Assistant Scenic Artist
    Miniature Scale Sets (not props or modellers)
    Assistant Miniature Scale Sets (not props or modellers)

Publicity Department
    Publicity Director (Editorial)
    Publicity Director (Pictorial)
    Specialist Publicity Writer
    Publicity Studio Representative
    Administrative Assistant (Head Office Publicity)
    Publicity Representative (Pictorial)

Administrative Assistant (Pictorial)
Studio Representative Trainees

Post-Production Script Department
A.C.T. grades employed on this work.

(2) SHORT FILM PRODUCTION
(a) All A.C.T. grades recognised for feature films
(b) All clerical grades employed by producers who do not own or operate front film studios.

(3) LABORATORIES
All grade of employees, including clerical workers.

(4) NEWSREEL
(a) All A.C.T. grades recognised for feature films and shorts, except for clerical workers.
(b) Newsreel clerical workers working at film laboratories.
(c) Assistant News Editor, Contact man, Lettering Artist, Filler-in.

(5) CARTOON, DIAGRAM, FILM STRIPS
(a) **Cartoons**
Supervising Director
Unit Director
Story Department Story Man
In-Betweener and Clean-up
Key Artist, Junior
Key Artist, Senior
Background and Lay-out
Colourist
Tracer

(b) **Diagrams**
Supervising Director
Unit Director
Key Artist, responsible for planning
Key Artist, not responsible for planning
Diagram Artist
Background Artist
Title Artist
Title Artist (not engaged on aerograph and background work)
Rostrum Camera Operator
Assistant Rostrum Camera Operator

(c) **Film Strips**
(1) A.C.T. grades employed in this work as recognised for Short films, Cartoon and Diagram films
(2) Research Worker, Chief Planning Artist, Negative Retoucher, Planning Artists, Artists, Assistant Artists, Planning Letterers, Lettering Artists, Stockkeeper.

Appendix C

Film Technicians: Numbers and Percentage by Gender, Decade, and Production Category

	Post Production (%)	Art & Effects (%)	Research, Development, & Publicity (%)	Camera, Sound, & Stills (%)	Cartoon & Diagram (%)	Floor (%)	Office (%)	Totals by Decade (%)
1930 F	92 (18.2)	0 (0.0)	6 (20)	14 (1.7)	0 (0)	69 (26.1)	1 (12.5)	182 (10.3)
1930 M	414 (81.8)	122 (100)	24 (80)	811 (98.3)	10 (100)	195 (73.9)	7 (87.5)	1583 (89.7)
1930 All	506	122	30	825	10	264	8	1765
1940 F	581 (32.6)	109 (20)	116 (33.2)	80 (5.9)	235 (46.7)	317 (32.6)	119 (75.3)	1557 (27.5)
1940 M	1199 (67.6)	436 (80)	233 (66.8)	1276 (94.1)	268 (53.3)	654 (67.4)	39 (24.7)	4105 (72.5)
1940 All	1780	545	349	1356	503	971	158	5662
1950 F	148 (25.3)	46 (22.7)	36 (24)	17 (3.89)	92 (44.2)	136 (36)	14 (60.9)	489 (24.6)
1950 M	438 (74.7)	157 (77.3)	114 (76)	420 (96.1)	116 (55.8)	242 (64)	9 (39.1)	1496 (75.4)
1950 All	586	203	150	437	208	378	23	1985
1960 F	125 (15.9)	72 (21.2)	35 (25)	10 (1.43)	26 (28.9)	174 (30.5)	26 (60.5)	468 (17.6)
1960 M	659 (84.1)	267 (78.8)	105 (75)	687 (98.6)	64 (71.1)	396 (69.5)	17 (39.5)	2195 (82.4)
1960 All	784	339	140	697	90	570	43	2663
1970 F	143 (18.1)	65 (32.5)	57 (27.8)	30 (5.23)	124 (41.1)	254 (37.1)	28 (71.8)	701 (25.1)
1970 M	647 (81.9)	135 (67.5)	148 (72.2)	544 (94.8)	178 (58.9)	430 (62.9)	11 (28.2)	2093 (74.9)
1970 All	790	200	205	574	302	684	39	2794
1980 F	282 (28.6)	271 (42.1)	136 (44)	177 (17.3)	208 (45)	711 (52.8)	45 (71.4)	1830 (37.8)
1980 M	705 (71.4)	373 (57.9)	173 (56)	847 (82.7)	254 (55)	635 (47.2)	18 (28.6)	3005 (62.2)
1980 All	987	644	309	1024	462	1346	63	4835
Total F	1371 (25.2)	563 (27.4)	386 (32.6)	328 (6.7)	685 (43.5)	1661 (39.4)	233 (69.8)	5227
Total M	4062 (74.8)	1490 (72.6)	797 (67.4)	4585 (93.3)	890 (56.5)	2552 (60.6)	101 (30.2)	14477
Total by Category	5433	2053	1183	4913	1575	4213	334	19704

Notes

Introduction

1. Martha M. Lauzen, "The Celluloid Ceiling: Behind-the-Scenes Employment of Women on the Top 100, 250, and 500 Films of 2018," 2019, accessed Sept. 6, 2019, https://womenintvfilm.sdsu.edu/wp-content/uploads/2019/01/2018_Celluloid_Ceiling_Report.pdf. The scandal associated with Hollywood producer Harvey Weinstein and subsequent #MeToo campaign also brought issues of gender equality and power to the fore in 2017.

2. Erin Hill, *Never Done: A History of Women's Work in Media Production* (New Brunswick, NJ: Rutgers University Press, 2016); J. E. Smyth, *Nobody's Girl Friday: The Women Who Ran Hollywood* (Oxford: Oxford University Press, 2017).

3. Leo Rosten, *Hollywood: The Movie Colony, the Movie Makers* (New York: Arno Press, 1941).

4. Sue Harper, *Women in British Cinema: Mad, Bad, and Dangerous to Know* (London: Continuum, 2000), 4.

5. Sally Potter quoted in Sophie Mayer, *The Cinema of Sally Potter* (London: Wallflower, 2009), 140.

6. Frank Sainsbury, "Close-Ups, No. 8—The Johnstone Sisters," *Cine-Technician* (Oct.–Dec. 1940): 95.

7. John Farleigh, "Dressed for the Part," *Picturegoer*, Dec. 2, 1950.

8. Zoe Irving, "Gender and Work," in *Introducing Gender and Women's Studies*, 3rd ed., ed. Diane Richardson and Victoria Robinson (Basingstoke, Hampshire: Palgrave Macmillan, 2008), 164–65.

9. Farleigh, "Dressed for the Part."

10. Sarah Baker and David Hesmondhalgh, "Sex, Gender, and Work Segregation in the Cultural Industries," *Sociological Review* 63: S1 (2015): 25.

11. See Emma Griffin on "Mind the Gender Pay Gap," *BBC Radio 4* (broadcast March 12, 2019).

12. Arlie Russell Hoschchild, *The Managed Heart: Commercialization of Human Feeling* (Berkeley: University of California Press, 2003), 7.

13. Ibid., 8.

14. Harper, *Women in British Cinema*, 4.

15. Anne V. Coates, cited in *British Film Editors: The Heart of the Movie*, by Roy Perkins and Martin Stollery (London: British Film Institute, 2004), 178.

16. This is especially the case for employment in the twentieth century. See Irving, "Gender and Work," 164.

17. Penny Summerfield, "'They didn't want women back in that job!': The Second World War and the Construction of Gendered Work Histories," *Labour History Review* 63, no. 1 (1998): 95.

18. Virginia Woolf, *A Room of One's Own* (1929; Oxford: Oxford University Press, 2015), 50.

19. Catherine Martin, "Archival Research as a Feminist Practice," *New Review of Film and Television* 16, no. 4 (2018): 458.

20. Elizabeth Nielson, "Handmaidens of the Glamour Culture: Costumers in the Hollywood Studio System," in *Fabrications, Costume, and the Female Body*, ed. Jane Gaines and Charlotte Herzog (New York: Routledge, 1990), 170–71.

21. Raymond Williams, *Keywords: A Vocabulary of Culture and Society* (London: Fontana, 1983).

22. Christine Gledhill and Julia Knight, eds., *Doing Women's Film History: Reframing Cinemas, Past and Future* (Urbana: University of Illinois Press, 2015).

23. Vicki Mayer, Miranda J. Banks, and John Thornton Caldwell, eds., *Production Studies: Cultural Studies of Media Industries* (New York: Routledge, 2009), 2.

24. Robert C. Allen and Douglas Gomery, *Film History: Theory and Practice* (New York: McGraw-Hill, 1985), 41.

25. For a discussion of the link between histories of forgotten people and different types of records, see Andrew Prescott, "The Textuality of the Archive," in *What Are Archives? Cultural and Theoretical Perspectives: A Reader*, ed. Louise Craven, 31–52 (Abingdon, Oxon: Taylor and Francis, 2016).

26. Natalie Wreyford and Shelley Cobb, "Data and Responsibility: Toward a Feminist Methodology for Producing Historical Data on Women in the Contemporary UK Film Industry," *Feminist Media Histories* 3, no. 3 (2017): 109.

27. Caroline Williams, "Personal Papers: Perceptions and Practices," in Craven, *What Are Archives?*, 60.

28. These observations are indebted to discussions with Phyll Smith, who offered a fascinating account of the 1911 British census and the cinema workforce of clerks, usherettes, and projectionists at the HoMER "What Is Cinema History?" Conference, Glasgow (UK), June 24, 2015.

29. Sue Armitage, "The Stages of Women's Oral History," in *The Oxford Handbook of Oral History*, ed. Donald A. Ritchie (Oxford: Oxford University Press, 2011), 178–79. Full discussion is outside the bounds of this project, but Armitage provides a useful summary.

30. Polly Russell, "Using Biographical Narrative and Life Story Methods to Research Women's Movements: Sisterhood and After," *Women's Studies International Forum* 35 (2012): 132.

31. G. Stevenson, "The Forgotten Strike: Equality, Gender, and Class in the Trico Equal Pay Strike," *Labour History Review* 81, no. 2 (2016): 144.

32. Ann Skinner, interview, "Histories of Women and Work in the British Film and Television Industries Project," Learning on Screen Collection (hereafter "Histories of Women and Work"). Hill makes a similar point that the script supervisors' repeated references to "worry" and "care" when describing their jobs "provides insight into the overriding function such work served in production." Hill, *Never Done*, 13.

33. To access the resource, go to https://learningonscreen.ac.uk and click on "Teaching and Research," "Collections," "Women's Work in British Film and Television."

34. Susan Belbin and Caroline Hutchings, interviews, "Histories of Women and Work."

35. Sue Morgan, "Theorizing Feminist History: A Thirty-Year Retrospective," *Women's History Review* 8, no. 3 (2009): 382.

36. Caroline Ramazanoğlu, with Janet Holland, *Feminist Methodology: Challenges and Choices* (London: Sage, 2002), 16.

37. Joan Sangster, "Gendering Labour History across Borders," *Labour History Review* 75, no. 2 (2010): 157.

38. Joan Wallach Scott, "Feminism's History," *Journal of Women's History* 16, no. 2 (2004): 18.

Chapter 1. Organizing Work

1. Sarah Street, *British National Cinema* (London: Routledge, 1997).

2. This is especially pertinent for understanding the careers of costume designers and those in art direction functions, who were more likely than their camera operator counterparts to move between film and theater for employment.

3. Quoted in Iain Reid, "The Persistence of the Internal Labour Market in Changing Circumstances: The British Film Production Industry During and After the Closed Shop," unpublished PhD thesis, London School of Economics, 2008, 100.

4. For a full account of the ACT's history, see Michael Chanan, *Labour Power in the British Film Industry* (London: British Film Institute, 1976).

5. BECTU as a union merged again in 2017 with the Prospect trade union, which represents public and private sector professionals and is, at the time of publication, part of its communications, media, and digital division.

6. Cole quoted in Chanan, *Labour Power*, 28.

7. Reid, "Persistence of the Internal Labour Market," 101.

8. Sylvia Walby, *Patriarchy at Work: Patriarchal and Capitalist Relations in Employment, 1800–1984* (Minneapolis: University of Minnesota Press, 1986), 244.

9. Ibid., 138.

10. Anne Phillips and Barbara Taylor, "Sex and Skill: Notes towards a Feminist Economics," *Feminist Review*, no. 6 (1980): 79.

11. Sainsbury, "Close-Ups, No. 8," 95.

12. Unnamed respondent quoted in Association of Cinematograph, Television, and Allied Technicians (ACTT), *Patterns of Discrimination against Women in the Film and Television Industries* (London: ACTT, 1975), 37.

13. Report by the Sub-Committee of Representatives of Association of Cine-Technicians, Electrical Trades Union, National Association of Theatrical and Kine Employees, June 23, 1947 (copy in author's possession). On the continuity of film trades, see Reid, "Persistence of the Internal Labour Market," 18–19.

14. Rosten, *Hollywood*, 246.

15. Walby, *Patriarchy at Work*, 155.

16. ACTT, *Patterns of Discrimination*, 4.

17. Cited in Frances Galt, "'But it's an awfully, awfully slow process': Women and the Association of Cinematograph, Television, and Allied Technicians (ACTT), 1960–1989," unpublished PhD thesis, De Montfort University, 2018, 146.

18. This approach is made evident in the ACTT's self-authored history, *Action! Fifty Years in the Life of a Union* (London: ACTT, 1983), which makes declarations about the union's equal pay policy (67). Similar pronouncements were made in the union's journal, *The Cine-Technician*, at repeated intervals throughout the 1940s and 1950s, usually accompanying any discussion of women's work in the industry.

19. ACTT, *Patterns of Discrimination*, 14.

20. Ibid., 15.

21. Reid, "Persistence of the Internal Labour Market," 111.

22. Harper, *Women in British Cinema*, 5.

23. Harriet Bradley, "Gender and Work," in *The Sage Handbook of the Sociology of Work and Employment*, ed. Stephen Edgell, Heidi Gottfried, and Edward Granter (London: Sage, 2016), 77.

24. See Baker and Hesmondhalgh, "Sex, Gender, and Work Segregation," 23–36.

25. For further expansion, see Reid, "Persistence of the Internal Labour Market." Will Atkinson and Kevin Randle make a useful point about how much scholarship on the present-day cultural industries, including film, draws too rigid a distinction between a "stable past" and a "flexible present" when, in reality, historical working conditions were more fluid than has been widely recognized. See Will Atkinson and Kevin Randle, "Working below the Line in the Studio System: Exploring Labour Processes in the UK Film Industry, 1927–1950," University of Hertfordshire, Business School Working Papers, 2013, 18.

26. Commercial television in Britain was a closed shop—in other words, film technicians had to be ACTT members to secure work—but for those employed by the BBC, ACTT membership was optional, as the union had no negotiating rights with the BBC, a state-owned corporation. By the early 1970s, the ACTT's television branch included about fourteen hundred BBC members. See ACTT, *Patterns of Discrimination*, 34–36, for a discussion of the ACTT and the BBC.

27. For a brief discussion, see Reid, "Persistence of the Internal Labour Market," 118. Moreover, projectionists in labs and newsreels were members of ACT while those employed in cinemas belonged to NATKE.

28. To date the only surviving fragments of NATKE's records that have come to light are held at the V&A (Victoria & Albert) Theatre and Performance Collections (London), the University of Warwick, and the London Metropolitan University, but they lack the range and scope of the ACT material.

29. See Reid, "Persistence of the Internal Labour Market," 134.

30. In this category I placed audiovisual technicians at universities and roles at companies such as Thorn-EMI, mainly dating from the 1970s and 1980s onward.

31. In assessing the main business of a company, I was assisted by sources including Grace's Guide to British Industrial History (www.gracesguides.co.uk), Brian McFarlane's Encyclopedia of British Film (London: Methuen, 2003), and the library and databases of the British Film Institute.

32. As a point of contrast, four thousand applications were received from women in the film processing laboratories (representing one-quarter of laboratory applications), and close to nine thousand applications in commercial television came from women (representing around one-third of all applications in television).

33. Useful descriptions of departments, their functions, and key staff can be found in Oswell Blakeston, Working for the Films (London: Focal Press, 1947), and Elizabeth Grey, Behind the Scenes in a Film Studio (London: Phoenix House, 1967), sources I have drawn on in this research.

34. For further discussion, see Melanie Bell, Feminist Media Histories 4, no. 4 (2018): 33–56.

35. Hill, Never Done, 197–99.

36. On this point, see Gledhill and Knight, Doing Women's Film History, 4.

37. Harper, Women in British Cinema, 162–63.

38. For further information, see Harper, Women in British Cinema, and Jill Nelmes and Julie Selbo, eds., Women Screenwriters: An International Guide (Basingstoke, Hampshire: Palgrave Macmillan, 2015).

39. For a discussion of this in the Hollywood context, see Hill, Never Done, 195.

40. Harper, Women in British Cinema, 187.

41. Others jobs included in Art and Effects are the property department and wardrobe staff, represented by NATKE. The art department was one of the largest with a higher proportion of staff in NATKE.

42. Betty Pierce, "The Work of the Film Architect, No. 2. The Drawing Office," Official Architect (Oct. 1950): 573.

43. Sue Bruley, Women in Britain since 1900 (New York: St. Martin's Press, 1999), 125.

44. Harper, Women in British Cinema, 226.

45. Valerie Charlton, "The Pythons, a Jabberwocky, and Me," Village Raw, accessed June 7, 2019, https://www.villageraw.com/portfolio/the-pythons-a-jabberwocky-and-me/.

46. ACTT, Patterns of Discrimination, 37.

47. See Blakeston, *Working for the Films*, 135.

48. See Marilyn Stafford Photography, https://www.marilynstaffordphoto graphy.com, accessed Sept. 4, 2019.

49. For the purposes of this study, I included all "cross-grade technicians" (men and women) under the Camera, Sound, and Stills category on the grounds that it did give women the opportunity to undertake camera and sound roles. The increase in women's participation rates is, in part, a function of how I have classified the data, and the figures should be understood in this context. I discuss the reality of technical opportunities for women in film co-ops in more detail in chapter 6.

50. *Cartoon for Commercials*, 1957, pamphlet in possession of interviewee Pamela Masters, "Histories of Women and Work."

51. The migration wave peaked in 1966 and women outnumbered men. Carl Bridge, Robert Crawford, and David Dunstan, eds., *Australians in Britain: The Twentieth-Century Experience* (Clayton, Vic.: Monash University e-Press, 2009).

52. Australian Women's Archives Project 2014, "Anne Jolliffe," *The Encyclopedia of Women and Leadership in Twentieth-Century Australia*, accessed April 26, 2019, http://www.womenaustralia.info/leaders/biogs/WLE0417b.htm

53. See the glossary in Perkins and Stollery, *British Film Editors*, for helpful descriptions (238–40).

54. Harper, *Women in British Cinema*, 231.

55. Cited in Richard Farmer, Laura Mayne, Duncan Petrie, and Melanie Williams, *Transformation and Tradition in 1960s British Cinema* (Edinburgh: Edinburgh University Press, 2019).

56. ACTT, *Patterns of Discrimination*, 39.

57. Perkins and Stollery, *British Film Editors*, 227–28.

58. Alex Anderson, interview in Ann Ross Muir, *A Woman's Guide to Jobs in Film and Television* (London: Pandora Press, 1987), 100–104.

Chapter 2. The 1930s

1. Linda Wood, *British Films, 1927–1939* (London: BFI National Library, 2009), 137. The BFI report categorizes "features" as over seventy minutes in length.

2. A total of 295 new production companies were registered in the UK between 1925 and 1932. Margaret Dickinson and Sarah Street, *Cinema and State: The Film Industry and the British Government, 1927–84* (London: British Film Institute, 1985), 39.

3. Tim Bergfelder, Sue Harris, and Sarah Street, *Film Architecture and the Transnational Imagination: Set Design in 1930s European Cinema* (Amsterdam: Amsterdam University Press, 2007), 80.

4. Ibid., 81.

5. Ibid. Carrick's studies about working methods were published in the 1940s and built on his work in British studios from the late 1920s onward.

6. Dickinson and Street, *Cinema and State*, 40.

7. Bergfelder et al., *Film Architecture*, 81.

8. Bruley, *Women in Britain*, 68.

9. Ibid., 70.

10. Women were not permitted to work more than ten hours a day or more than six hours of overtime per week. "Factories Act 1937," accessed Jan. 29, 2018, http://www.legislation.gov.uk/ukpga/1937/67/section/73/enacted.

11. For an overview of wages for women in a range of jobs, see Juliet Gardiner, *The Thirties: An Intimate History* (London: HarperCollins, 2010), 557–59.

12. For an overview of women screenwriters during the 1930s, see Harper, *Women in British Cinema*; and Nelmes and Selbo, *Women Screenwriters*.

13. The marriage bar at the BBC lasted until 1944 although it was never uniformly employed. For a full discussion, see Kate Murphy, "A Marriage Bar of Convenience? The BBC and Married Women's Work, 1923–39," *Twentieth-Century British History* 25, no. 4 (2014): 533–61.

14. Iain Reid, "Trade Unions and the British Film Industry, 1930s–80s," in *The Routledge Companion to British Cinema History*, ed. I. Q. Hunter, Laraine Porter, and Justin Smith (Abingdon, Oxon: Routledge, 2017), 253.

15. Picturegoer Weekly, *The Picturegoer's Who's Who and Encyclopaedia of the Screen To-Day*, foreword by George Arliss (London: Odham's Press, 1933).

16. Antonia Lant, with Ingrid Periz, eds., *Red Velvet Seat: Women's Writing on the First Fifty Years of Cinema* (London: Verso, 2006), 547–682.

17. Ibid., 555.

18. Isadore Silverman, "Women behind the Screen," *Picturegoer*, May 13, 1931, 18.

19. Mary Field, "Why Women Should Make Films," *Film Weekly*, Oct. 10, 1931, 8.

20. Auriol Lee, "Women Are Needed in British Films," *Film Weekly*, Aug. 8, 1932, 7.

21. "An Elstree or Hollywood for Japan?," British Pathé, 1931, https://www.youtube.com/watch?v=ZSmkaJkuhcE; and "The Prince in Filmland," British Pathé, 1932, https://www.youtube.com/watch?v=V_dsvOFrcQw.

22. Hill, *Never Done*, 58.

23. M. Haworth-Booth, "The Place for Women in the Film Studios," *Picturegoer*, Nov. 16, 1935, 15.

24. "Clothes and the Film," *Film Weekly*, May 28, 1931, 12.

25. Harper, *Women in British Cinema*, 213. Harper claims that Zinkeisen was the only woman costume designer in the 1930s.

26. Cathleen Mann was a portrait painter of some note whose work was regularly exhibited at the Royal Academy through the 1930s. In 1926 she became, through marriage, the eleventh marchioness of Queensbury, and some of her screen credits are in this name. C. Sykes and B. Whitworth, "Mann [*married name* Follett], Cathleen Sabine [*other married name* Cathleen Sabine Douglas, marchioness of Queensberry] (1896–1959)," *Oxford Dictionary of National Biography*, Sept. 23, 2004, accessed Aug. 15, 2019, https://www.oxforddnb.com/view/10.1093/ref:odnb/9780198614128.001.0001/odnb-9780198614128-e-34852.

27. See Catherine A. Surowiec, "Anthony Mendleson, Ealing's Wardrobe Wizard," in *Ealing Revisited*, ed. Mark Duguid, Lee Freeman, Keith Johnston, and Melanie Williams (London: Palgrave Macmillan, 2012), 111–24.

28. For a detailed discussion of manufacturing and finishing in Hollywood studios, and the gender and ethnicity of the workforce, see Elizabeth Nielson, "Handmaidens of the Glamour Culture: Costumers in the Hollywood Studio System," in *Fabrications, Costume, and the Female Body*, ed. Jane Gaines and Charlotte Herzog (New York: Routledge, 1990), 160–79.

29. Adrian Brunel, *Filmcraft: The Art of Picture Production* (London: George Newnes, 1933), 59.

30. E. G. Cousins, "Eve and Her Fig Leaves," *Picturegoer*, June 27, 1931, 22, 24; "Clothes and the Film," *Film Weekly*, 12.

31. Frank Shaw, "If I Was Santa Claus at Elstree," *Picturegoer Christmas Annual, 1931* (London: Odham's Press), 55.

32. Adrian Brunel, *Film Production* (London: George Newnes, 1936), 63.

33. Brunel, *Filmcraft*, 59.

34. Gordon Conway, "Frocks for Films," *The Bioscope British Film Number 1928*, 244. See "Gordon Conway Hompage [*sic*]," *Women and Silent British Cinema*, https://womenandsilentbritishcinema.wordpress.com/the-women/gordon-conway-hompage/.

35. See Nathalie Morris, "What We'll Be Wearing in the Future (If Classic Sci-Fi Films Got It Right)," Nov. 5, 2014, accessed Feb. 7, 2018, http://www.bfi.org.uk/news-opinion/news-bfi/features/what-we-ll-wearing-future-classic-sci-fi-films.

36. Gordon Conway, "Dressing the Talkies," *Film Weekly*, Sept. 2, 1929, 7. Here Conway's approach to the relationship between costume and story is an early example of the "handmaiden to the story" orthodoxy that now characterizes practitioners' discussions of their craft. See Melanie Williams, "The Girl You Don't See: Julie Harris and the Costume Designer in British Cinema," *Feminist Media Histories* 2, no. 2 (2016): 71–106.

37. Gordon Conway, "Fashions for the Films," *Picture Show*, April 28, 1928, quoted in Raye Virginia Allen, *Gordon Conway, Fashioning a New Woman* (Austin: University of Texas Press, 1997), 121; Conway, "Frocks for Films."

38. Bergfelder et al., *Film Architecture*, 82.

39. For Conway's comments on performance, see "Frocks for Films." For the photographic qualities of fabric, see Conway, "Dressing the Talkies."

40. Conway, "Dressing the Talkies."

41. Gordon Conway 1928–29 Press Books, cited in Allen, *Gordon Conway*, 109.

42. Conway, "Dressing the Talkies."

43. Allen, *Gordon Conway*, 131–32.

44. Ibid., 110.

45. Ibid., 107.

46. Ibid., 112.

47. Ibid.

48. Ibid., 130.

49. Ibid., 265–66.

50. Cited in ibid., 152.

51. Allen makes a similar claim, arguing that Gaumont-British was "ambivalent" about Conway's vision and the place of costume design more generally in film production at this time. Allen, *Gordon Conway*, 266. Although other women designers such as Doris Zinkeisen produced several important publications about costume design, these were focused on the stage. More generally there was a lack of critical mass around film costume debates of the type that characterized art direction at this time, factors that have contributed to its absence in film scholarship.

52. Recorder, "Cine Profile of Teresa Bolland," *Cine-Technician* (Aug. 1953): 97.

53. For a detailed discussion of continuity with specific reference to those working with director David Lean, see Melanie Williams, "The Continuity Girl: Ice in the Middle of Fire," *Journal of British Cinema and Television* 10, no. 3 (2013): 603–617.

54. In comparison, there are references to male continuity supervisors in Hollywood in David Lean's private papers. See Williams, "Continuity Girl," 613.

55. Nathalie Morris, "Alma Reville," in Nelmes and Selbo, *Women Screenwriters*, 621.

56. Alison Selby-Lowndes, "Women & the ACT," *Cine-Technician* (July-Aug. 1938): 58. Selby-Lowndes herself worked in continuity, joining the union in 1936 at age twenty-three as continuity assistant for two pounds per week.

57. Martha Robinson, *Continuity Girl* (London: Robert Hale, 1937); Meg Bennett, "The Continuity Girl," in Brunel, *Film Production*, 144–47; Toni Roe, "Script Girl," *Cine-Technician* (Aug.-Oct. 1936): 48.

58. Kay Mander, "The Cutter's Fifth Column," *Cine-Technician* (Oct.–Dec. 1940): 89.

59. Roe, "Script Girl," 48.

60. Phyllis Crocker, "The Continuity Girl," in *Working for the Films*, ed. Oswell Blakeston (London: Focal Press, 1947), 147; Roe, "Script Girl," 6.

61. Crocker, "Continuity Girl," 149.

62. Mander, "Cutter's Fifth Column," 89.

63. Phyllis Crocker, cited in Williams, "Continuity Girl," 606.

64. Roe, "Script Girl," 48.

65. Skinner, interview, "Histories of Women and Work."

66. Meg Bennett, "The Continuity Girl," in Brunel, *Film Production*, 144–47.

67. Ibid.

68. Crocker, "Continuity Girl," 150.

69. Mander, "Cutter's Fifth Column," 89.

70. Angela Allen, "Did I have peas on my fork?," interview, *Script Supervisors UK*, accessed Aug. 12, 2019, http://www.scriptsupervisors.co.uk/page12.htm.

71. Research on David Lean's working partnership with his continuity girls suggests that Allen's experience may be more common than has been widely acknowledged. For a description of Lean's working relationship with his script supervisors, see Williams, "Continuity Girl." Erin Hill also records how experienced continuity girls like Peggy Robertson guided inexperienced directors away from, for example, an overreliance on panning and tracking shots. Hill, *Never Done*, 185.

72. Alma Young quoted in Hill, *Never Done*, 180.

73. See Erin Hill for a discussion of Robertson in *Never Done*, 179–81. For Reville's emotional labor on Hitchcock shoots, see Nathalie Morris, "The Early Career of Alma Reville," in *Hitchcock Annual* (New York: Columbia University Press, 2006), 1–31.

74. Bennett, "Continuity Girl," 144.

75. Skinner, interview, "Histories of Women and Work."

76. Ibid.

77. For descriptions of Tilly Day's agency, see Williams, "Continuity Girl," 608.

78. Crocker, "Continuity Girl," 148; Kay Mander, interview, Sept. 28, 1988, BECTU History Project, https://historyproject.org.uk/interview/kay-mander.

79. Phyllis Ross, "Continuity," in "'Women Talking': A Symposium on the Part Played by Women Technicians in Film Production," Kinematograph Section, Royal Photographic Society of Great Britain, 1946, 15.

80. Roe, "Script Girl," 48.

81. Ross, "Continuity," 16.

82. Alma Reville, "Cutting and Continuity," *Motion Picture News*, Jan. 13, 1923, 10.

83. An additional sixty women were employed in processing roles at Britain's leading film laboratories in the 1930s, mainly Pathé, Kays, Denham, Elstree, and Humphries, at similar wages. For further information about these women, consult the "Histories of Women and Work" database at https://learningonscreen.ac.uk/womenswork/.

84. Siân Reynolds, "The Face on the Cutting Room Floor: Women Editors in the French Cinema of the 1930s," *Labour History Review* 63, no. 1 (1998): 68.

85. Reville, "Cutting and Continuity," 10.

86. Crisp quoted in Reynolds, "Face on the Cutting Room Floor," 68.

87. Reynolds, "Face on the Cutting Room Floor, 77–78.

88. Thelma Myers, "Cutting and Editing," in "'Women Talking,'" 19.

89. Kristen Hatch, "Cutting Women: Margaret Booth and Hollywood's Pioneering Female Film Editors," *Women Film Pioneers Project,* ed. Jane Gaines, Radha Vatsal, and Monica Dall'Asta, Center for Digital Research and Scholarship, Columbia University Libraries, New York, Sept. 27, 2013, accessed Aug. 14, 2019, https://wfpp.cdrs.columbia.edu/essay/cutting-women/.

90. Reynolds, "Face on the Cutting Room Floor," 67.

91. Morris, "Early Career of Alma Reville," 3.

92. British editor Sid Cole claimed that film companies paid different rates of pay depending on the "prestige" of the film. Sidney Cole, interviews, July 9, 1987, March 14, 1987, BECTU History Project, https://historyproject.org.uk/interview/sidney-cole.

93. Roy Perkins and Martin Stollery, *British Film Editors: The Heart of the Movie* (London: BFI Publishing, 2004), 66–67.

94. Hill, *Never Done*, 193.

95. By 1946 these had mushroomed to six positions in total: supervising editor, editor, dubbing editor, assembler (first assistant), second assistant cutter, and laboratory contact.

96. Perkins and Stollery, *British Film Editors*, 67.

97. For a further discussion of editors' wages, see Rachel Low, *Filmmaking in 1930s Britain* (London: George Allen and Unwin, 1985), 31.

98. Freda Bruce Lockhart, "Lady with Scissors," *Film Weekly*, Oct. 9, 1932, 14.

99. Michael Balcon, *Michael Balcon Presents . . . A Lifetime of Films* (London: Hutchinson, 1969), 111.

100. Myers, "Cutting and Editing," 21–22.

101. Honess quoted in Perkins and Stollery, *British Film Editors*, 166. See also Harper, *Women in British Cinema*, 230. BAFTA is the British Academy of Film and Television Arts, an independent arts charity formed in 1947.

102. Mary Harvey, interview, Nov. 6, 1996, BECTU History Project, https://historyproject.org.uk/interview/mary-harvey-welford.

103. Teddy Darvas, interviews, Nov. 8, 1991, Nov. 27, 1991, Jan. 22, 1992, BECTU History Project, https://historyproject.org.uk/interview/teddy-darvas. Darvas, who went to the same school as Connell, remembered her as "a very bright student."

104. Hill, *Never Done*, 193. While Hill's example is of Paramount in the 1920s, chapter 4 examines the ongoing sexist culture of Britain's editing rooms in the 1940s, 1950s, and beyond.

105. Myers, "Cutting and Editing," 21–22.

106. Selby-Lowndes, "Women & the ACT," 58.

107. Ibid.

108. This equates to an extra 25 percent in wages for technicians working the night shift compared to their peers working day shifts. Erin Hill has shown how there was similar occupational segregation in Hollywood's laboratories, with men assigned to "stages of the process involving heavy machinery (large drying racks . . .), individual judgement (timing of exposure, negative density, and so on) and technological knowledge (developing and transfer machines)." Hill shows how as the studio system developed, and especially with the coming of sound, work in film processing was reorganized with women relegated to negative cutting as well as print assembly and examining. Hill, *Never Done, 79.*

109. Sainsbury, "Close-Ups, No. 8," 94–95.

110. This is approximately six times the pay of a domestic servant; see Bruley, *Women in Britain*, 62.

111. Sainsbury, "Close-Ups, No. 8," 95.

112. Lean quoted in Perkins and Stollery, *British Film Editors*, 66.

113. Sainsbury, "Close-Ups, No. 8," 95.

114. Alice (Queenie) Turner, interview, April 27, 1993, BECTU History Project, https://historyproject.org.uk/interview/alice-queenie-turner.

115. Ibid.

116. Edward Dmytryk quoted in Hill, *Never Done*, 190.

117. Turner, interview, BECTU History Project.

118. Margaret Thomson, interviews, Aug. 23, 1989, March 27, 1990, Jan. 18, 1996, BECTU History Project, https://historyproject.org.uk/interview/margaret-thomson.

Chapter 3. The 1940s

1. Sarah Street, *British National Cinema* (London: Routledge, 1997), 11.

2. For wartime cinema attendance figures, see ibid., 12.

3. "Conscription and Reserved Occupations," *Cine-Technician* (July-Aug. 1939): 48–49.

4. Reid, "Trade Unions and the British Film Industry," 254.

5. Association of Cinematograph, Television, and Allied Technicians (ACTT), *Action! Fifty Years in the Life of a Union* (London: Pear Publications, 1983), 21.

6. See Reid, "Trade Unions and the British Film Industry," 254.

7. Jo Fox, "To Be a Woman: Female Labour and Memory in Documentary Film Production," *Journal of British Cinema and Television* 10, no. 3 (2013): 586.

8. Bert Craik, "Make Way for Women," *Cine-Technician* (Nov.-Dec. 1942): 126.

9. Ibid.

10. Kay Mander, "For Women Technicians," *Cine-Technician* (Aug.-Sept. 1940): 72.

11. Bert Craik, "Equal Pay for Equal Work," *Cine-Technician* (July-Aug. 1946): 100–101.

12. Women remained highly visible in the laboratory workforce as negative cutters, in positive assembly, and as positive joiners.

13. Editor Freddie Wilson, cited in Perkins and Stollery, *British Film Editors*, 178.

14. Rank's ambitions were short-lived. Continuity girl and, later, producer Ann Skinner started her career in Rank's publicity department in 1955 only to find herself unemployed within a year when the department closed.

15. Also profiled were documentary director Budge Cooper, editor Thelma Myers, and Hazel Wilkinson from the Navy Film Section. The notes from the symposium were later published; see "Women Talking," 2–29.

16. A report of the event in *Kinematograph Weekly* described the topic of women in film production as "the theme of an unusual meeting" (Nov. 16, 1944, 46).

17. In this respect, the film industry was no different from any other, with Penny Summerfield finding that "[w]omen's wartime access to 'men's work' was extremely limited." Summerfield, *Reconstructing Women's Wartime Lives* (Manchester: Manchester University Press, 1998), 3.

18. James Chapman, *The British at War: Cinema, State, and Propaganda, 1939–1945* (London: I. B. Tauris, 1998), 139–40.

19. ACTT, *Action!*, 21.

20. Cartoon and diagram work demanded a larger crew (workers in paint and trace, animation, script, rostrum camera, etc.), but both forms had a much smaller workforce than features.

21. Craigie, cited in Fox, "To Be a Woman," 593. For reflections on Thomson, see "Women at Work," Studio Review, *Kinematograph Weekly*, Oct. 2, 1952, 10. The term "blue stocking" was used pejoratively to describe an intellectual woman.

22. See Lant, *Red Velvet Seat*, 563.

23. *Cine-Technician* (May-June 1943): 61. Although the motion was defeated, it did lead to a debate about the union encouraging younger members in the

production workforce to serve on the council. The difference between Thomson's and Grierson's approaches may be due to generational difference.

24. See Ros Cranston, nonfiction curator at the British Film Institute. At the time of this writing (2019), new scholarship on Jill Craigie is being undertaken by Lizzie Thynne, Yvonne Tasker, and Sadie Wearing. *Jill Craigie: Film Pioneer*, accessed June 19, 2019, https://www.jillcraigiefilmpioneer.org.

25. Mary Beales was married to documentary director Michael Orrom; Yvonne Fletcher to Paul Fletcher, managing director of the documentary unit Greenpark; and Budge Cooper to documentarian Donald Alexander. See Gledhill and Knight on how women's contribution to film production may be "obscured by more publicly visible or self-promotional male partners." Gledhill and Knight, *Doing Women's Film History*, 4.

26. For a useful biographical overview of Thomson's work, see Sarah Easen, "Margaret Thomson," in *Encyclopedia of the Documentary Film*, vol. 3, ed. Ian Aitkin (London: Routledge, 2006), 1318–19.

27. *Documentary News Letter*, vol. 6, 1943, 181.

28. "British Films Instruct New York Gardeners," report from a brochure issued in New York by the Museum of Modern Art, reproduced in *Documentary News Letter*, vol. 4, 1943, 201.

29. Thomson, interview, BECTU History Project.

30. Ibid.

31. Quoted in Patrick Russell, *Children Learning by Experience* (1947), accessed April 6, 2018, http://www.screenonline.org.uk/film/id/582557/index.html.

32. Thomson, interview, BECTU History Project.

33. Thomson credits Denis Forman with describing the film as cinema verité. Thomson, interview, BECTU History Project.

34. Ibid.

35. Marion Grierson, interview, Oct. 2, 1989, BECTU History Project, https://historyproject.org.uk/interview/marion-grierson-taylor. For letters between Grierson and Evelyn Spice (1938), see Fox, "To Be a Woman," 592.

36. Thomson, interview, BECTU History Project. Fox makes a similar point in her discussion of the "sisterly comradeship" evident in letters between Evelyn Spice and Marion Grierson in the 1930s. Fox, "To Be a Woman," 592. Documentary film culture of the interwar years was recognized for its collective/community ethos, not least because of its socialist underpinnings, but relationships between women, who have been peripheral to the history of the movement, may have been particularly acute.

37. Patrick Russell, "Who's Driving?: Peter Pickering," in *Shadows of Progress: Documentary Film in Post-War Britain*, ed. Patrick Russell and James Piers Taylor, 274–75 (London: British Film Institute, 2010).

38. Summerfield, *Reconstructing Women's Wartime Lives*, 7.

39. Beales earned screen credits for *March to Aldermaston* (1959) and *The Secret Pony* (1970).

40. Mander, interview, BECTU History Project; Grierson quoted in Fox, "To Be a Woman," 593.

41. James Chapman, *The British at War: Cinema, State, and Propaganda, 1939–45* (London: I. B. Tauris, 1998), 140.

42. For discussion of the AFPU, see Chapman, *British at War*; Kay Gladstone, "The AFPU—The Origins of the British Army Combat Film," *Film History* 14, nos. 3/4 (2002): 316–31; and Keith Buckman, "The Royal Air Force Film Production Unit, 1941–45," *Historical Journal of Film, Radio, and Television* 17, no. 2 (2006): 219–44.

43. "Naval Film Unit," *Documentary News Letter*, Aug. 1941, 154.

44. Wilkinson, "Women Talking," 26.

45. Ibid., 27.

46. While Wilkinson's account focuses on the navy, she estimates that women in the other service film units "are doing jobs very similar to ours," and there is some corroborating evidence for this statement. In Buckman's research on the Royal Air Force Film Unit, he quotes cinematographer Christopher Challis's recollection that in a roll call of the unit's staff conducted in January 1942, eight of the unit's twenty-three staff were "airmen and *airwomen* cutters, typists, drivers and a photographer." Buckman, "Royal Air Force Film Production Unit," 221; emphasis added.

47. Roly Stafford, oral history interview no. 22094, Imperial War Museum Collections, https://www.iwm.org.uk/collections/item/object/80020604.

48. Wilkinson, "Women Talking," 23.

49. Joe Mendoza, "Me and Mulberry": Royal Naval Instructional Film Unit, June 7, 2004, accessed April 13, 2018, http://www.bbc.co.uk/history/ww2peopleswar/stories/37/a2717237.shtml.

50. Wilkinson, "Women Talking," 26.

51. Rebecca Harrison, "The Coming of the Projectionettes: Women's Work in Film Projection and Changing Modes of Spectatorship in World War II British Cinemas," *Feminist Media Histories* 2, no. 2 (2016): 47–70.

52. Wilkinson, "Women Talking," 27.

53. Ibid., 25; Richard Wallace, Rebecca Harrison, and Charlotte Brunsdon, "Women in the Box: Female Projectionists in Post-War British Cinemas," *Journal of British Cinema and Television* 15, no. 1 (2018): 46–65.

54. For further discussion, see Laurie Ede, "Art in Context: British Film Design of the 1940s," in *The New Film History*, ed. James Chapman, Mark Glancy, and Sue Harper (Basingstoke, Hampshire: Palgrave Macmillan, 2007), 73–88.

55. Carmen Dillon, interviews, June 23, 1993, May 6, 1994, Sept. 30, 1994, BECTU History Project, https://historyproject.org.uk/interview/carmen-dillon.

56. Lehmann had an established reputation in British visual culture as an artist and illustrator.

57. Carmen Dillon, interview in Brian McFarlane, *An Autobiography of British Cinema* (London: Methuen, 1997), 177.

58. Betty Pierce, "The Work of the Film Architect, No. 4. Decoration, Furnishing, and Trick Effects," *Official Architect*, Dec. 1950, 697.

59. Copies of *Official Architect* are held in the library of the Royal Institute of British Architects (London). Interviews with Peggy Gick are available through the BECTU History Project website.

60. Betty Pierce, "The Work of the Film Architect, No. 2. The Drawing Office," *Official Architect*, Oct. 1950, 573.

61. Ibid., 574.

62. Ibid., 573.

63. Laurie N. Ede, "Conversations with Edward Carrick," *Journal of British Cinema and Television* 2, no. 1 (2005): 133.

64. Peggy Gick, interview, April 22, 1997, BECTU History Project, https://historyproject.org.uk/interview/peggy-gick.

65. Ian Dalrymple, "The Crown Film Unit, 1940–43," in *Propaganda, Politics, and Film, 1918–45*, ed. N. Pronay and D. W. Spring (London: Macmillan, 1982), 216.

66. Gick, interview, BECTU History Project.

67. Ibid.

68. Ibid.

69. Catherine de la Roche, "The Stars Behind the Camera: Carmen Dillon," *Picturegoer*, July 16, 1949, 14.

70. Dillon, interview, BECTU History Project.

71. Carrick, quoted in Ede, "Art in Context," 78.

72. Lynne Walker, ed., *Women Architects: Their Work* (London: Sorella Press, 1984), 19.

73. Gick, interview, BECTU History Project.

74. There are references to illustrations by Gick appearing in "The Builder" in 1943 and 1950, but I have been unable to trace these through the library of the Royal Institute of British Architects.

75. Bert Craik, "Equal Pay for Equal Work," *Cine-Technician* (July–Aug. 1946): 100–101.

Chapter 4. The 1950s

1. Sue Harper and Vincent Porter, *British Cinema of the 1950s* (Oxford: Oxford University Press, 2003), 37.

2. Street, *British National Cinema*, 15–17.

3. ACTT, *Action!*, 161.

4. Steve Chibnall and Brian McFarlane, *The British "B" Film* (London: Palgrave Macmillan, 2009), 42.

5. This demand continued until the end of the 1950s, with British and American companies battling it out through the decade to produce "B" features to meet the supporting-program quota. See Chibnall and McFarlane, *British "B" Film*, 20–59.

6. Harper and Porter, *British Cinema*, 244.

7. Reid, "Persistence of the Internal Labour Market," 118–20.

8. Teresa Bolland, Cine Profile by "Recorder," *Cine-Technician* (Aug. 1953): 97.

9. Peggy Anderson, "The Strange Life of a Production Secretary," *Cine-Technician* (Dec. 1953): 162–63.

10. See editor Helga Cranston's assertion that "as a member of A.C.T., . . . the question of differentiation between the work of men and women is unheard of,"

comments that demonstrate the official position of the union on women's work. "Women in Conference," *Cine-Technician* (July 1954): 138.

11. Jane Lewis, *Women in Britain since 1945* (Oxford: Blackwell, 1992), 73.

12. Claire Langhamer, "Feelings, Women, and Work in the Long 1950s," *Women's History Review* 26, no. 1 (2017): 77–92.

13. Bruley, *Women in Britain*, 123.

14. "A.C.T. News," compiled by "Middy," *Cine-Technician* (July-Aug. 1952): 90.

15. For marriage patterns in 1950s Britain, see Bruley, *Women in Britain*, 131.

16. See Viola Klein, *Britain's Married Women Workers* (London: Routledge and Kegan Paul, 1965). 15.

17. For a discussion of secretaries in the British context, see Gillian Murray, "Taking Work Home: The Private Secretary and Domestic Identities in the Long 1950s," *Women's History Review* 26, no. 1 (2017): 62–76.

18. See the "Secretaries Conference at PERA," news item, broadcast on Midland Regional news, discussed in Murray, "Taking Work Home," 69.

19. David C. Cousland, "The Production Manager," in *Working for the Films*, ed. Oswell Blakeston (London: Focal Press, 1947), 69–70.

20. Ibid., 70, 73.

21. Skinner, interview, "Histories of Women and Work."

22. Ibid.

23. Sheila Collins, interview, Oct. 20, 1987, BECTU History Project, https://historyproject.org.uk/interview/sheila-collins.

24. Ibid.

25. Bolland, Cine Profile by "Recorder."

26. Hill, *Never Done*, 136.

27. Kevin Brownlow, *David Lean: A Biography* (London: Faber and Faber, 1997), 364.

28. Ibid., 361, 326.

29. Skinner, interview, "Histories of Women and Work."

30. Darvas, interview, BECTU History Project. That Darvas remembers these acts of kindness so acutely suggests the importance they played in his professional life, not only helping him secure work in a rapidly freelancing economy but also saving him from some of the humiliations that came through unemployment, perhaps more keenly felt for men, who were expected to be breadwinners.

31. Brownlow, *David Lean*, 314.

32. Pamela Mann-Francis, interview, Jan. 6, 1994, BECTU History Project, https://historyproject.org.uk/interview/pamela-mann-francis-nee-mann.

33. Ibid.

34. See Skinner, interview, "Histories of Women and Work."

35. Hill, *Never Done*, 162.

36. Oral history does not reveal what Mann-Francis felt at the time, only how she later framed the experience. Langhamer found a similar structure of feeling in her research on women who worked as secretaries in the 1950s. As these women recalled the emotional labor they had undertaken in the execution of

their professional role, what came through in their life writing was "an underlying anger sublimated at the time but emerging over subsequent years." Claire Langhammer, "Feelings, Women, and Work in the Long 1950s," *Women's History Review* 26, no. 1 (2017): 87.

37. Steve Chibnall, "Banging the Gong: The Promotional Strategies of Britain's J. Arthur Rank Organisation in the 1950s," *Historical Journal of Film, Radio, and Television* 37, no. 2 (2017): 245–46. Entries in trade publications such as *The British Film and Television Year Book, 1955–56*, ed. Peter Noble, bear witness to women's presence as publicity directors, including Mary Dipper at Romulus Films, Jacqueline Ward at Wilcox-Neagle Productions, and Susan Storer at Charter Films, a company led by brothers John and Roy Boulting.

38. John B. Myers, "Film Publicist," in Blakeston, *Working for the Films*, 182.

39. Skinner, interview, "Histories of Women and Work."

40. Myers, "Film Publicist," 183.

41. Jez Stewart, "Staff Snapshot—1946: Part 1," accessed June 26, 2018, http://halasbatchelor75.co.uk/staff-snapshot-1946-1/. URL unavailable as of Nov. 2, 2020, but see *Great Women Animators*, compiled by Skye Lobell, accessed Nov. 2, 2020, http://greatwomenanimators.com/category/1940s-animation/.

42. As an example of the central position that women animators occupied at the studio, eleven of the eighteen animators who worked on the instructional film *Handling Ships* (1945) were women.

43. *A Moving Image, Joy Batchelor 1914–91: Artist, Writer, and Animator* (London: Southbank Publishing, 2014).

44. *Cartoon for Commercials*, 1957, pamphlet in possession of interviewee Pamela Masters, "Histories of Women and Work."

45. Kirsten Thompson, "'Quick—Like a Bunny!' The Ink and Paint Machine, Female Labor, and Color Production," *Journal of Animation Studies*, Feb. 3, 2014, accessed July 20, 2018, https://journal.animationstudies.org/kirsten-thompson-quick-like-a-bunny/.

46. See Daisy Yan Du, "Socialism and the Rise of the First Camerawoman in the History of Chinese Animation," animationstudies 2.0 (blog.animationstudies.org), accessed Oct. 10, 2017; Ruth Richards, "The Women of Studio Ghibli," animationstudies 2.0 (blog.animationstudies.org), accessed Oct. 23, 2017; Diane Wei Lewis, "Shirage and Women's Flexible Labor in the Japanese Animation Industry," *Feminist Media Histories* 4, no. 1 (2018): 115–41.

47. Mindy Johnson, *Ink and Paint: The Women of Walt Disney* (New York: Hyperion, 2017), 13.

48. Hill, *Never Done*, 81.

49. Johnson, *Ink and Paint*, 13.

50. Jill Clark, interview by son Christopher Clark, May 19, 2014, personal copy in author's possession.

51. Ibid.

52. Thompson, "'Quick—Like a Bunny!'"

53. Ibid.

54. Clark, interview.

55. Masters, interview, "Histories of Women and Work."

56. Quoted in Thompson, "'Quick—Like a Bunny!'"

57. Disney ran paint application classes at its studios and published evaluation criteria for its painters. Johnson, *Ink and Paint*, 102.

58. Ibid.

59. Masters, interview, "Histories of Women and Work."

60. Clare Kitson, "A Woman's Place," in *Moving Image*, 27.

61. Masters, interview, "Histories of Women and Work."

62. In Clare Kitson's account, all of the women had been to art school but many of the men had not. Kitson, "Woman's Place," 27.

63. Ibid.

64. Jez Stewart, "The Mystery of the Disappearing Women," accessed June 26, 2018, http://halasbatchelor75.co.uk/where-did-they-go/. URL unavailable as of Nov. 2, 2020, but see *Great Women Animators*, compiled by Skye Lobell, accessed Nov. 2, 2020, http://greatwomenanimators.com/category/1950s-animation/.

65. Kitson, "Woman's Place," 26.

66. Freddie Wilson, "A Museum of Recollection," *Guild of British Film Editors Journal*, no. 53, 1979; cited in Perkins and Stollery, *British Film Editors*, 178.

67. Perkins and Stollery, *British Film Editors*, 178. The Archers production company was a partnership between Michael Powell and Emeric Pressburger.

68. Ibid., 179.

69. Ibid., 178.

70. For a discussion of women editors and feature filmmaking, see Harper, *Women in British Cinema*.

71. Kitty Marshall, interview, Feb. 1, 1988, BECTU History Project, https://historyproject.org.uk/interview/kitty-marshall-hermges.

72. Kitty Wood, interview, June 9, 1987, BECTU History Project, https://historyproject.org.uk/interview/kitty-wood-morrison.

73. Monica Mead, interview, "Histories of Women and Work."

74. Lusia Krakowska, interview, Jan. 23, 1998, BECTU History Project, https://historyproject.org.uk/interview/lusia-krakowska-mrs-arendt.

75. While working freelance also characterized men's experiences in the industry, the opportunities available were highly gendered, with men having access to a greater number of positions, including camera, sound, and lighting, that were closed to women.

76. Wood, interview, BECTU History Project.

77. Russell and Taylor, *Shadows of Progress*, 80–81.

78. Marshall, interview, BECTU History Project.

79. Ibid.

80. Mead, interview, "Histories of Women and Work."

81. Marshall, interview, BECTU History Project.

82. Wood, interview, BECTU History Project.

83. Mead, interview, "Histories of Women and Work."

84. Ibid.; Coates quoted in Ann Ross Muir, *A Woman's Guide to Jobs in Film and Television* (London: Pandora Press, 1987), 107.

85. Krakowska, interview, BECTU History Project.

86. Michael Brooke, "Sunday by the Sea," BFI Screenonline, accessed July 22, 2019, http://www.screenonline.org.uk/film/id/1379437/index.html.

87. Krakowska, interview, BECTU History Project.

88. Wood, interview, BECTU History Project.

89. Mead, interview, "Histories of Women and Work."

90. Ibid. Mead later qualified that this was "too broad an answer."

91. Krakowska, interview, BECTU History Project. Mead probably benefited professionally by being married to a cameraman.

92. In addition to the more than forty women joining the union as editors in the 1950s were one hundred women who joined in assistant editor or trainee roles. For further information about these women, consult the "Histories of Women and Work" database at https://learningonscreen.ac.uk/womenswork/.

Chapter 5. The 1960s

1. Mark Banks and Kate Oakley, "UK Art Workers, Class and the Myth of Mobility," in *The Routledge Companion to Labor and Media*, ed. Richard Maxwell (New York: Routledge, 2006), 170–79.

2. See Richard Farmer, Laura Mayne, Duncan Petrie, and Melanie Williams, *Transformation and Tradition in 1960s British Cinema* (Edinburgh: Edinburgh University Press, 2019).

3. Sue Harper and Vincent Porter, *British Cinema of the 1950s: The Decline of Deference* (Oxford: Oxford University Press, 2003), 244.

4. Margaret Dickinson and Sarah Street, *Cinema and State: The Film Industry and the British Government, 1927–84* (London: BFI, 1985), 227.

5. Ibid., 233.

6. Sarah Street, *British National Cinema* (Abingdon, Oxon: Routledge, 1997), 20–21.

7. Reid, "Persistence of the Internal Labour Market," 127.

8. ACTT, *Patterns of Discrimination*, 36.

9. Harper, *Women in British Cinema*, 102.

10. Pamela Power, interview, "Histories of Women and Work."

11. *Film Fanfare*, nos. 2 & 3 (1956), accessed Oct. 2, 2018, https://www.british pathe.com/video/film-fanfare-no-2-3/query/film+fanfare+no+2.

12. Julie Harris, "Costume Designing," *Films and Filming*, Nov. 1957, 17.

13. Langley Moore had done much to bring costume to the attention of the general public through a six-part series she wrote and presented for the BBC in 1957 titled "Men, Women, and Clothes."

14. Shirley Russell obituary, *Daily Telegraph*, March 13, 2002.

15. See "Dressing Up Lawrence," *Evening Standard*, Nov. 12, 1969; "Mrs. Ken Russell," *Sunday Times*, Dec. 12, 1971; Gordon Gow, "Them and Us," interview with Shirley Russell, *Films and Filming*, Oct. 1977, 14.

16. Jocelyn Rickards, *The Painted Banquet: My Life and Loves* (London: Weidenfeld and Nicolson, 1987), 58; Russell in Gow, "Them and Us," 15.

17. Angela Neustatter, "Whip Hand," *Guardian*, July 20, 1977, 9.

18. Ibid.

19. Hill, *Never Done*, 130.

20. Russell quoted in Gow, "Them and Us," 15.

21. Rickards, *Painted Banquet*, 89; Phyllis Dalton, interview transcript, Feb. 11, 2000, BECTU History Project, https://historyproject.org.uk/interview/phyllis -dalton, 27.

22. Dalton, interview, BECTU History Project.

23. Russell quoted in Gow, "Them and Us," 13.

24. NATKE was the National Association of Theatrical and Kine Employees, the union representing cinema staff (projectionists and others). Wardrobe and the property department came under NATKE's remit because these roles had links with theater.

25. ACT interunion agreement, 1947.

26. John Farleigh, "Dressed for the Part," *Picturegoer*, Dec. 9, 1950, 17. Murray worked for thirty years in the British film industry; her screen credits include *The African Queen* (1951), *The Prince and the Showgirl* (1957), *This Sporting Life* (1963), and the "Carry On" franchise (a series of thirty-one comedies, all with titles beginning with the words "Carry On.").

27. "Costume Design: A Definition," Sept. 16, 1981, ACTT Archive, Clapham, London, box III/file no. 87, "Art Department 1983." The very fact that some designers were driven to make this statement highlights how film producers in the 1980s were beginning to recruit wardrobe personnel, on lower wages, to costume their films.

28. The British Film Institute also holds the Robert and Barbara Clark Collection. Wardrobe mistress Barbara Clark (who also earned screen credits as Cecilia Gray) was active in the film industry between 1950 and the 1970s, although much of the collection relates to her husband, makeup artist Bob Clark, rather than her working practices.

29. Jo Botting, "From Sinatra to *Rollerball*," interview with Julie Harris, National Film Theatre, 2002, accessed Oct. 5, 2018, http://old.bfi.org.uk/features/interviews /harris.html.

30. Ibid.

31. Jane Hamilton, interview, "Histories of Women and Work."

32. Dalton, interview, BECTU History Project.

33. Ibid.

34. Ibid. Here Dalton is recalling Adamson's work on *The Message* (1976).

35. Nielson, "Handmaidens of the Glamour Culture," 170–71.

36. Dalton, interview, BECTU History Project.

37. Ibid.

38. Nielsen, "Handmaidens of the Glamour Culture," 166–67. See also Hill, *Never Done*, 77.

39. Rosemary Burrows, interview by Matthew Sweet, *The Film Programme*, BBC Radio 4, Aug. 27, 2010, accessed Nov. 19, 2018, https://www.bbc.co.uk/sounds/play/bootgx3t.

40. Ibid.

41. Ibid.

42. Burrows now specializes in wardrobe for epics, most recently *Gladiator* (2000) and *Alexander* (2004).

43. Russell quoted in Gow, "Them and Us," 16.

44. Kirsty Sinclair Dootson, "'The Hollywood Powder Puff War': Technicolor Cosmetics in the 1930s," *Film History* 28, no. 1 (2016): 122.

45. Hill, *Never Done* (68). See also Lant, *Red Velvet Seat*, for hairdressing being listed in industry how-to manuals as one of the most popular jobs for women by the late 1920s (55).

46. Harry Davo, "The Art of Make-Up," *Cine-Technician* (May 1935): 12; *The Picturegoer*, 1936, 58.

47. See Robert and Barbara Clark Collection, British Film Institute; Walter Schneiderman, interview, Feb. 19, 2013, BECTU History Project, accessed Nov. 16, 2018, https://historyproject.org.uk/interview/walter-schneiderman. Schneiderman worked at many of the British studios during his long career and also worked with leading Hollywood stars including Bette Davis, Kirk Douglas, and Denzel Washington.

48. Skill Set Film Production Workforce Survey, 2008, https://www.screenskills.com/media/1412/creative_media_workforce_survey_report_2008.pdf.

49. Schneiderman, interview, BECTU History Project.

50. See Linda de Vetta, interview, "Histories of Women and Work."

51. Peggy Rignold, interview, May 29, 1995, BECTU History Project, https://historyproject.org.uk/interview/peggy-hyde-chambers-nee-rignold.

52. Christine Allsop, interview with her mother, Connie Reeve, Oct. 2015 (personal correspondence with the author).

53. Ibid.

54. Jean Steward, interview, "Histories of Women and Work."

55. Ibid.

56. Linda de Vetta, interview, "Histories of Women and Work."

57. Ibid.

58. Allsop, personal correspondence with author. "Television girls" is an oft-repeated phrase in interviews with women, suggesting that women makeup artists could not be separated from their gender in discussions about their labor.

59. Mary Hillman, interview, April 12, 2011, BECTU History Project, https://historyproject.org.uk/interview/mary-hillman. That Hillman was visibly upset recalling the incident suggests the level of ill feeling that was directed toward her and her team at the time. NATKE's president supported her because her appointment was legitimate; she was a member in good standing with the union and had previously worked with Alan Parker and the film's producer, Alan Marshall.

60. Ibid.

61. However, de Vetta would claim that her proudest professional achievement was aging Jeremy Irons from eighteen to eighty in *The House of the Spirits* (1993).

62. Linda de Vetta, personal collection. De Vetta and her makeup box were sufficiently eye-catching to warrant studio photography, although how widely circulated the image was is unknown.

63. Linda de Vetta, interview, "Histories of Women and Work."

64. Ibid.

65. Bowie Films was headed by Les Bowie, who had worked as a scenic artist in British studios since the 1940s. He started his own company in 1950, which created miniatures, mechanical devices, trick photography, and matte paintings, and was best known for its work on Hammer films, starting with *The Quatermass Experiment* (1955) and including *One Million Years BC* (1966). McFarlane, *Encyclopedia of British Film*, 76.

66. ACTT, *Action!*, 129.

67. An additional three women puppeteers were recruited at other, smaller companies.

68. Mary Turner, interview with Richard Farrell, *Andersonic* 19, no. 0 (2015): 6.

69. Ibid., 9.

70. Cuff was a talented painter; her work earned a place at the Summer Exhibition of the Royal Academy in 1967, and she was offered an exhibition at the Paris Salon, which she turned down because she was working on Kubrick's *2001*. Her father knew costume and set designer Olga Lehmann and had worked on early television commercials, giving him connections with Shepperton Studios. See Joy Cuff, interview, "Histories of Women and Work."

71. She would later work with Bob Cuff on the matte paintings for *Adventures of Baron Munchausen* (1988) and *Erik the Viking* (1989), creating fantastical worlds of imagination.

72. Cuff, interview, "Histories of Women and Work."

73. Ibid.

74. David Hughes, *The Complete Kubrick* (Penguin: Random House, 2001), Kindle edition.

75. Cuff, interview, "Histories of Women and Work."

76. Ibid.

77. Ibid.

78. Ibid.

79. Why Kubrick should agree to this is unknown and Cuff does not speculate. It may well be that the cost of the extra hires was small compared to the overall budget, and Kubrick was keen to retain the skills of not only Cuff but her colleague Bob Cuff as well.

80. Cuff, interview, "Histories of Women and Work."

81. Ibid. See also John Caldwell on the "dragon-lady style toughness" as a recurring trope in descriptions of women in powerful roles. John Caldwell, *Production Culture* (Durham, NC: Duke University Press, 2008), 54.

82. See Harper, *Women in British Cinema*, 191. For an interview with Young on her experience of the British film industry, see "The Young and the Restless Dead," *Fangoria*, no. 144, July 1995, where she explains, "I was just cross much of the time . . . when I didn't get a job because I was a woman."

83. Cuff, interview "Histories of Women and Work."

84. Alison Payne, "'It hit us like a whirlwind': The Impact of Commercial Television Advertising in Britain, 1954–1964," unpublished PhD thesis, Birkbeck College, University of London (2016).

85. Cited in ibid., 207. The ACTT union later acknowledged the important role that the commercials sector played in keeping technicians in work, saying it was "one of the largest consistent employers of film production resources" and alongside television documentaries "sustained the industry in volume of work." See ACTT, *Action!*, 117.

86. Pamela Power, interview, "Histories of Women and Work."

87. Wood, interview, BECTU History Project.

88. Gick, interview BECTU History Project.

89. Ibid.

90. Ibid.

91. Mann-Francis, interview, BECTU History Project. Interviewer Alan Lawson's comments are revealing: "I thought you just stopped [filmmaking]," implicitly meaning feature filmmaking, but Mann-Francis saw commercials as an important part of her professional life.

92. Mann-Francis, interview, BECTU History Project.

93. Payne, "Impact of Commercial Television," 214.

94. Ibid. There are few extant sources beyond trade publications to explore this further.

95. Power, interview, "Histories of Women and Work." For the history of the common uptake of this equipment in Britain, see Perkins and Stollery, *British Film Editors*, 146, 164.

96. Power, interview, "Histories of Women and Work."

97. Ibid.

98. Ibid.

99. Ibid.

100. On the issue of women's financial independence, matte artist Joy Cuff makes a similar point about the challenges she faced obtaining a mortgage for her house in the 1960s, despite earning more than her husband at the time. For further accounts, see Arthur McIvor, *Working Lives: Work in Britain since 1945* (Basingstoke, Hampshire: Palgrave Macmillan, 2013), 97.

Chapter 6. The 1970s and 1980s

1. Street, *British National Cinema*, 20.

2. Ibid., 21.

3. Cited in Galt, "Women and the ACTT," 137.

4. Ibid.

5. Advertisements promoting the event were run in *Film and Television Technician* in November 1974.

6. Similar events were run in subsequent years with the National Film School launching a suite of short training courses in the early 1980s, including "Film Familiarisation Course for Ethnic Minorities and Women." For a full discussion, see Galt, "Women and the ACTT," 227.

7. Templeman quoted in Theresa Fitzgerald, "Now About These Women," *Sight and Sound* 58, no. 3 (1986): 191–94. In 1972 Myles, along with Laura Mulvey and Claire Johnston, co-programmed the "Women's Event" at the Edinburgh Film Festival, the first festival in the UK and Europe to focus entirely on the work of women filmmakers. See Katherine Kamleitner, "Closing the Gaps: Researching the Women's Event at the Edinburgh International Film Festival 1972," March 27, 2018, accessed Dec. 10, 2018, https://womensfilmandtelevisionhistory .wordpress.com/2018/03/27/closing-the-gaps-researching-the-womens-event-at -the-edinburgh-international-film-festival-1972/; Lynda Myles, conversation with the author, Dec. 6, 2018.

8. John Cook, "Channel 4 and British Cinema," in McFarlane, *Encyclopedia of British Film*, 113–14.

9. Moya Burns quoted in, "Women in Focus," *In Camera* (Spring 1992): 4; Melanie Chait, interview in Anne Ross Muir, *A Woman's Guide to Jobs in Film and Television* (London: Pandora Press, 1987), 290.

10. The union was also subjected to an inquiry by the Monopolies and Mergers Commission in 1988, which was critical of its "closed shop" policy. The union not only responded by softening its entry criteria but also actively looked to increase its membership base this decade to ensure its survival.

11. See Una Moles, "Danger! Women at Work," *Film Base News*, Feb./March 1943, 16–17; Flora Gregory, "Jobs for the Girls," *AIP & Co*, Jan.–Feb. 1986): 24–28.

12. Sarah Benton, interview, cited in Galt, "Women and the ACTT," 179–80.

13. Diane Tammes, interview, Aug. 19, 2008, BECTU History Project, https:// historyproject.org.uk/interview/diane-tammes.

14. Ibid. Such beliefs were reported as common in the industry at this time. The researchers who compiled the *Patterns* report (1975) referred to this as the "woman driver syndrome"—in other words, the belief that women cannot "get on" with machinery. *Patterns*, 9.

15. Cited in Galt, "Women and the ACTT," 163.

16. Fitzgerald, "Now About These Women," 192. Parsons's fellow recruits included Conny Templeman (director), Jenni (Jennifer) Howarth (writer), and Toni de Bromhead (documentarian).

17. Parsons, in Fitzgerald, "Now About These Women," 193.

18. Parsons quoted in "Women in Focus," 5.

19. "Alex and Chyna," *British Cinematographer* 20 (2004): 37.

20. Ibid.

21. "Women in Film," *Eyepiece* 14, no. 1 (1993): 11.

22. Campbell quoted in Muir, *Woman's Guide*, 119.

23. Tammes, interview, BECTU History Project.

24. ACTT, *Patterns of Discrimination*, 37.

25. Reid, "Persistence of the Internal Labour Market," 183.

26. "Women in Film," *Eyepiece*, 11.

27. Catherine Coulson quoted in Burns, "Women in Focus," 19.

28. Genevieve Davies cited in Gregory, "Jobs for the Girls," 26.

29. "Rising to the Challenge: An Interview with Sue Gibson," *Exposure*, Spring 1998: 10.

30. Susan Jacobson, "Clapper Loader," in Barbara Baker, ed., *Let the Credits Roll: Interviews with Film Crew* (London: Aston House Press, 2005), 137.

31. Gibson interview in Dominic Timms, "A Woman's Place," *Televisual*, May 1997, 27; Davies quoted in Gregory, "Jobs for the Girls," 26.

32. Gibson quoted in Timms, "A Woman's Place," 28.

33. Campbell quoted in "Women in Focus," 17.

34. Gibson quoted in "Women in Film," 10.

35. Martha M. Lauzen, "Where Are the Film Directors (Who Happen to Be Women)?," *Quarterly Review of Film and Video* 29, no. 4 (2012): 311.

36. *Film and Television Technician*, Feb. 1983, 5.

37. Terry Wragg from Leeds Animation Workshop had a similar experience when she attended union meetings in the 1980s, describing it as "a closed shop, absolute power . . . a boys' club with a few token women." Yvonne Tasker, "An Interview with Terry Wragg on the Work of the Leeds Animation Workshop," *Feminist Media Histories* 2, no. 2 (2016): 122–32. Wragg and other women do acknowledge the importance of key men like Roy Lockett who were instrumental in getting accreditation for the workshops.

38. Nuala Campbell quoted in Muir, *Woman's Guide*, 119. Grips are responsible for moving and installing camera equipment on the shoot.

39. Burns, "Women in Focus," 4.

40. Ibid.

41. Penny Eyles, interview, "Histories of Women and Work."

42. Cited in Reid, "Persistence of the Internal Labour Market," 183.

43. Dominic Timms, 'A Woman's Place', *Televisual*, May 1997, 27–28.

44. Duncan Petrie, *The British Cinematographer* (London: BFI. 1996), 3.

45. See "Seven Questions with Marleen Gorris, Director of Mrs. Dalloway," *IndieWire*, Feb. 23, 1998, accessed Nov. 26, 2018, https://www.indiewire.com/1998/02/seven-question-with-marleen-gorris-director-of-mrs-dalloway-83082/.

46. Gibson quoted in Timms, "A Woman's Place," 27; "Women in Film," 10.

47. Gibson quoted in Timms, "A Woman's Place," 27.

48. Ibid.

49. Ibid., 4.

50. Ibid.

51. Martha M. Lauzen, "Kathryn Bigelow: On Her Own in No-(Wo)Man's Land," *Camera Obscura* 26, no. 3 (78) (2011): 147.

52. Interviews with Gibson also demonstrate the feminine and masculine duality that Lauzen finds in interviews with Bigelow. For example, Gibson is described as a "tough operator" who likes control and has a singular vision, a masculine edge that is softened by references to the interview taking place while she relaxes in her "lovely north Dorset home." (see Gibson, in "Rising to the Challenge" and in Timms, "A Woman's Place," and *Exposure*).

53. Campbell quoted in Muir, *Woman's Guide*, 119–20.

54. Chait quoted in Muir, *Woman's Guide*, 291–92.

55. "Alex and Chyna," 37.

56. "Rising to the Challenge," 11; and Timms, "A Woman's Place," 20.

57. Parsons quoted in Muir, *Woman's Guide*, 53; Tammes quoted in Muir, *Woman's Guide*, 56.

58. Galt, "Women and the ACTT," 164.

59. This is not to claim that Billie Williams's cinematography isn't noteworthy, but rather that a cinematographer who happened to be a woman would not as readily been offered the job.

60. Campbell quoted in Muir, *Woman's Guide*, 120.

61. Margaret Dickinson, "Workshop Movement," in McFarlane, *Encyclopedia of British Film*, 743.

62. There is evidence that this is beginning to change. At the time of press, doctoral research is beginning to examine women in the workshop movement and their connections with female-led film collectives.

63. Gopaul quoted in Margaret Dickinson, ed., *Rogue Reels: Oppositional Film in Britain, 1945–90* (London: BFI, 1999), 308; Elaine Drainville, interview, History of Women in Film and Television.

64. Amber had a "defined membership, a structure and agreed policies on pay and working methods," while the "formal structure and patterns of work" of the Black Audio Film Collective are more those of a cooperative than a collective. For an overview, see Dickinson, *Rogue Reels*, 207.

65. Dickinson, *Rogue Reels*, 205.

66. Ibid., 315.

67. Ibid.

68. Martin quoted in *Rogue Reels*, 252.

69. Leeds Animation Workshop had to contend with a male artist who created storyboards that reproduced gender stereotypes, depicting a male character being served tea by a female character in a frilly apron. In Wragg's account this created a split in the group, as the male artist insisted the image was funny rather than derogatory, a situation that was resolved only when the artist left and formed another company. See Wragg's interview with Tasker in *Feminist Media Histories*, 127.

70. Muir, *Woman's Guide*, 309. "The Women's Unit" was comprised of Sarah Noble and Cassandra McGrogan, with Noble making *Site One: Holy Loch* (1985) and McGrogan *Your Health's Your Wealth* (1990). Noble died in 1987. For a wider discussion of the work of the Edinburgh Film Workshop, see Robin MacPherson,

"Radical and Engaged Cinema," in *Directory of World Cinema: Scotland*, ed. Bob Nowlan and Xach Finch (Bristol, UK: Intellect, 2015), 31–45.

71. Murray Martin interviewed by Margaret Dickinson in Dickinson, *Rogue Reels*, 247–62.

72. Ibid.

73. Gillian Lacey quoted in Jayne Pilling, ed., *Women and Animation: A Compendium* (London: BFI, 1992), 36.

74. Terry Wragg, interview, "Histories of Women and Work."

75. Ibid.

76. Ibid.

77. The precedent of an all-female crew was supported by the ACTT union—one response to years of criticism regarding the limited opportunities for women in film—under a special agreement between the ACTT and the funders of the BFI. The film was made under workshop conditions, with all members of the crew paid thirty pounds per day, including actress Julie Christie, at the time a leading British star. See Sally Potter in conversation with Sheila Johnston, "Like Night and Day," *Monthly Film Bulletin*, May 1984, 141.

78. Elaine Drainville, interview, "Histories of Women and Work."

79. Antonia Lant, "Women's Independent Cinema: The Case of Leeds Animation Workshop," in *Fires Were Started: British Cinema and Thatcherism*, 2nd ed., ed. Lester D. Friedman (London: Wallflower, 2006), 179.

80. Joan Goodman, "Woman's Point of Contact, *The Times*, Jan. 13, 1983.

81. Marcel Berlins, 'Digging for Real Gold in the Hills, *The Times*, May 7, 1984.

82. Ibid.

83. Ibid.

84. Elaine Drainville, interview, "Histories of Women and Work." Rushton was a leading voice in sound recording; see "Mic "'em Up," *Black Filmmaker* 3, no. 9 (2000): 9.

85. Drainville also makes the point that an all-female crew was not a given but had to be argued for with the union. Chait, she said, was "very determined" to push it through, arguing that a film about lesbians should be made by women. *Veronica* and *Gold Diggers* do seem to have set a precedent, and a small number of films (educational documentaries and fictional shorts) began to appear in the following years, including *Cue for Change* (1986, dir. Margaret Dickinson, ACT Films), which was intended to encourage schoolgirls into nontraditional roles in the television industry. Others include *Co-ops at Work* (1986) and *London Story* (1986, dir. Sally Potter), which used a female-majority crew.

86. At this time, the group was known as the "Leeds Nursery Film Group" and was an ad hoc group of women making a film about one of the key demands of the women's liberation movement. It later became Leeds Animation Workshop and men worked in the group, but differences of opinion over gender stereotyping in their films led to it becoming an all-women workshop.

87. Terry Wragg, interview, "Histories of Women and Work."

88. Ibid.

89. Drainville, interview, "Histories of Women and Work."

90. Ibid.

91. Wragg, interview, "Histories of Women and Work."

92. Drainville, interview, "Histories of Women and Work."

93. Ibid.

94. Blackwood and Attille were founding members of the group; their union membership forms show Blackwood joining as a "researcher" and Attille in the role of assistant camera, both at two hundred pounds per week in 1983.

95. ACTT, "Grant-Aided Workshop Production Declaration (Abridged), in Dickinson, *Rogue Reels*, 166.

96. Manthia Diawara, "Power and Territory: The Emergence of Black British Film Collectives," in Friedman, *Fires Were Started*, 125–35.

97. For figures, see Reid, "Persistence of the Internal Labour Market," 143.

98. Martina Attille, in Jim Pines, Martina Attille, Maureen Blackwood, et al., "The Passion of Remembrance," *Framework* 32/33 (1986): 102.

99. Maureen Blackwood, in ibid., 97.

100. Martina Attille and Maureen Blackwood, "Black Women and Representation," in *Films for Women*, ed. Charlotte Brunsdon (London: BFI, 1986), 203.

101. "Programme Notes," *Tate Film*, "Rewind: Sankofa, Martina Attille: *Dreaming Rivers*," Nov. 2, 2015. Attille was also a member of the visual arts forum Black Women Artists Study Group (1995–1997) and had a central presence in the visual arts community, being documented in imagery produced by important Black women artists like Sonia Boyce. The workshops that Attille and Blackwood delivered should also be understood in the wider context of the Black arts movement and the feminist avant-garde and important exhibitions like *The Thin Black Line*, which took place in London in 1985. See Fiona Carson and Claire Pajackowska, eds., *Feminist Visual Culture* (Edinburgh: Edinburgh University Press, 2000), 32.

102. Pines et al., "Passion of Remembrance," 101.

103. Ibid., 103.

104. Karen Alexander, "Mothers, Lovers, and Others," *Monthly Film Bulletin* 56, no. 669 (Oct. 1989): 314–18. The film won Best Film at the Black Filmmakers Hall of Fame in 1990.

105. Ibid.

106. Ibid.

107. Ibid.

108. Wheeler Winston Dixon, "Maureen Blackwood, Isaac Julien, and the Sankofa Collective," *Film Criticism* 20.1/2 (Fall/Winter 1995–96): 131–43.

109. Maureen Blackwood interview in "Home from Home," *Black Film Bulletin* 1, nos. 3–4 (1993/94): 26.

110. Sirkka-Liisa Konttinen, talk on the film *Keeping Time* and *Step by Step*, Side Gallery Talks & Interviews, *Amber*, Nov. 27, 2016, accessed Feb. 4, 2019, https://www.amber-online.com/collection/keeping-time-talk-27-11-16/.

111. Sirkka-Liisa Konttinen, interview, 2002, British Library, Sound and Moving Image Collection.

112. Konttinen, talk on *Keeping Time*.

113. Konttinen, interview, British Library.

114. Sirkka-Liisa Konttinen, *Step by Step* (Newcastle: Bloodaxe Books, 1989), 5.

115. Ibid.

116. Konttinen, talk on *Keeping Time*.

117. Ibid.

118. Ibid.

119. Ibid. See also Konttinen, interview, British Library.

120. Konttinen, *Step by Step*, 117–18.

121. Ibid.

122. Denise Butters quoted in ibid., 103.

Epilogue

1. Scott, "Feminism's History," 18.

2. Virginia Woolf, *A Room of One's Own* (1929), in Virginia Woolf, *A Room of One's Own and Three Guineas* (Oxford: Oxford University Press, 2015), 43.

3. Patrick Russell, obituary, "Anne Balfour-Fraser," *The Guardian*, Aug. 21, 2016, accessed May 31, 2019, https://www.theguardian.com/film/2016/aug/21/anne -balfour-fraser-obituary

4. Anonymized participant of the "Trailblazing Women On and Off Screen" symposium, University of Greenwich, June 29, 2017.

5. Ibid.

6. The conference, titled "Multivoicedness and European Cinema: Representation, Industry, and Politics," was held by the Film Section of the European Communication, Research, and Education Association (ECREA) in November 2017 at University of College Cork, Ireland.

Select Glossary

Background Artist (Cartoon and Diagram)

Those in this role were responsible for drawing and painting the variety of background settings (buildings, objects, landscape) against which the action took place, working from original designs provided by the chief animator. It was a mid-ranking job in the production hierarchy, two levels down from the chief animator, and above the in-betweener and paint and trace.

Clapper Loader (Camera) (equivalent to second assistant camera)

One of the most junior roles in the camera crew, the clapper loader's main duties were managing the clapper board or film slate (which noted key information about the scene being recorded, vital for the editing team) and loading the correct film stock into the camera magazine. This involved liaising with the director of photography about the type of film stock required, making a judgment about how much stock would be needed for each scene, loading it into the magazine, and unloading after shooting was finished. If the magazine wasn't properly closed, the day's rushes could be lost; if the wrong film stock was loaded, the exposure was compromised (known as "fogging"). The clapper loader supported the camera operator and focus puller, making sure the correct lens was at hand when required, looking after equipment and stock, and ordering supplies and repairs when necessary.

Continuity Girl (or script supervisor) (Floor)

The director's "right hand," the continuity girl was on the studio floor throughout rehearsal and shooting and was responsible for ensuring continuity between takes. She did this by recording detailed information about scene setups (dialogue, movement, position, and effects) and used this to prompt the director and artists when necessary. She also prepared progress reports, viewed the rushes, and acted as the key point of contact for the director, artists, camera crew, and editor during shooting.

Draftswoman (Art Department)

Those in this role were responsible for interpreting the art director's original designs (expressed through rough sketches and verbal instructions) and transposing them into proper working drawings (scale blueprints) from which the construction team could build the film's sets. The drawings had to include detailed instructions about finishes, movable parts, cutouts for window views, and any other special requirements. Draftswomen needed skills in perspective drawing and a knowledge of architecture and a variety of period styles.

Editor, Assistant Editor, and Negative Cutter (Postproduction)

The editor was responsible for assembling the filmed scenes through cutting and joining, taking out and inserting frames to add pace, drama, and rhythm to the action. Scenes were cut and reworked many times, with discussion between the editor, director, and others at daily screenings, before the final cut was achieved (known as the "workprint" or "cutting copy").

The assistant editor organized the cutting room, cleaned equipment, cataloged cut film (known as "logging the rushes") using the numbers along the side of the film as a guide, and performed some of the more routine cuts to gain experience.

The cutting copy would be sent to the laboratory, where the negative cutter would find the corresponding negatives (using the numbers as a guide) and cut the negative to match the print.

Focus Puller (Camera) (equivalent to first assistant camera)

The focus puller worked with the camera operator to manually control the focus of a camera's lens during shooting. They had to accurately calculate the distance of the camera to the subject, recalculate the distance as the subject moved around in the scene, and adjust the focus of the lens accordingly as the camera tracked backward and forward.

In-Betweener (Cartoon and Diagram)

A type of junior animator's role, the in-betweener was responsible for the drawings that came between the key drawings or frames. Their work was essential to give the impression of a smooth, fluid transition between images.

Matte Artist/Painter (Art Department)

Matte painting was a technique where artists painted "locations" on sheets of glass that were then integrated with live-action footage as seamlessly as possible. It was typically used for elaborate backgrounds, fantasy worlds, or for settings that were too expensive to film in real life. Before digital techniques were available, matte artists were skilled in drawing and painting and, like all artists, had a keen understanding of composition, color, tone, depth of field, and perspective.

Paint and Trace (Cartoon and Diagram)

Tracing involved copying the paper drawings produced by animators onto cels, using a variety of materials (pens, nibs, wax pencils) depending on the style of line required. Each individual cel was hand-painted in accordance with a specified color scheme for characters and props. A thin, specially mixed paint was used (to give the kind of opaque finish a camera could pick up), and because this paint was difficult to work with, painters had to work quickly and accurately. A consistent "look" across multiple cels relied on the paint and tracer's skilled brushwork and ability to overlap contrasting colors.

Production Secretary (Floor)

An organizer and problem solver, those in this office-based role helped to coordinate and manage the logistics of film production across its different departments. This involved ensuring that equipment, props, costumes, sets, and extras were in place for shooting, ordering any travel permits and catering, and generally making sure the operational side of film production ran as smoothly as possible.

Index

Page numbers in *italics* refer to images.

Melanie Bell is an associate professor of film and media at the University of Leeds. Her books include *Julie Christie: Stardom and Cultural Production* and *Femininity in the Frame: Women and 1950s British Popular Cinema*.

WOMEN AND FILM HISTORY INTERNATIONAL

The University of Illinois Press
is a founding member of the
Association of University Presses.

University of Illinois Press
1325 South Oak Street
Champaign, IL 61820-6903
www.press.uillinois.edu